Wales

100 Remarkable Vistas

I dedicate this book to three inspirational Earth science teachers:

the late Arthur Harris, Cyfarthfa Castle Grammar School, Merthyr Tudful,
and two former members of staff of University College London,
Dr Eric Robinson and Emeritus Professor Eric H. Brown, my research supervisor and academic mentor

First impression: 2017

The publishers wish to acknowledge the support of Cyngor Llyfrau Cymru

Cover photograph: Siân Elis-Gruffydd
Design: Richard Ceri Jones

ISBN: 978-1-78461-449-2

Published and printed in Wales on paper from well-maintained forests by
Y Lolfa Cyf., Talybont, Ceredigion SY24 5HE

website www.ylolfa.com
e-mail ylolfa@ylolfa.com
tel 01970 832 304
fax 832 782

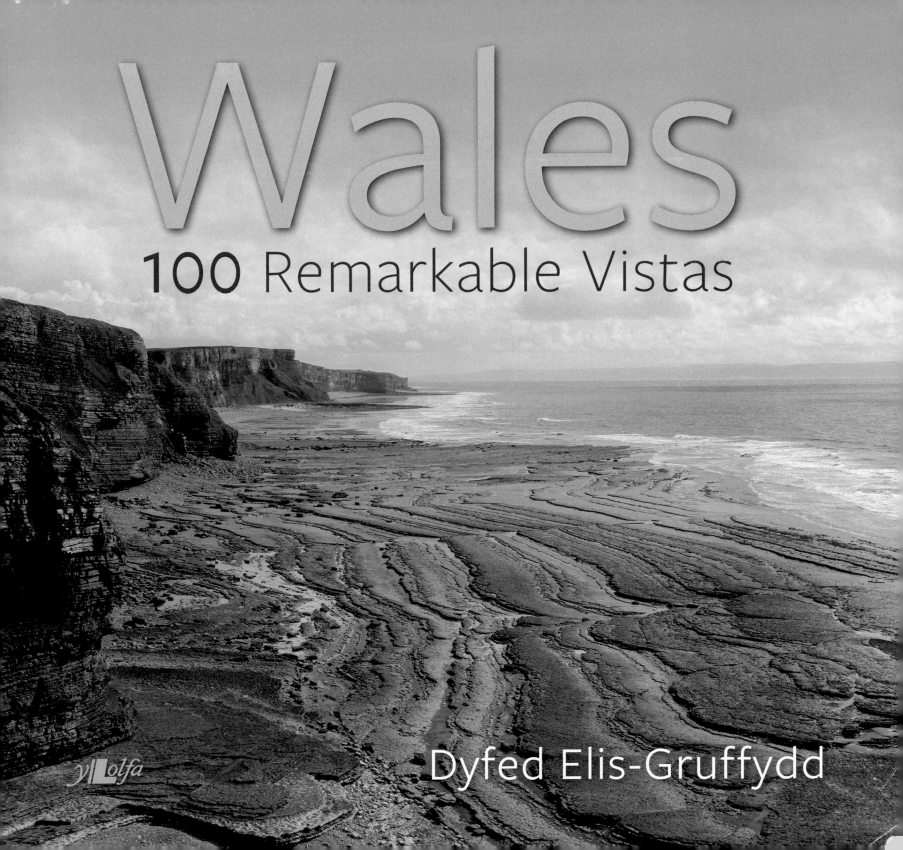

Wales

100 Remarkable Vistas

Dyfed Elis-Gruffydd

y Lolfa

Wales: 100 Remarkable Vistas

Foreword

Hen Gymru fynyddig, paradwys y bardd,
pob dyffryn, pob clogwyn, i'm golwg sydd hardd,
Trwy deimlad gwladgarol, mor swynol yw si
ei nentydd, afonydd i mi.

Old land of mountains, the paradise of bards,
each cliff and each valley and loveliness guards,
Through love of my country, so charmed will be
its streams, and its rivers to me.

Second verse of the Welsh National Anthem, 'Hen Wlad fy Nhadau'. It's quoted in an article entitled 'Exploring geological language in the Welsh landscape' by Elinor Gwynn and published in *Earth Heritage*, Addendum 2, Spring 2017.

'*Trwy ddrych y bardd neu'r llenor neu'r paentiwr y gwelaf ddarn o wlad... Ni buasai i mi ddim diddanwch wrth groesi'r darn moel hwnnw o wlad rhwng Dolgellau a Ffestiniog, onibai fy mod yn gweld y moelydd llwm trwy ddrych y bardd [R. Williams Parry].*' 'Through the eyes of a poet or author or artist I view the landscape... For me there would be no delight whilst crossing that barren stretch of land between Dolgellau and Ffestiniog, if I were not able to see the bare mountaintops through the eyes of poet [Robert Williams Parry, one of Wales' most notable twentieth-century poets]. So said Aneirin Talfan Davies in his book, *Crwydro Sir Gâr* (1970); 'Wandering Carmarthenshire'. Acceptable though his perspective may be, it is nevertheless a restrictive outlook, for the Welsh landscape is a product of its geological history and the processes that have fashioned its incredibly varied topography. The rocks and minerals of Wales have, over the ages, determined the location of specific industrial activities, have influenced its wildlife habitats and left their stamp on the archaeological riches of Wales and its architectural heritage. The country's three National Parks, five Areas of Outstanding Natural Beauty, and 14 Heritage Coasts, in particular, bear testimony to past and present erosional and depositional processes that have shaped the Welsh landform and now pose a challenge to its people as a consequence of human-induced global warming, which will, amongst other things, threaten the very existence of its coastal settlements – the home of the majority of its twenty-first century inhabitants – as sea level continues to rise.

However, although I unashamedly view the land through the eyes of an Earth scientist, I'm neither oblivious nor unmindful of alternative perspectives, as readers will discover. The task of selecting and visiting a mere 100 vistas proved to be both challenging and pleasurable. Challenging because it was necessary to ensure an even spread of sites the length and breadth of Wales, and pleasurable because it prompted me to visit locations which, prior to the preparation of the book, were *terra incognita*. Although many of the vistas are undeniably attractive, they were chosen not on the basis of their natural beauty but rather their remarkableness and accessibility. Most should be within reach of the majority of readers.

Welsh place-names and Ordnance Survey Grid References

In Wales several places have Welsh and English names (Aberteifi, Cardigan; Caerdydd, Cardiff; Caergybi, Holyhead; Trefaldwyn, Montgomery; Yr Wyddfa, Snowdon; Ynys Môn, Anglesey) or Welsh names and English renditions (Caerffili, Caerphilly; Merthyr Tudful, Merthyr Tydfil). Both appear on road-signs and over much of the country Welsh place-names rightly take precedence and appear above the English names. Since I live my life habitually, if not exclusively, through the medium of Welsh, my mother tongue, Welsh names are infinitely preferable. However, in the case where two names are in use, first use of the English name is followed by the Welsh name in brackets. Hopefully, English-speaking readers will not only respect the indigenous Welsh names, which now do appear on Ordnance Survey 1:25,000 and 1:50,000 topographical maps, but also make every effort to pronounce them correctly.

Acknowledgements

The Grid References set alongside the title of each one of the 100 vistas discussed allow those readers not familiar with the geography of Wales to locate each place with the aid of the relevant 1:25,000 Ordnance Survey map.

Words common in Welsh place- and feature-names

aber: river mouth or confluence

afon: river

bwlch: col, pass

castell: castle

chwarel: quarry

clogwyn: cliff

craig (creigiau): rock(s), cliffs

coed: trees, wood

crib: ridge

cwm: a narrow, steep-sided, glaciated valley

dyffryn: valley

glyn: valley, vale

llan: church

llyn (llynnoedd): lake(s)

melin: mill

moel (foel): a bare summit

morfa: salt-marsh, saltings

mynydd (mynyddoedd): mountain(s)

nant (nentydd): stream or valley

ogof: cave

pont: bridge

tarren: escarpment, cliff

traeth: beach

trwyn: headland

twyn (twyni): sand dune(s)

ynys: island

I'm greatly indebted not only to Garmon and Lefi Gruffudd, Managing Director and Commissioning Editor, respectively, of Y Lolfa for asking me to undertake the writing of this book, but also to English Editor Eirian Jones for her invaluable advice and editorial exactitude, and Ceri Jones for the format and design of the volume. I owe a good deal to the support of several members of Cymdeithas Edward Llwyd – especially Mal James, Crwbin – and Capel Mair, Aberteifi, especially to those few good friends who have been a constant source of vital encouragement. I'm also grateful to Gillian Clarke for granting me permission to include her poem 'Six Bells, 28 June 1960'. As usual, I owe a debt of gratitude to my wife, Siân, for her unfailing advice and help, for taking a number of the photographs which appear in the book, for joining me on several of the excursions, and above all for her patience.

Dyfed Elis-Gruffydd
Summer 2017

Maes Mawr Quarry and Mona Marble

(Chwarel Maes Mawr a Marmor Môn) SH 363908

Were it not for what it represents, the collection of boulders amongst trees and bushes in the centre of the field situated about 200 metres south-west of Ebenezer chapel, on the outskirts of the nucleated village of Llanfechell, is truly unremarkable. Few walkers following the public footpath alongside the south-western edge of the field would scarcely give the rocks a second thought. They do, however, denote the site of Maes Mawr quarry, an excavation that would have been, without doubt, a talking point amongst the villagers in 1806 or thereabouts, when George Bullock (1782–1818), a sculptor and cabinet maker of Liverpool, decided to purchase it for the princely sum of £1,000. At the time, slate quarrymen in Penrhyn quarry, near Bethesda, were paid 1s. 6d. (7½ p) a day!

The rock quarried at Maes Mawr was known as Mona Marble, a prized and very attractive decorative stone when cut and polished. But despite its name, it is not a true marble – a limestone transformed into marble under the influence of intense heat and pressure – but a dark-coloured igneous rock metamorphosed into serpentinite (serpentine). Of probable late Precambrian age, the serpentinite, mainly dull purple or greenish in colour but often veined and multicoloured, outcrops in three main areas: between Llanfechell and Mynachdy, near the north-west tip of Anglesey; on Holy Island (Ynys Gybi) between Four Mile Bridge (Pontrhydybont) and Rhoscolyn; and in places on mainland Anglesey in the vicinity of Caergeiliog. But the Maes Mawr quarry and that near Bodior mansion, Rhoscolyn, were the two most important sources of Mona Marble. Samuel Lewis, author of *A Topographical Dictionary of Wales* (1833), asserted that the Llanfechell 'marble' was 'of very superior quality ... equal in the brilliancy and variety of its colours to the finest specimens of Italy'. On the other hand, Angharad Llwyd, antiquary and author of *A History of the Island of Mona ...* (1833),

Verd antique (left)

Fireplace of purply serpentinite, Penrhyn Castle (© The National Trust)

9

adjudged a 'prize essay' at the Royal Beaumaris Eisteddfod in August 1832, claimed that 'the finest quarry of the beautiful variegated marble called verd antique' was that near Bodior, adding that 'The specimens obtained [there], in diversity and brilliancy of colour, surpass every other'.

The Maes Mawr quarry was opened during the second half of the eighteenth century but it was at its most productive during the early years of the nineteenth century. In 1813, George Bullock settled in London where he established the Mona Marble Works, Maes Mawr 'verd antique' (green serpentinite) being shipped to the city via the nearby port of Cemais. In order to promote his ambitious venture, advertisements and articles appeared in the press singing the praises of Mona Marble and the products fashioned therefrom. In an article entitled 'Mona Marble: Characterization and Usage',

Monument to W.O. Stanley of Penrhos, St Cybi's Church

published in *Stone in Wales* (2005), geologist Jana Horák cites several examples of the use made of the green serpentinite, including a fireplace in Towneley Hall Art Gallery and Museum, Burnley, and ecclesiastical monuments in St Cuthbert's, Halsall, and St Luke's, Farnworth. Of particular interest is the commission that Bullock received in 1816, for he was asked to prepare 'a magnificent table of green marble, which was sent to [Napoleon] Bonaparte, when at St. Helena', his island home following his deportation in 1815. The 'green marble' in question was, according to Llwyd, obtained from the quarries near Rhoscolyn. And when at Trentham Hall, on the outskirts of Stoke-on-Trent, a mansion demolished in 1912–13, Llwyd herself encountered 'a beautiful chimney piece, made of Mona marble, found at Rhôs Colyn'.

Given that its overmantel was designed by Bullock before his death in 1818, the purple serpentinite used to construct the fireplace in Speke Hall, a sixteenth-century mansion on the shores of the Mersey, near Liverpool, probably came from Maes Mawr. During the 1820s and 1830s use was made of the same decorative stone in some of the rooms of Penrhyn Castle, near Llandygái. Most impressive is the magnificent fireplace in one of the keep's bedrooms.

In the absence of any references to the Maes Mawr quarry after the late 1830s, it would appear that quarrying had come to an end during that decade. However, it was reopened briefly in the 1980s to secure a quantity of purple serpentinite to renovate the Speke Hall fireplace.

In contrast to the Maes Mawr quarry, that near Rhoscolyn was worked on occasions until the late 1890s. For example, during internal renovation work in Worcester Cathedral in the 1860s, the architect, Sir Gilbert Scott, made use of 'verd antique' for the round columns supporting the pulpit. The last reference to the quarry is to be found in *The Geology of Anglesey* (1919): 'It was', said author Edward Greenly, 'quarried many years ago, and was used again in 1897 for the Stanley monument (W.O. Stanley of Penrhos; 1802–84)' in St Cybi's Church, Holyhead (Caergybi). The ostentatious Italian Renaissance chest of Carrara marble rests on polished, rectangular blocks of Mona Marble.

Site of Maes Mawr quarry, Llanfechell (right)

Mynydd Trysglwyn

(Mynydd Parys) SH 438905

The only grave in Wales designated a Regionally Important Geodiversity Site is that of Edward Greenly who died in Bangor in 1951 and was buried in the graveyard of Llangristiolus Church, Anglesey (Ynys Môn). It's a fitting tribute to a geologist who devoted over 20 years of his life to studying and mapping the geology of the island, a labour of love that resulted in the publication of his masterpiece, *The Geology of Anglesey*, by the Geological Survey of Great Britain in 1919. Anglesey, wrote Greenly, is blighted by two desolate wilderness areas, one natural and the other of man's making: Newborough (Niwbwrch) and Mynydd Parys (147 m). An undeserved observation in the case of Newborough, but few would challenge his assessment of Mynydd Parys copper mine for, as recalled by Jan Morris in her book entitled *The Matter of Wales* (1984), the place 'looks like a huge long-disused rubbish dump, or perhaps the remains of some fearful explosion – covered all over with grey, red, brown, orange and yellow deposits, surrounded by an air of bitter exhaustion, and riddled everywhere, among its struggling heather, with perilous shafts and galleries'.

The kaleidoscopic colours are attributable to the combination of metalliferous ores in the area's rocks, especially pyrite (iron sulphide), chalcopyrite (copper and iron sulphide), sphalerite (zinc sulphide) and galena (lead sulphide). The origin of the sulphides was something of a mystery to Greenly and remains the subject of much debate, but it's thought that they were deposited in the rocks on or below the sea floor by circulating mineral-rich hot water generated during a period of Ordovician volcanic activity, some 450 million years ago.

Copper ore, in particular, was sought-after even in prehistoric times. Although it's known that Bronze Age people dug for ore on Mynydd Trysglwyn, some 4,000 years ago, and that the valuable mineral was also known to the Romans, the Mynydd Parys mine (named after the Parys family, constables of Caernarfon Castle during the reign of Harry IV) was at its most productive during the late eighteenth century and the first half of the nineteenth century, following the discovery of the 'Great Lode', a rich vein of copper ore in March 1768. At the time, the enterprise, a combination of three mines – Parys, Mona and Morfa Du – was producing about 3,000 tonnes of ore a year and employing about 1,500 men, women (including the so-called 'copper ladies', employed to separate the valuable ore from the waste rock) and children.

The most notable feature of the mine was the 'Great Opencast', a vast open-cast pit which was worked for copper ore and may have formed in part as a result of the collapse of countless shafts sunk near the summit of Mynydd Parys. In time, however, it became necessary to dig ever deeper in order to acquire commercial quantities of the ore and during the first half of the nineteenth century in excess of 50 shafts were sunk to a maximum depth of 320 metres, 173 metres below sea level. But the ore's low grade, drainage difficulties, the spiralling costs of deeper mining, the falling price of copper and the importation of cheaper foreign ores all contributed to the end of mining operations by the late 1890s.

Environmentally the demise of what was once the biggest copper mine in Europe was a blessing. The pollution, experienced first-hand by both David Thomas (better known by his bardic name, Dafydd Ddu Eryri; 1759–1822) and Thomas Pennant (1726–98) during the last quarter of the eighteenth century, was horrendous. For

The windmill was built in 1878

Thomas, crossing the mountain was a loathsome experience for it was perpetually enveloped in a cloud of 'sulphurous smoke'. Pennant too spoke of the 'Suffocating fumes of the burning heaps of copper [that] arise in all parts, and extend their baneful influence for miles around. In adjacent parts vegetation is nearly destroyed; even the mosses and lichens of the rocks have perished.' Writing in 1849, Samuel Lewis (c.1782–1865) complained about the noise, adding that 'the reverberated roar of frequent explosions of gunpowder used in blasting the rock, added to the dismal scene an effect truly appalling'.

The noise and noxious fumes are a thing of the past but not so the toxic, acidic waters and poisoned land. Nevertheless, the alluring ugliness of the mine's surreal 'lunar' landscape continues to attract not only numerous visitors, but also makers of science-fiction television programmes and films, such as *Doctor Who* and *Mortal Kombat: Annihilation* (1997). Such activities take place within sight of the head-frame of Morris Shaft, sunk to a depth of 300 metres by Anglesey Mining plc, owners of the westernmost part of Mynydd Parys, between 1988 and 1990. To this day mineral exploration continues and resources of mainly copper and zinc ores, together with significant quantities of lead, silver and gold, are estimated at 6.5 million tonnes. If the price of copper and zinc were to rise, mining on Mynydd Parys may well resume. Indeed, in September 2017 a BBC Wales news item reported that due to the worldwide shortage of zinc the mine may reopen in 2020.

Morris Shaft

Mynydd Bodafon

SH 472854

To claim, as many do, that Mynydd Bodafon (178 m) is the highest 'mountain' on the island of Anglesey (Ynys Môn) is somewhat confusing. It is, however, factually correct, for the highest point in the county of Anglesey is Holyhead Mountain (220 m; Mynydd Twr) on Holy Island (Ynys Gybi), which in reality is no longer an island since the land in the vicinity of the old ford at Four Mile Bridge (Pontrhydybont, 'the bridge of the ford's bridge') has long since been reclaimed from the sea. To add to the confusion, some would argue that only eminences above 600 metres (2,000 feet) are mountains, whilst those below the qualifying height are merely hills.

The term used by Edward Greenly, author of *The Geology of Anglesey* (1919), to describe Mynydd Bodafon and Holyhead Mountain, in addition to the other seven conspicuous hills – Bwrdd Arthur (164 m), Mynydd Crafgoed (155 m), Mynydd Llwydiarth (150 m), Mynydd Nebo (168 m), Mynydd Eilian (177 m), Mynydd Parys (147 m) and Mynydd y Garn (170 m) – is 'monadnock', a word in the vocabulary of some of the native tribes of North America for an isolated hill rising above a gently rolling plain. The term is wholly appropriate, because the monadnocks of Anglesey and Holy Island, islands of hard, resistant rocks that have withstood erosion, stand

proud of an extensive, undulating, hummocky platform whose surface is nowhere more that 85 metres above sea level.

Bobi Jones, author of *Crwydro Môn* (1957), one of a series of county-based, Welsh-language travel books published between 1952 and 1985, asserted that Mynydd Bodafon, a craggy, 1.5-kilometre-long ridge, was 'the oldest mountain in Wales, if not in Europe'. The summit, he added, 'was the oldest in Anglesey, quartzite, a rock that was once sandstone but has been recrystallized and hence it is immensely hard'. During the 1950s and for many subsequent years, the quartzite of Mynydd Bodafon and Holyhead Mountain was deemed to be of Precambrian age but to suggest that the rock was amongst the oldest in Europe was a gross exaggeration. After all, geologists prior to the publication of Bobi Jones' book were well

Llyn Bodafon

aware of much older rocks in Scandinavia. By today, however, it's doubtful whether the fine-grained, white quartzite pre-dates Cambrian times, the period of Earth history that dawned 542 million years ago.

With the exception of heather and gorse, shallow rooted in patches of thin, peaty soil, the summit of Yr Arwydd, the highest point of Mynydd Bodafon, is bare compared to the terrain surrounding Llyn Bodafon, a small, shallow lake south of Penycastell (169 m), the second highest of the monadnock's three summits. Schist – a metamorphic rock that splits into thin irregular plates – is the basis of the greener oasis. The rock's propensity to disintegrate more readily than quartzite, coupled with its covering of glacial

boulder-clay, has resulted in the formation of richer soil. Equally striking is the contrast between the rocky, wind-swept upland and its surrounding patchwork of green fields and woodland.

But Mynydd Bodafon's lack of stature is relative, because a panorama second to none awaits walkers who choose to follow the grassy path to the summit of Yr Arwydd. To the west lies Holyhead Mountain; east-north-eastwards it's possible to glimpse the rocky shores of Porth Helaeth, near Moelfre, where the *Royal Charter*, with its cargo of gold, was wrecked during the severe storm of 26 October 1859; whilst to the south-east are the high summits of Snowdonia (Eryri).

A less attractive element of the panorama, north of Yr Arwydd, is

the scarred landscape of Mynydd Parys, once the world's largest copper mine. But it's wind turbines that have incurred the wrath of some of the island's residents. Trysglwyn, a short distance south of Mynydd Parys, is one of three large wind farms in northern Anglesey; the second is located near Cemaes, and the third, and largest, between Llyn Alaw reservoir and Mynydd Mechell. The three together are capable of generating enough clean electricity to satisfy the demands of about 10,500 homes, equivalent of about 70 per cent of all the island's homes. However, in the opinion of supporters of Anglesey Against Wind Turbines, an organization committed 'to oppose any further erection of commercial on-shore wind turbines', such structures are 'unreliable, inefficient, noisy,

unsightly and damaging to our wildlife'. That assertion prompted the Advertising Standards Authority to rebuke the organization for its misleading adverts and unfounded claims.

Ironically, wind turbines in the form of windmills have been a feature of Anglesey's landscape ever since the eighteenth and nineteenth centuries. Almost fifty are known to have been built and employed to mill locally-grown grain. The majority closed in the early years of the twentieth century but Melin Llynnon, built in 1775, survives as the only working windmill in Wales producing stone-ground wholemeal flour using organic wheat. The substantially intact tower of Melin Llidiart, one of the oldest windmills, stands a short distance south of Mynydd Bodafon.

South Stack and Holyhead Mountain

(Ynys Lawd a Mynydd Twr) SH 202823

Until 1828, when a rope bridge was erected across the strait between Ynys Lawd and the larger Holy Island (Ynys Gybi), the only way of accessing the site of the South Stack lighthouse, completed in 1809, was either by boat or aerial ropeway. Fortunately, in the case of Edward Greenly (1861–1951), author of *The Geology of Anglesey* (1919), a 24-year-long project which he had begun in 1895, he was able to access the small island by way of a later iron bridge in order to marvel at 'The great cliffs that ... are among the finest on the British coasts'. Sir John Smith Flett, appointed Director of the Geological Survey of Great Britain in 1920, was also much impressed for, after visiting Ynys Lawd in the company of Greenly in 1907, he

Intricately folded layers of sandstone and mudstone

was at pains to stress that 'There can hardly be a finer section in the British Isles for the study of both great and minute folding [and], of the relations of the one to the other'.

Only from a boat is it possible to appreciate fully the remarkable contortions in the cliffs between Ynys Lawd and Ellin's Tower that speak of enormous ancient pressure in the Earth's crust. Greenly was well aware of that fact and 'after several failures to obtain a boat to go along that dangerous coast', he was fortunate to have been given an opportunity, on one occasion, to join 'the Holyhead Steam Lifeboat' out on exercise, although sketching the folded strata 'bit by bit, from the lifeboat in a somewhat heavy rolling sea' proved problematic! Today, an unforgettable experience awaits those visitors who are prepared to descend the 400 steps down the 110-metre-high cliff, pausing here and there to study the intricate folds, before visiting the lighthouse on the island beyond the aluminium bridge opened in 1997.

The alternating beds of rusty-looking sandstone and bluish-grey mudstone record the deposition of once horizontal layers of sand and mud on the floor of an ancient sea. Although the rocks have maintained their layered appearance, the powerful compressive forces that folded the strata were also responsible for superimposing on the larger upfolds and downfolds a bewildering pattern of minor folds and smaller wrinkles.

Traditionally, most of the rocks of Anglesey and Holy Island, including those of Ynys Lawd, were considered to be Precambrian in age, attributable to that inordinately long first chapter in the history of the Earth that came to an end 542 million years ago. Indeed, until relatively recently, geologists were of the opinion that they occupied the largest area of Precambrian rocks in Britain, south of the Scottish Highlands. But not any more. The presence of trace fossils, the tracks of burrowing worms in the layered rocks prompted others to suggest that they were formed sometime after 542 million

Ellin's Tower

But for those visitors with eyes set on more distant horizons, the rocky summit of Holyhead Mountain, a mere 1.5 kilometres from Ynys Lawd, is the place to be. From within the bounds of Caer y Tŵr, a late Iron Age hillfort and site of a Roman signal station, it is possible, on a clear day, to espy Cumbria, Isle of Man (Ynys Manaw), Ireland (Iwerddon) and Snowdonia (Eryri). The height and barrenness of Holyhead Mountain is attributable to the hardness and resistance of shining-white Holyhead Quartzite, a rock of Cambrian age, some 10 million years younger than the South Stack strata upon which it rests. The quartzite's hardness also proved to be of commercial value, for it was used not only to construct the 2.4-kilometre-long, outer-harbour breakwater of Holyhead (Caergybi) – the longest in Europe – between 1847 and 1873, but also to manufacture fire bricks over a period of about 70 years. Following its closure in 1973, the site of the former brickworks became part of the Holyhead Breakwater Country Park, opened in 1990.

Holyhead breakwater

years ago. That is now confirmed, because small zircon crystals in the rocks of South Stack have yielded a radiometric date of 522 million years, indicating that the strata – in addition to many of the other supposed Precambrian rocks of Anglesey and Holy Island – were deposited during Cambrian times (542–488 million years ago) and later deformed during a period of continental collision and mountain building some 400 million years ago.

Standing on the very edge of the coastal cliffs a short distance south of Ynys Lawd is Ellin's Tower, a castellated folly built in 1868 by W.O. Stanley – Member of Parliament for Anglesey (1837–44) and an antiquarian of wide reputation – as a summer retreat for his wife, Ellin, a keen observer of bird life. Ever since its restoration in the 1980s, the tower has become a focal point of the RSPB South Stack reserve. Equipped with binoculars and telescopes, it offers visitors spectacular views of seabird colonies – including guillemots, razorbills and fulmars on narrow, cliff ledges, and puffins on the grassy slopes above the cliffs – during the breeding season.

Ynys Llanddwyn

SH 387627

Since it's only cut off from the adjoining afforested mainland for a few hours at high water, Ynys Llanddwyn (the island of Dwynwen's church) is more properly described as a peninsula, a narrow neck of land projecting into the sea. Delightful though it is today, the island to which Dwynwen decided to retire during the fifth century lost its charm and isolation in the late fourteenth century, when severe storms initiated the formation of extensive sand dunes that choked not only the port and settlement of Newborough (Niwbwrch), but also nearby agricultural land. In time, Newborough Warren, now part of the Newborough Warren and Ynys Llanddwyn National Nature Reserve at the southern tip of Anglesey (Ynys Môn), developed into one of the largest and finest dune systems in Britain. Those dunes nearest to Ynys Llanddwyn lie hidden under Corsican pines planted between 1947 and 1963. Amongst the trees, now the haunt of red squirrels, is the craggy ridge of Cadair y Cythraul (c.40 m) that was in the time of Dwynwen part of an elongated island, twice the length of the present peninsula, situated between the estuary of the river Cefni and Abermenai.

It was on that wind-swept island that Dwynwen experienced the solitude she sought after her lover, Maelon Dafodrill, broke off their engagement. According to one version of the legend, God, who punished Maelon by turning him into a block of ice, granted his broken-hearted fiancée three wishes: that Maelon be thawed; that she would be able to hear the prayers of those suffering the pangs of lovesickness; and that she would be allowed to live the solitary life

Yr Eifl and the old lighthouse

of a nun on the island. Following her death, the church of Llanddwyn and a nearby holy well became a place of pilgrimage frequented by Welsh lovers wishing to commune with Dwynwen, the patron saint of lovers, whose feast day is celebrated on 25 January. It is claimed that the ruined sixteenth-century church stands on the site of Dwynwen's sanctuary and because of its spiritual, historical and cultural significance, work undertaken in 2012 cleared those sections of the building obscured under a cover of blown sand and repaired the arch above the chancel window that had collapsed during the late 1940s or early 1950s.

However, Carl Rogers, author of the official guidebook, *The Isle of Anglesey Coastal Path* (2005), insists that not all visitors are drawn to this part of Anglesey's coastline simply to learn more about Dwynwen. A greater attraction in the minds of many is the glorious, sandy expanse of Traeth Llanddwyn, especially at low tide, and the breathtaking panorama of the Llŷn peninsula, viewed from the tip of Ynys Llanddwyn: the three striking summits of Yr Eifl (564 m) and the chain of ancient volcanic hills extending south-west towards Morfa Nefyn and Portin-llaen.

To the pilots living in the row of four early nineteenth-century cottages at the southern end of Ynys Llanddwyn, the view was all too familiar because it was they who were responsible for guiding vessels, *en route* to the ports of Caernarfon and Y Felinheli, safely through the ever-changing pattern of channels between the treacherous sand banks of Abermenai. In addition to building the cottages, the Caernarfon Harbour Trustees were also responsible for constructing Tŵr Mawr in 1824, a whitewashed tower not dissimilar in form to the windmills that were once a feature of Anglesey's landscape. Four years after its construction, it became a lighthouse when a lantern was placed in an extension to the ground floor of the tower. The light was extinguished in the early 1970s and replaced by a lantern placed atop a small tower on the island opposite the cottages.

Compared to the rich flora of Newborough Warren forming the eastern half of the National Nature Reserve (it boasts over 500 different species, including many rare orchids and the dune helleborine [*Epipactis dunensis*] in dune slacks, its only habitat in Wales), Ynys Llanddwyn is species poor. Nevertheless, it's not bereft of wild flowers. Above the rocky shore grow patches of squill (*Scilla verna*) in spring, and bloody crane's-bill (*Geranium sanguineum*), rock samphire (*Crithmum maritimum*), rock sea-lavender (*Limonium binervosum*) and sea spleenwort (*Asplenium marinum*) in summer.

But if Newborough Warren is the botanical paradise, Ynys Llanddwyn was identified as a geological paradise by Edward Greenly, author of *The Geology of Anglesey* (1919). The colour and texture of the various rock types, especially those in the sandy bays near the old lighthouse, are truly remarkable. There, multicoloured mudstones and sandstones are mixed with black volcanic rocks, red jasper and white limestone. Furthermore, the pillow lava, reminiscent of piles of misshapen pillows, forming the islets at the northern end of Ynys Llanddwyn, are amongst the finest examples in Britain. The pillows, the product of submarine volcanic eruptions, were believed to be Precambrian in age (pre-550 million years ago) but that is now in doubt following the discovery of possible Cambrian microfossils in the red jasper between the pillows.

Pillow lavas of possible Cambrian age (542–488 million years ago), almost as fresh as when formed

Anglesey Column, Llanfair Pwllgwyngyll

(Tŵr Marcwis, Llanfair Pwllgwyngyll) SH 536715

In his book, *Blwyddyn yn Llŷn* [A Year in Llŷn] (1990), the poet, R.S. Thomas (1913–2000), ventured to state that the 'Llŷn peninsula is no more than a part of Wales, a platform from which to see the remainder'. Others disparagingly maintain that Anglesey (Môn) too is merely a platform from which to admire the grandeur of Eryri, the mountains of Snowdonia. The assertion is baseless. Nevertheless, to climb the 115 steps of the spiral stair to the top of the Anglesey Column would be a waste of time and energy were it not for the awe-inspiring panorama of Eryri viewed from the platform encircling the statue of Henry William Paget, of Battle of Waterloo fame. The 34-metre-high Greek Doric column – set atop Cerrig-y-borth, a craggy hillock overlooking Menai Strait – was completed in 1816–17 but the four-metre-high bronze statue of Paget, Earl of Uxbridge and later 1st Marquess of Anglesey, was not erected until 1860.

Between the limestone headland of the Great Orme (Y Gogarth) to the north-east and the granite hills of Yr Eifl to the south-west, rise the summits of Y Carneddau, Y Glyderau, Yr Wyddfa (Snowdon) and the Nantlle ridge above lowland Arfon. Despite their splendour, they are but the eroded remains of the Caledonian Mountains, an ancient mountain chain of Alpine proportions whose remnants are also to be found in Spitsbergen, Scandinavia, Scotland, Greenland (Grønland), Newfoundland, and the northern section of the Appalachian Mountains of eastern North America. They were uplifted when two ancient continents, situated about 30° south of the equator, collided with one another. For some 100 million years the so-called Iapetus Ocean separated the two landmasses but, between 450 million and 400 million years ago, the ocean gradually closed, a movement that triggered an era of violent volcanic activity

Menai Strait, Britannia bridge and the mountains of Snowdonia (right)

that peaked during Ordovician times, about 450 million years ago.

In Wales, the continental collision caused the enormously thick pile of mudstones and sandstones that had accumulated on the sea floor during Cambrian, Ordovician and Silurian times to be squeezed, torn, broken and uplifted in the jaws of the tectonic vice. The Ordovician volcanic rocks, which have profoundly influenced the Snowdonian landscape, were subject to the same treatment. Furthermore, the powerful compressive forces transformed much of the mudstone into slate, the raw material of an extractive industry that has made an enduring impression on the landscape of north-west Wales, especially in the vicinity of the northernmost slate

quarrying centres of Bethesda, Llanberis and Nantlle, and in and around Blaenau Ffestiniog and Corris further to the south.

The same earth-crunching forces fractured the rocks. Many faults were newly-formed but other older tears were reactivated, such as the complex Menai Strait Fault System, which effectively forms the boundary between Anglesey and mainland Wales. In time, this zone of fractured rocks influenced the formation of the Menai Strait, whose broad, river-like appearance is reflected in its Welsh name, Afon Menai.

With the exception of that portion of the waterway between the Britannia rail and road bridge and Y Felinheli, the 25-kilometre-long

Menai Strait and the granite hills of Yr Eifl

strait is a combination of two old river valleys, one river flowing north-east and the other south-west, but both excavated along lines of broken bedrock. Their valleys were deepened further by the erosive power of ice, flowing south-west across Anglesey and the neighbouring mainland during the Last Glaciation. As the ice melted and retreated about 17,000 years ago, large volumes of meltwater not only deepened further still the two valleys, but also excavated the deep channel between the Britannia bridge and Y Felinheli. But the Menai Strait, as viewed from Paget's vantage point atop the Anglesey Column, did not assume its present appearance until about 7,000 years ago when the post-glacial rise in sea level flooded both valleys and the linking meltwater channel. As a result, Anglesey became an island.

The tower itself is built of Carboniferous limestone, quarried at Moelfre on the east coast of Anglesey and imported via the tiny harbour of Pwllfanogl, alongside which stands the former home of

Sir Kyffin Williams, the Welsh nation's premier twentieth-century landscape and portrait artist. Although formed some 350 million years ago, the blue-grey limestone is comparatively young and of little interest when compared to the nature and age of the rock of international interest on which the Doric column stands. Blueschist, a rare type of metamorphic rock not encountered anywhere else in Britain, is formed by the transformation of basalt, volcanic rocks of similar composition and sediments under the influence of high pressures and relatively low temperatures. The rock, dated to about 590–580 million years ago, represents a slice of ocean-floor crust of Precambrian age. Because of its uniqueness, the land around the base of the tower has been designated a Site of Special Scientific Interest, which means that the blueschist, whose colour is attributable to the presence of the blue mineral, glaucophane, should not be hammered by unscrupulous, souvenir-seeking geologists or members of the public.

The Great Orme mines

(Mwyngloddiau'r Gogarth) SH 771831

Goodness knows what possessed J.A. Steers (1899–1987), who spent his entire illustrious academic career in the Department of Geography, University of Cambridge, to assert in his *magnum opus, The Coastline of England & Wales* (1946), that 'The north coast of Wales does not present any particularly interesting features'. To claim that the two, impressive Carboniferous limestone headlands of the Great Orme (Y Gogarth) and Little Orme (Trwyn y Fuwch), flanking the seaside town of Llandudno, are of no particular note beggars belief. Nevertheless, he was correct to point out that the Great Orme, 'with its magnificent cliffs' was originally an island, 'later joined to the mainland by an isthmus of blown sand'.

It was on that unprepossessing stretch of sand that Llandudno first developed, especially following the completion of the Chester–Holyhead Railway in 1849. Fourteen years later, what is now the largest seaside resort in Wales, was described as 'Queen of the Welsh Resorts', famed for its wide promenade backed by a curving line of grand hotels, its 700-metre-long late nineteenth-century pier, and the Great Orme Tramway opened in July 1902.

The development of the fashionable resort was matched by the gradual decline and closure of the Great Orme mines that were, during the nineteenth century, the most productive copper mines of mainland Wales. Mining was centred upon the Pyllau ('pits') valley on

Llandudno between the Great Orme and Little Orme

the headland's south-east-facing slopes and there, at a height of about 150 metres above sea level, near the tramway's halfway station, stood both the Old and New Mine whose shafts plunged to a depth below sea level. Chalcopyrite, a brassy-coloured sulphide of copper and iron, was the main ore dug and it was to be found in veins following faults and fissures in the limestone. It appears that the New Mine, first mentioned in 1807, closed c.1840 but the Old Mine, which was probably established in the seventeenth century, remained open until about 1881. During the nineteenth century, it's estimated that the mines produced about 50,000 tonnes of copper ore, the bulk of which was exported to Amlwch on the north coast of Anglesey (Ynys Môn), where it was smelted together with low-grade Mynydd Parys ore.

In 1831 and again in 1849, miners working in the Pyllau mines discovered signs of ancient workings which, at the time, were attributed to the Romans. However, in 1987, landscaping work designed to eradicate the industrial scars of the nineteenth century, unearthed signs of mining activity much older than the Roman period. As thousands of tonnes of spoil that had accumulated around the old shafts were removed, those involved in the clearance

The Bronze Age mine and entranceway to the subterranean passageways

Blue-green malachite (right)

operations uncovered ancient shafts and tunnels containing bone tools, hammer stones and charcoal. By carbon dating the bones and charcoal it became apparent that the earliest mining took place during the Bronze Age, some 4,000 years ago. Over the past 20 years, further exploratory work by archaeologists, engineers and cavers revealed the existence of a large 20-metre-deep opencast copper mine, together with a network of narrow tunnels and one large underground chamber. It's thought that the smallest excavations were the work of children. Other than the possible use of fire-setting (the shattering of heated rock by dousing it with water), which would explain the presence of charcoal, the only tools at the disposal of both children and adults labouring in the terrifyingly cramped passageways were antler picks and hammer stones (about 2,400 were found), wave-eroded cobbles collected from local beaches. What led to the discovery of the copper ore remains a mystery but, in all probability, it was the presence of verdigris on exposed rock surfaces that first drew the attention of Bronze Age miners to its existence, for the emerald green colouration is indicative of the presence of malachite, a carbonate

of copper, which may form as a result of the oxidation of chalcopyrite.

Without doubt, the Great Orme Bronze Age copper mine is an archaeological site of international importance and, since it opened to the public in 1991, hundreds of thousands of visitors have marvelled at the prodigious accomplishments of prehistoric peoples. It's a site like no other anywhere in Britain, if not the world, for in 2005 it was awarded the title of 'The Largest Prehistoric Copper Mine in the World' by the Guinness World Record team! Within a stone's throw of the mine, Maes y Facrell National Nature Reserve is the site of another unique feature, for nowhere else in Britain is it possible to encounter wild cotoneaster (*Cotoneaster cambricus*, known appropriately in Welsh as *cotoneaster y Gogarth*), amongst a rich flora of rare, lime-loving wild flowers. First discovered in 1783, it's the headland's most noteworthy plant, whose presence, according to naturalist William Condry, is attributable to 'an October fieldfare arriving on the Orme and leaving on some ledge a dropping containing seeds that were in a berry the bird had swallowed in the mountains of Scandinavia the previous day'!

The Great Orme's limestone headland and Llandudno's pier

Talacre and Point of Ayr

(Talacre a'r Parlwr Du) SJ 125848

Were it not for the imposing, rock-solid limestone promontory of the Great Orme (Y Gogarth), Point of Ayr (Y Parlwr Du or Trwyn Talacre), fashioned from soft clays and shingle ridges at the easternmost extremity of the north Wales coast, could claim to be the northernmost headland of mainland Wales. Nearby lies the untidy seaside village of Talacre, an 'ideal family resort' for those who wish to be within easy reach and earshot of multifarious attractions, including amusement arcades, pubs and clubs, cafés and fish-and-chip shops, caravan parks, the salt-marsh and dunes of a Royal Society for the Protection of Birds (RSPB) nature reserve, a Site of Special Scientific Interest (SSSI), a gas terminal, and what was the site of the most well-known colliery of the north-east Wales coalfield!

The Point of Ayr colliery stood alongside the shore of the Dee estuary (Dyfrdwy), to the south of the headland, on land reclaimed from the sea. All attempts during the 1860s and 1870s to locate workable coal-seams, which lay for the most part deep beneath the estuary and open sea, proved fruitless. Success came in the 1890s when miners of the Point of Ayr Colliery Company discovered good seams of house and steam coal. As a result, a second shaft was sunk to a depth of 200 metres in order to exploit the legacy of luxuriant tropical forests that cloaked the land during late Carboniferous times, about 310 million years ago. After the nationalization of the coal industry in 1947, a third shaft was sunk to a depth of 275 metres and in no time at all the colliery, which employed over 700 men, was

Point of Ayr gas terminal (above)
Dee estuary and Connah's Quay power station (facing)

Talacre Warren dunes and lighthouse

producing over 200,000 tonnes of coal a year. During its final years, the pit's entire output was pulverized and transported by train to Fiddlers Ferry power station, near Warrington, whilst the miners and other local folk burnt Staffordshire coal! In the early 1990s it was said that there were sufficient reserves 'to last another century' but the colliery, the last deep pit of the north-east Wales coalfield, closed in August 1996.

For several years part of the colliery's headgear stood forlorn in Greenfield Heritage Park, Holywell (Parc Treftadaeth Maes Glas, Treffynnon), but was moved and re-erected alongside the A548 near Ffynnongroyw, a former coalmining village close to the old coalmine. Unfortunately, it was not possible to place the memorial, unveiled in September 2014, on the site of the colliery because prior to its final closure the land had already been acquired by the developers of the Point of Ayr gas terminal. It's there that natural gas, discovered in the

1990s in the 240-million-year-old Triassic sandstone formations deep below the floor of Liverpool Bay, comes ashore via a 33-kilometre-long pipeline from the drilling platforms of the Celtic gas fields. Following treatment, the gas is transported through a 27-kilometre-long pipeline to a power station at Connah's Quay (Cei Connah), near the head of the Dee estuary.

Viewed from the path that follows the top of the sea embankment to the south of Talacre, the gas terminal's gleaming network of pipes and stacks is in stark contrast to the sandbanks, mudflats and dunes of the RSPB Dee Estuary–Point of Ayr Nature Reserve, edged on their landward side by salt-marsh. The estuary is one of the most important in Britain and Europe for its populations of waterfowl and waders. It's also a refuge for many thousands of migratory birds in winter. Waders such as oystercatchers, curlews, knots, redshanks, bar-tailed godwits, black-tailed godwits and dunlins are best seen on an incoming tide when they move landwards whilst eating their fill of invertebrates living within the mud and sand beneath their feet.

In fact, the RSPB nature reserve is part of Gronant Dunes and Talacre Warren SSSI reached by following the sea embankment to the old Point of Ayr lighthouse, marking the entrance to the treacherous Dee estuary. Built in 1776 but much altered around 1820, it was decommissioned in 1883 and replaced by a lightship moored north of the entrance to the Dee channels. Both the lighthouse and sand dunes, traceable as far west as Prestatyn, are built on a foundation of numerous gravel ridges that are part of the Point of Ayr spit. The dunes, in particular, are of special scientific interest for they are one of the last remaining unspoilt and intact system that once extended along the length of the north Wales coast, before they were, in the words of naturalist William Condry, 'spoilt by a vast sprawl of bungalows, shanties and caravans'. Chief amongst the dunes colourful floristic treasures are the orchids – early marsh-orchid (*Dactylorhiza incarnata*), northern marsh-orchid (*Dactylorhiza purpurella*) and southern marsh-orchid (*Dactylorhiza praetermissa*) – which thrive on the floor of slacks, low-lying depressions between marram (*Ammophila arenaria*) covered dunes, a grass whose extensive system of creeping underground stems allows it to thrive under conditions of shifting sands and high winds.

The Vale of Clwyd caves

(Ogofâu Dyffryn Clwyd) SJ 015710

The Palaeolithic caves of Wales are a rare and precious archaeological and cultural resource. Of the twelve most important sites only three are in north Wales and two of them are in the Vale of Clwyd. On either side of the broad, agricultural valley it's possible to trace the broken and faulted outcrop of the Carboniferous limestone, which accumulated in the warm, tropical seas of Carboniferous times, some 350 million years ago. And wherever the distinctive blue-grey rock is encountered, caves abound, some of which have yielded the earliest evidence of humanity in Wales.

By far the most important of all the Palaeolithic caves of Wales is Pontnewydd Cave, which lies hidden amongst the trees at the foot of a limestone cliff, some 50 metres above the northern banks of the river Elwy and about nine kilometres from its confluence with the river Clwyd, near St Asaph (Llanelwy). As emphasized by Stephen Green and Elizabeth Walker, joint authors of *Ice Age Hunters: Neanderthals and Early Modern Hunters in Wales* (1991), Pontnewydd Cave, a site not open to the public and used as an ammunition store during the Second World War, is of international importance: 'It is the most north-westerly earlier Palaeolithic site in

The entrance to Pontnewydd Cave

Ffynnon Beuno and Cae Gwyn Caves, Tremeirchion

Europe and it has produced the oldest human teeth ever found in Britain. Indeed, it is one of only two sites to have produced early human remains in Britain.'

The cave's contents were first examined by geologists during the 1870s and 1880s but the most important excavations were undertaken by archaeologists from the National Museum of Wales between 1978 and 1995. In the depths of the cavern 19 teeth came to light, together with part of a child's upper jaw; the remains of at least five individuals, two of them children, who spent time in the cave about 230,000 years ago. However, the human occupation of the site is seen as perhaps no more than brief and seasonal. The Neanderthal inhabitants of Pontnewydd – the earliest people of Wales – were part of one branch of the human evolutionary tree that is thought to have died out some 36,000 years ago. Modern humans (*Homo sapiens*) shared a common ancestor with Neanderthal people but did not evolve from them.

In addition to human bones, those of wild animals such as bear, rhinoceros, wolf, leopard and bison, together with stone tools, were also recovered. Such evidence suggests that the people who periodically sheltered in the cave were Lower Palaeolithic hunter-gatherers, that sought their prey in the Elwy and Clwyd valleys during one of the interglacial periods that characterized the Great Ice Age, which dawned about 2.6 million years ago and has yet to come to a close. The stone tools included hand axes, scrapers and sharp flakes fashioned mainly from hard igneous rocks and flints, glacial erratics that were transported into the area by glaciers whose source lay in the mountains of Snowdonia, or possibly the Lake District, during a glacial period predating 230,000 years ago.

Near the village of Tremeirchion, on the eastern side of the Vale of Clwyd and about seven kilometres east of Pontnewydd Cave, are the Ffynnon Beuno and Cae Gwyn caves, which contained human tools attributable, in all probability, to the Early Upper Palaeolithic period, some 30,000–35,000 years ago. The contents of the two caves were examined during the 1880s by a team of excavators under the direction of Dr Henry Hicks, a Welsh-speaking doctor and highly-gifted amateur geologist who hailed from St Davids (Tyddewi). In a layer of sediment on the floor of both caves were the bones of woolly rhinoceros, woolly mammoth, ox and hyena,

intermingled with flint tools. Outside the two caves, the same layer was covered by glacial deposits – sand, gravel and clay containing fragments of marine shells – deposited by an ice sheet flowing south from the Lake District and north-west Scotland.

Thanks to Hicks, some of the animal bones discovered during his team's research work were placed in the hands of various colleges and museums, including Manchester Museum who, in 1971, arranged for the carbon dating of one mammoth bone. On the basis of the date, it is known that the mammoth was wandering the Vale of Clwyd, in the company of other animals, during the increasingly cold climate that characterized the valley some 21,500 years ago. About 1,500 years later, at the peak of the Last Glaciation, the entire area was overrun by the ice sheet that deposited the glacial deposits sealing the mixed layer of animal bones and flint tools outside Ffynnon Beuno and Cae Gwyn caves. The flint tools predate the mammoth bone, indicating that the people that fashioned them departed the valley well before the onset of the glaciation.

Given the archaeological and geological importance of the two caves, it's a pity that neither Bangor University nor St Beuno's College, Tremeirchion, retained the collection of bones that they too received from Henry Hicks.

St Beuno's College, Tremeirchion

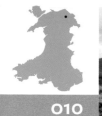

The Clwydian Hills and Vale of Clwyd

(Bryniau Clwyd a Dyffryn Clwyd) SJ 152655

Despite the unquestionable beauty of all five Areas of Outstanding Natural Beauty (AONB) in Wales – Anglesey (Ynys Môn), Llŷn Peninsula (Llŷn), Clwydian Range and Dee Valley (Bryniau Clwyd a Dyffryn Dyfrdwy), Wye Valley (Dyffryn Gwy) and Gower (Gŵyr) – not one can ascribe its natural beauty solely to the action of natural processes. Two of the most conspicuous features of the Clwydian Range and Dee Valley AONB, designated in 1985 and enlarged in 2011 to include that part of the Dee valley between Corwen and Chirk (Y Waun), are their heather moors and hill forts, both of which are attributable to man's activities.

The splendour of today's vista from the summit of Moel Llys-y-coed (c.465 m) is very different to that of 10,000 years ago. At that time, most of the Clwydian hills, including Moel Fama(u) (554 m), would have been clothed with trees. The pollen record obtained from a peatbog on the summit of Moel Llys-y-coed reveals that the heather moor began to spread between 10,000 and 6,000 years ago, when Mesolithic and Neolithic peoples first set about clearing the native woodlands, a task which continued apace during the succeeding Iron Age and Middle Ages. Woodland was replaced by heather moor, together with grassland, bracken and heather

Moel Arthur and Penycloddiau

Moel Fama(u)

(*Calluna vulgaris*), whose purple flowers carpet and enliven the hills in late summer. Growing amongst the heather are spreads of bilberry (*Vaccinium myrtillus*), small deciduous bushes noted for their tasty, blue-black berries ready to devour midsummer, and western gorse (*Ulex gallii*), whose bright yellow flowers add a splash of colour in late summer–early autumn. Ironically, however, afforestation and agricultural land 'improvement' schemes have been responsible for the loss of some 40 per cent of the semi-natural heather moorland since the Second World War.

Besides the heather moorland, Iron Age hill forts are a conspicuous feature of the hills. Moel Arthur (456 m), a steep-sided, conical hill immediately north of Moel Llys-y-coed, is crowned by a small, roughly circular fort defended by two strong banks and ditches on its weaker northern side but by a single rampart where the hill-slopes are steepest. To reach Penycloddiau (440 m), the finest of the Clwydian hill forts, involves a short (2.5 km) but energetic walk northwards from Moel Arthur along a section of Offa's Dyke Path. The stronghold commands vast prospects over the Dee and Wirral (Cilgwri) in the east and over the Vale of Clwyd and Snowdonia (Eryri) in the west. But it's the size of the 21-hectare hill

fort, one of the largest in Wales, which astonishes visitors. Its defences, consisting largely of a single, grass-covered rampart set between an inner and outer ditch, are over two kilometres in length. With the exception of the partially excavated fort atop Moel Hiraddug, not one of the remaining five Clwydian hill forts have been the subject of thorough archaeological examination, but it has been suggested that each one was the territorial centre of a domain that extended across the vale and beyond, so that the occupants of each fort would have similar natural resources at its disposal.

South of Moel Llys-y-coed, Moel Fama(u), the highest hill of the Clwydian range, was never a hill fort but its summit is crowned by the area's 'most iconic silhouette', the ruin of the Jubilee Tower, built in 1810–12 to celebrate the jubilee of King George III's accession to the throne. The original, 26-metre-high structure was the first Egyptian-style monument to be constructed in Britain but, providentially, the obelisk that stood on the massive, square podium was blown down during a gale in 1862. Partially restored in 2013, the monument's one redeeming feature is its podium, which offers a superb vista of the Vale of Clwyd.

Aptly described by the eighteenth-century naturalist and antiquarian Thomas Pennant as a 'plain ... of matchless fertility', nowhere is its fertile floor more than about 40 metres above sea level. In the opinion of Welsh-language poet and journalist Gwilym R. Jones (1903–93), who spent the greater part of his life in Denbigh (Dinbych), the vale is 'Britain's Garden of Eden' where 'God's imprint is evident on its Welsh clay floor'. The clay in question is part of a sequence of glacial sediments deposited on top of the vale's Triassic rock floor during the retreat of the ice sheet that overran almost the whole of Wales, 20,000 years ago.

Blocks of red Triassic sandstone, deposited in the form of desert dunes, some 225 million years ago, are evident in the walls of several of the buildings in Ruthin (Rhuthun), including the thirteenth-century castle that overlooks the river Clwyd. In contrast, the Clwydian hills flanking the vale are fashioned from mudstones and sandstones that accumulated on the floor of a deep Silurian sea, about 420 million years ago. The Vale of Clwyd Fault, that marks the boundary between the juxtaposed Triassic and Silurian rocks, is also responsible for the impressive west-facing scarp of the hills.

Dyffryn Clwyd

Bryn Trillyn, Mynydd Hiraethog

SH 947591

Between the Conwy valley (Dyffryn Conwy) and Vale of Clwyd (Dyffryn Clwyd) in north-east Wales lies Mynydd Hiraethog (sometimes known as the Denbigh Moors), an undulating upland plateau, much of it over 400 metres above sea level, which is underlain by Silurian mudstones and sandstones. Cleric and writer Walter Davies (better known as Gwallter Mechain), who prepared agricultural surveys for the Board of Agriculture during the 1810s, described the area as 'one of the most extensive and dreary wastes in the principality'. English author Thomas Roscoe was similarly unimpressed. 'Moors stretching along in almost interminable tracts with scarcely a tree to offer obstruction to the winds of heaven', was how he characterized Hiraethog in his travel book, *Wanderings and Excursions in North Wales* (1836). Much more recently, M. Skuse, in an article entitled 'Hiraethog', published in *Rural Wales* in 2001, inexplicably described the area as 'one of the very last unspoilt wild places in Wales'. It's nothing of the sort. The landscape is a relatively modern creation. The panorama from the summit of Bryn Trillyn (496 m), a hill which rises no more than about 50 metres above the surrounding extensive tract of open access land alongside the A543 between Denbigh (Dinbych) and the A5 at Pentrefoelas, is dominated by vast plantations of alien conifers, Llyn Brenig reservoir and heather moorland, once managed as grouse moor but now abandoned.

Bryn Trillyn, heather moorland, coniferous plantations and Llyn Brenig reservoir

The planting of coniferous trees on many of the heather moors of Hiraethog began in the early years of the nineteenth century, but Hiraethog Forest, which incorporates Clocaenog Forest, is a twentieth-century creation, made up of a mix of Norway spruce, pine and larch. It clothes over 6,000 hectares, including Bronze Age cairns, the remains of summer dwellings (*hafotai*), which had become permanently settled in the post-medieval period, and the lands of former upland farms. But nature conservationists can console themselves by reminding visitors that the alien forest, one of the largest coniferous plantations in Wales, is a stronghold of the endangered red squirrel.

Within a radius of three kilometres of Bryn Trillyn ('the hill of three lakes'), Llyn Aled, Llyn Brân (both transformed into reservoirs) and Llyn y Foel-frech fill depressions excavated into the country rock by an ice sheet that flowed north-eastwards across the upland during the Last Glaciation. All three, however, are small when compared to the two twentieth-century reservoirs, namely Alwen (completed in 1921) and Brenig (completed in 1976), one of the largest inland lakes in Wales. Since all the reservoirs are now popular centres of open-air activities, they are in the minds of many acceptable intrusive landscape features. Far more contentious and controversial is the introduction of wind turbines across Mynydd Hiraethog. Tir Mostyn and Foel Goch wind farms, near the eastern shores of Llyn Brenig, have been operational since 2015 and other schemes are under consideration.

Compared to the indelible imprint of forestry plantations,

Ruins of Gwylfa Hiraethog

reservoirs and wind turbines, the visual impact of the shooting lodge, known as Gwylfa Hiraethog ('the watch-tower of Hiraethog'), which once stood on the summit of Bryn Trillyn was minimal. Nevertheless, that amazing two-storey, Jacobean building in sight of the nearby main road was, for many years, the most remarkable landmark of Hiraethog's bleak and windswept moors. It was the creation of Merseyside millionaire Hudson Ewbanke Kearley, a successful businessman who held several influential parliamentary posts following his election as Member of Parliament for Devonport in 1892. Built in 1908, two years before Kearley was elevated to the peerage as Baron Devonport in July 1910, the luxurious thirteen-bedroom mansion, which apparently replaced an earlier wooden chalet imported from Norway and known as Plas Pren ('the wooden mansion'), claimed to be the highest inhabited house in Wales and boasted the most extensive views of any house in Britain! It was a property that allowed Kearley to indulge in his favourite pastime of shooting grouse and entertaining distinguished guests, including Lloyd George.

For many years after Kearley sold his country retreat and estate in 1925, the lodge became the home of the estate gamekeepers until it was finally abandoned in the 1960s and left to decay. The dilapidated building, whose walls had been constructed of cement-rendered local stone with dressed stonework of Gwesbyr sandstone around window and door frames, is now an eyesore barely visible from the nearby A543.

Less apparent than the ruins of Gwylfa Hiraethog are the lines of shooting butts amongst the unmanaged heather- and bilberry-clad slopes of Bryn Trillyn. There, on the 'Glorious Twelfth [of August]' – the start of the shooting season – and on subsequent days, privileged guests would gather in anticipation of bagging as many red grouse as possible that nested amid the heather. Now that Gwylfa Hiraethog is no more, the only lasting symbol of the old shooting estates, once a characteristic feature of Hiraethog's landscape, are the tracts of semi-natural heather moorland, formerly carefully managed for the enjoyment of Hudson Ewbanke Kearley and his ilk.

Dressed blocks of Gwesbyr sandstone

41

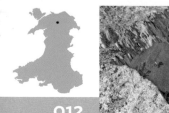

Ffos Anoddun, Betws-y-coed

SH 801542

Following the completion of the A5, the mail coach London–Holyhead road created early in the nineteenth century, many of the early tourists who flocked to Betws-y-coed at the confluence of the rivers Conwy and Llugwy were in search of the picturesque, of landscapes characterized by rugged wildness. By mid-century the village was already home to a substantial group of painters and by the 1880s artistic visitors galore were on the lookout for natural wonders and locations where they could identify with Nature itself. It was an area replete with scenic delights, spectacles to satisfy the most curious and venturesome of visitors.

A pothole in the Conwy's bedrock channel

One of the most well-known attractions on the Llugwy was Swallow Falls, the literal English translation of Rhaeadr y Wennol, which is itself an incorrect rendition of Rhaeadr Ewynnol ('foaming falls'), an apt description of what is in reality a succession of small falls and rapids. If that failed to please, the rapids and the waterfall on the rivers Lledr and Machno, respectively – both tributaries of the Conwy – were notable lures south of Betws. So too were Rhaeadr y Graig Lwyd ('waterfall of the grey rock', now known as Rhaeadr Conwy, a literal English translation of Conwy Falls) and Ffos Anoddun, 'the deep defile' a short distance downstream of the waterfall, which greatly impressed George Borrow.

To appreciate the secluded, picturesque gorge through which, to quote Borrow, the Conwy flows noisily 'amongst broken rocks, which chafe it into foam' when in flood, a descent to river bank via a slippery, stone staircase, largely carved from slate, is essential. However, the visitor will not discover the whereabouts of the defile under the shade of beech and oak trees by following signs labelled 'Ffos Anoddun'. From Pont yr Afanc, the early nineteenth-century single span bridge that carries the A470 across the Conwy, every sign directs walkers to 'Fairy Glen', an inappropriate touristy designation coined in the nineteenth century, in all probability, in the belief that it would attract English-speaking visitors to the supposed mysterious otherness of 'Wild Wales'.

Although Ffos Anoddun and all the famed waterfalls in the neighbourhood of Betws-y-coed are currently part of the Conwy's catchment area, that was not the case in the dim and distant past. The rivers Llugwy, Lledr and Machno, including the upland course of the Conwy south-west of Pentrefoelas, were once part of the upper reaches of the Dee (Dyfrdwy), a river that flowed through the wide, dry valley between Pentrefoelas and Cerrigydrudion, and on towards Llangollen and the Welsh border, following what is now the path of the A5. In the meantime, that section of the Conwy between Trefriw

and the sea was busily extending its course southwards along the line of a major fault, a line of weakness traceable from Conwy town in the north to beyond Pont yr Afanc in the south. In time, the river captured the Llugwy, Lledr, Machno and what is now the uppermost course of the Conwy, depriving the Dee of its headwaters.

A notable feature of the four diverted rivers are the smooth, circular potholes that characterize their rocky beds and striking examples, both large and small, are to be seen by walking the footpath that follows the banks of the Conwy between Ffos Anoddun and its confluence with the Lledr. Such potholes, which often contain pebbles, are formed by the abrasive action of pebbles and cobbles that have been spun rapidly by eddies, particularly when the river is in flood. Although it's possible that some of the potholes have been formed by the erosive action of the Conwy, the large cauldron-like pothole at Pont yr Afanc, a landform unlike no other elsewhere in Wales, suggests that many of them are glacial rather than fluvial features.

The impressive cauldron came to light following improvements to the A470 between Pont yr Afanc and Betws-y-coed in the early 2000s. It's situated near the foot of the steep, east-facing slopes of the Conwy valley and at a height well beyond the reach of the river. It appears that it was formed by a torrent of meltwater, armed with pebbles, cobbles and boulders, which rushed headlong downslope at a time when the ice sheet that had covered the entire area at the peak of the Last Glaciation, 20,000 years ago, was beginning to melt and thin. In all probability, rivers of sub-glacial meltwater were also responsible for carving at least some of the potholes in bedrock river channels in the vicinity of Betws-y-coed and elsewhere in upland Wales.

In Norway glacial potholes are called *jettegryte*, 'giants' cauldrons', namely '*crochanau'r cewri*' in Welsh, a termed coined by the Reverend D. Lloyd Jones of Llandinam, author of 'Crochanau'r Cewri', an article published in the Welsh-language journal *Cymru* in 1903, which includes a description of such features and other glacially-sculptured landforms. Jones, son of John Jones, Tal-y-sarn, one of Wales' most powerful preachers, was a gifted amateur geologist who penned many excellent geological articles before his untimely death in 1905, aged 62.

The glacial pothole alongside the A470 near Pont yr Afanc

The Lakes of Cowlyd, Geirionydd and Crafnant

013

(Llynnoedd Cowlyd, Geirionydd a Chrafnant) SH 738633

The high cliffs and rocky nature of the western slopes of the Conwy valley (Dyffryn Conwy) clearly indicate that most of the rocks from which they have been carved are very different in character to those underlying the gentler and greener eastern valley side. East of the Dyffryn Conwy Fault, a major tear traceable through the middle of the valley, the upland is fashioned from Silurian mudstones and sandstones, strata that are nowhere near as hard and resistant to erosion as the Ordovician volcanic rocks (lavas and ashes) and slates of the rugged hill-country and mountains to the west of the fault. Because of the area's ruggedness, roads are few and drivers of a nervous disposition should think twice before venturing to follow the initial steep, narrow and tortuous lane that heads from Trefriw and on to Cwm Brwynog, 'the marshy valley', and Llyn Cowlyd.

Beyond the ridge of Cefn Cyfarwydd (503 m), the road descends into Cwm Brwynog, once known as Cwm Cawlwyd (Cowlyd), the habitat of the wise 'Owl of Cwm Cawlwyd' who was quizzed by Arthur's messengers as to the whereabouts of Mabon son of Modron. The incident is recorded in the early twelfth-century prose tale recorded in the Mabinogion (*The Mabinogion* [2007], translation by Sioned Davies), and in its response the omniscient owl offers the following brief account of the valley's wooded history: 'When I first came here the large valley was a wooded glen, and a race of men came there, and it was destroyed. And the second wood grew in it, and this wood is the third.' But today the valley is treeless, marshy and deserted, and farms such as Brwynog Uchaf, situated at the terminus of the road, were abandoned and fell into ruins in the early years of the twentieth century.

Llyn Cowlyd

Cwm Brwynog

remarkable attribute is its anomalous location, for it fills an elongated rock basin that lies athwart the watershed between Nant y Benglog (the upper Llugwy valley between Llyn Ogwen and Capel Curig) and Dyffryn Conwy. The upper end of the lake stands about 110 metres above the floor of Nant y Benglog, whilst its lower end is some 500 metres above the rock floor of Dyffryn Conwy near Dolgarrog, which itself is at least 130 metres below sea level! That part of the watershed between Penllithrig-y-wrach and Creigiau Gleision was breached by a powerful flow of ice, as the upper layers of the Nant y Benglog glacier escaped eastwards and joined the Dyffryn Conwy glacier, at the peak of the Last Glaciation, 20,000 years ago.

Though smaller lakes, both Crafnant (22 metres deep) and Geirionydd (15 metres deep) occupy similar glacial breaches to the east and west of Mynydd Deulyn (400 m) – 'mountain of the two lakes' – south-east of Llyn Cowlyd. Llyn Geirionydd, clearly visible from the tortuous country road high above Trefriw on the return journey from Cwm Brwynog, is particularly attractive. On Bryn y Caniadau, a hillock overlooking the lake, stands a monument purporting to mark the grave of the sixth-century poet Taliesin, whilst the lake shore was the setting for Arwest Glan Geirionydd, a festival established by William John Roberts (1828–1904) in 1863 to

From Brwynog Uchaf a level gravel trackway and public footpath follows the banks of 'the black river' – afon Du – as far as the Llyn Cowlyd dam wall, a reservoir completed in 1921 and set between the craggy slopes of Penllithrig-y-wrach (c.700 m) to the north-west and Creigiau Gleision (634 m) to the south-east. Llyn Cowlyd, at a height of about 365 metres, is not only the longest of the lakes of Snowdonia (Eryri), but also the deepest. Its depth (67.7 m) was measured by Thomas John Jehu, a native of Llanfair Caereinion, who was appointed Professor of Geology and Mineralogy in the University of Edinburgh in 1913, 11 years after publishing his bathymetrical study of Snowdonia's lakes. However, since the rock basin within which the lake waters lie is partially filled with lake sediments, its depth clearly exceeds 68 metres.

In spite of its depth and length (c.2.75 kms), Llyn Cowlyd's most

46

Dam wall of Llyn Cowlyd and glacial breach

rival the official National Eisteddfod, whose increasing use of English he resented. Better known by his bardic name, Gwilym Cowlyd, Roberts was a native of Trefriw and his all-Welsh Arwest was held annually over a period of 40 years.

Although 'a little paradise' in the opinion of Alun Llywelyn-Williams, author of the travel book *Crwydro Arfon* [Wandering through Arfon] (1959), Llyn Geirionydd is not a favourite haunt of fishermen. Whilst Llyn Cowlyd contains brown trout and Arctic char, and Llyn Crafnant is renowned for its stock of brown and rainbow trout, there are few, if any, fish in Llyn Geirionydd. Their absence is attributed to the lake's polluted waters, poisoned by metal-mine effluent. Waste tips of the Pandora mine, which closed *c*.1912, form the foundation of the car park and picnic site at the head of the lake.

Llyn Geirionydd and Bryn y Caniadau

014

Penrhyn Slate Quarry, Bethesda

(Chwarel y Penrhyn, Bethesda) SH 622650

The Reverend W.S. Symonds, author of *Records of the Rocks* (1872), written specifically for amateur geologists who, like himself, enjoyed their leisure hours amongst rocks, was in no doubt whatsoever that the 'celebrated slate quarries of Penrhyn are among the wonders of North Wales'. Unsurprisingly, perhaps, quarry manager John J. Evans would have agreed wholeheartedly with Symonds' assertion, for in his Welsh-language paper entitled 'Daeareg Ardal Bethesda' [The Geology of the area around Bethesda], published in 1884, he claimed that the slates produced under his supervision were, in all probability, the product of the finest vein of slate in the world! Furthermore, the quarry which Richard Pennant, later Baron Penrhyn, developed in the 1780s could, by the end of the nineteenth century, claim to be the world's largest slate quarry, an astonishing chasm about 1.6 kilometres long and 370 metres deep.

The arduous and dangerous task of winning the slate was undertaken on step-like galleries, over 20 in all and each about 18 to 21 metres above the one below. Introduced in 1799 the gallery system, served by a complex network of tramways, enabled large numbers of quarrymen to work on the same slate vein at different heights, whilst some of the gallery names, such as Crimea (1854–6) and Sebastopol (1854–5), relate to the time when they were first opened. Throughout the nineteenth century, Penrhyn was one of the most productive slate quarries in the world and during the 1860s and 1870s its workforce of over 3,000 men – almost all Welsh speaking, which prompted historian A.H. Dodd to describe slate quarrying as 'the most Welsh of Welsh industries' – were annually producing over 100,000 tonnes of mainly roofing slates of unsurpassed quality.

One of Pennant's main achievements was the construction of a tramway, affectionately known as *y lein fach*, 'the little line', that linked the quarry to Porth Penrhyn, the harbour on the shores of the Menai Strait (Afon Menai). Although completed in 1801, the use of horses to pull loaded wagons proved ineffectual and inefficient. Between 1874 and 1876 a railway was built and because its track-bed was less steep than the tramway, steam engines were capable of pulling tens of heavily loaded wagons to the harbour and the empties back to the quarry, 168 metres above sea level. The roofing slates were mainly destined for the towns and cities of England, such as Liverpool, Birmingham, Bristol and London but large quantities were also despatched to Scotland and Ireland and aslo exported worldwide to places such as Hamburg, Trieste, Boston and New Orleans.

Penrhyn Quarry is located at the north-eastern end of the Cambrian slate belt which extends some 20 kilometres between Pen-y-groes, south of Caernarfon, to Bethesda. The slate is part of the so-called Llanberis Slate Formation, rocks which originally accumulated as layers of mud, together with occasional layers of coarse sand on the floor of a sea between 540 and 520 million years ago. In time the mud was transformed into mudstones and the sand into sandstones, but 100 million years elapsed before the

Braichmelyn, on the outskirts of Bethesda, and the Penrhyn Quarry

mudstones were converted into slate. The transformation was the product of a collision between two continents that once lay on opposite shores of the ancient Iapetus Ocean in which the deposits of Cambrian age had accumulated. Within the jaws of that tectonic vice the mudstones were folded and squeezed to such a extent that the resultant slate could be readily split into thin sheets along parallel cleavage planes that were often at right angles to the original layers of mudstone.

In the quarry there are three main workable and commercially important veins of slate, separated by two relatively thin layers of coarse sandstone. Most of the slates are reddish-purple in colour but some are blue and others are green. Although few and far between, the green slates in particular do contain specimens of fossil trilobites, crustaceans that flourished and scuttled about on the floor of the Cambrian seas. They were first discovered by two of the quarrymen in 1887.

With the exception of Alexandra Quarry on the flanks of Moel Tryfan, north of Dyffryn Nantlle, which is involved in processing slate waste, Penrhyn is now the only remaining working quarry along the Cambrian slate belt; its nearest neighbour, the huge Dinorwig Quarry, whose workshops form the core of the National Slate Museum (Amgueddfa Lechi Cymru) near Llanberis, finally closed in 1969. However, Welsh Slate Ltd, the current owners of Penrhyn Quarry, still produce an impressive range of products for external use, such as roofing slates, slate paving and cladding, and internal purposes, such as slate tiles, hearths and worktops. Quarrying also produced a prodigious quantity of slate waste. Penrhyn's tips, in addition to the water-filled chasm that Zip World's adventurous visitors can hurtle across at a speed of 100 miles an hour, are part of the legacy of an industry that has left an indelible imprint on the landscape of north-west Wales.

Zip World's new headquarters, which include a restaurant, viewing area and shop, opened in 2017 © Zip World

Nant Ffrancon

SH 637630

015

'I do assure the traveller, who delights in wild nature, that a visit ... up Nant Frankon [*sic*], from Bangor, will not be repented': so said naturalist Thomas Pennant and author of *Tours in Wales* (1778 and 1781). Poised above the head of the valley is Llyn Ogwen whose waters cascade, not over Ogwen Falls – an oft-heard misnomer – but down Rhaeadr y Benglog, a waterfall under the shadow of Pen y Benglog, a befitting description of ice-scoured rocks reminiscent of a *penglog*, the rounded shell of the human skull. Beyond the cascade, Pennant was struck by the near flat valley bottom 'surrounded with mountains of a stupendous height ... the tops of many edged with pointed rocks'.

Nant Ffrancon – also known as Dyffryn Ogwen – is one of the most impressive glacial troughs of Snowdonia (Eryri) and is unequalled elsewhere in Wales. Through it runs the A5, the mail coach road created to improve communications with Ireland, via Holyhead (Caergybi). Designed by the brilliant Scottish civil engineer Thomas Telford (1757–1834), nowhere does its gradient exceed 1 in 22, a modest declivity compared with 1 in 6 along parts of a track established in 1791 to provide a link between the Penrhyn slate quarry, at Bethesda, and the estates of quarry owner Richard Pennant, later Baron Penrhyn, at Capel Curig. That trackway, reckoned by Thomas Pennant to be 'the most dreadful horse-path in Wales', followed the foot of the valley's western slopes as far as the steep climb between Blaen-y-nant (*c*.220 m), at the head of Nant Ffrancon, and the shores of Llyn Ogwen (*c*.310 m). Telford, on the other hand, chose to locate his road, created early in the nineteenth century, across the steep, eastern valley-side slopes, a decision that posed problems not only during construction work, but ever since its completion.

Naturalist Edward Llwyd (or Lhuyd) was well aware of the inherent instability of the valley's steep-sided slopes. In a letter sent to botanist John Ray in February 1691, Llwyd recorded that residents of Nant Ffrancon 'find it necessary to rid their grounds often of the stones which the mountain floods bring down', recalling an instance in 1685 when

> part of a rock of one of the impendent cliffs ... became so undermined [by rain and subsurface water] that, losing its hold, it fell down in several pieces, and, in its passage down a steep and craggy cliff, dislodged thousands of other stones.

To this day, rockfalls and landslides do occur every now and again.

The upper reaches of Nant Ffrancon

Cwm-coch cirque and the pointed summit of Foel Goch (831 m)

Appearance-wise, the western valley-side slopes are in marked contrast to those on the eastern side. Between the summit of Y Garn (947 m), overlooking the upper reaches of Nant Ffrancon, and Carnedd y Filiast (c.820 m), south of the Penrhyn slate quarry, are six rocky amphitheatres (cirques), each sculpted by a glacier that fed the Nant Ffrancon glacier, when the Last Glaciation was at its peak 20,000 years ago. The presence of such glacial landforms solely on the uppermost western valley-side slopes is striking. The pattern is attributable to the fact that the snow, which subsequently gave rise to the glaciers, accumulated in cold, north-east-facing hollows beyond the reach of the sun's warm rays. Although all of Snowdonia's glaciers had disappeared by 15,000 years ago, small glaciers reformed in the six shady cirques during a brief, intensely cold period between 13,000 and 11,500 years ago.

For much of the 15,000 years that have elapsed since the peak of the Last Glaciation, a three-kilometre-long lake filled two, deep, rock basins gouged in the floor of Dyffryn Ogwen by the erosive power of the Nant Ffrancon glacier. Both basins have long since been infilled with gravel, clay and mud swept from the surrounding slopes, deposits which record the climatic and environmental changes that have occurred over the past 15,000 years.

The initial deposition of inorganic gravel and clay on the lake floor during the retreat of the Nant Ffrancon glacier was followed by a period of mud accumulation, an organic deposit containing the pollen of trees, such as dwarf birch (Betula nana), indicative of an ameliorating climate that came to an abrupt end 13,000 years ago. For a period of 1,500 years, when the mountains of Britain were once more in the icy grip of a short-lived glacial episode, the deposition of inorganic lake clays in place of organic mud signalled the temporary disappearance of trees. Tree pollen reappears in layers of organic mud deposited some 11,500 years ago, a change that heralded the increasing warmth of the post-glacial period. Trees recolonized the bare hillsides. Dwarf birch was first to reappear, followed by willow and pine, and finally oak and elm, subsequently cleared by man. Reed-swamp developed around the shrinking lake margins; shallow, open water gave way to peatbogs, drained by farmers over the centuries to create the rushy pastures through which the river Ogwen now meanders.

016

Cwm Idwal

SH 645595

Cwm Idwal occupies a special place in the annals of nature conservation in Wales. In 1954 it was designated a National Nature Reserve, the first in the country on account of its rich botanical and geological heritage that has been the subject of pioneering studies by famous naturalists, such as Edward Llwyd (or Lhuyd; 1660–1709) and Thomas Pennant (1726–98), and notable geologists, such as William Buckland (1784–1856), Adam Sedgwick (1785–1873) and his student, Charles Darwin (1809–82).

Ever since the days of the early pioneers, Clogwyn y Geifr, extending either side of the Devil's Kitchen (Twll Du; 'the black chasm'), described by Pennant as that 'horrible gap, in the centre of a great black precipice', has been a favoured location for those naturalists in search of botanical treasures. The cliffs and scree slopes at their base are the habitat of arctic-alpine plants; some flourishing on sheltered rock ledges and others hidden within the scree. Hereabouts and on other high, lime-rich ledges in Snowdonia,

Llyn Idwal and the summit of Pen yr Ole Wen (978 m). The lake is narrowest where a hummocky moraine extends across the floor of Cwm Idwal.

Llwyd discovered the Snowdon lily (later called *Lloydia* [now *Gagea*] *serotina* in his honour), a plant found nowhere else in Britain. The damp, calcareous ledges of Cwm Idwal are also one of the few places where mountain avens (*Dryas octopetala*) thrives at the southern edge of its British territory. The plant, which has given its name to the Younger Dryas, the cold period between 13,000 and 11,500 years ago that marked the end of the Last Glaciation, has small leaves similar to those of the oak and eight-petalled, white flowers surrounding a cluster of yellow anthers.

Most of Cwm Idwal's rocks are the product of violent, submarine volcanic eruptions that characterized the Ordovician period, about 450 million years ago. Amongst the rocks are thick flows of volcanic ash (ash-flow tuffs), in addition to lava flows, some of which are the

basis of patches of thin, calcareous soils and their associated rich arctic-alpine and mountain flora, and others that have resulted in the formation of acidic soils, less species rich. Less common than the volcanic rocks are bedded, sedimentary sandstones and siltstones containing fossils of creatures that lived in the sea, within which accumulated the products of underwater eruptions and those that occurred on short-lived volcanic islands.

About 50 million years after the cessation of Ordovician volcanic activity, the entire rock succession was folded and crumpled during a period of powerful earth movements that gave rise to a multitude of large and small folds, including the Snowdon syncline, a downfold whose downward sloping limbs are clearly evident either side of Pennant's 'horrible gap'. Near the head of Llyn Idwal, the Idwal Slabs

Llyn Idwal, Idwal Slabs and Snowdon syncline (left)

(Rhiwiau Caws), thick layers of ash-flow tuffs on which generations of apprentice rock climbers have honed their skills, are part of the syncline's south-eastern limb.

It was in Cwm Idwal that Charles Darwin served part of his geological apprenticeship under the guidance of his mentor, Adam Sedgwick, one of the founders of modern geology who was appointed Professor of Geology at the University of Cambridge in 1818. Their two-day stay in August 1831 was mainly spent searching for fossils. No mention was made of Cwm Idwal's magnificent glacial landforms for the simple reason that geologists in Britain knew nothing about the 'glacial hypothesis' until Louis Agassiz, a glaciologist and native of Switzerland, travelled to Britain in September 1840 with the intention of finding convincing evidence of past glacial activity, which he did following his visit to England, Scotland and Ireland, but not Wales.

In the meantime, however, William Buckland, who was appointed Reader of Geology at Oxford University in 1819, had been utterly convinced of the validity of the 'glacial hypothesis' following a visit to Switzerland and his friend Agassiz in 1838. Indeed, shortly after Agassiz departed Britain in December 1840, Buckland discovered incontrovertible evidence of glacial activity near Pont Aberglaslyn, between Beddgelert and Porthmadog. He recorded his revolutionary discovery in the Visitor's Book (now sadly lost) of the Goat Hotel, Beddgelert, on 16 October 1841. Two months later, he presented a paper entitled 'On the Glacia-Diluvial Phænomena in Snowdonia ...' before members of the Geological Society of London, including Darwin, describing the many glacial features and landforms that he had found in the valleys of Snowdonia and in the vicinity of Cwm Idwal.

Following the reading of Buckland's paper, Darwin revisited Cwm Idwal's grand glacial amphitheatre. There, by his own admission, 'Guided and taught by the abstract of Dr. Buckland's memoir', he too was now able to see the clear signs of past glacial activity. In his article, 'Notes on the Effects produced by the Ancient Glaciers of Caernarvonshire ...' (1842), he drew particular attention to the moraines at the upper and lower end of Llyn Idwal and to the ice-smoothed and scratched rocks around the lake's periphery. His valuable contribution to the glacial history of Cwm Idwal is remembered and applauded. Not so Buckland's pioneering study. That is largely overlooked and forgotten.

The panel of rock specimens outside the Ogwen Centre reads, 'Darwin's geological steps through Snowdonia – 1831'

Camau daearegol Darwin trwy Eryri - 1831

Snowdon and Cwm Dyli

017

(Yr Wyddfa a Chwm Dyli) SH 610544

In 1831, 65 years before the first train reached the summit of Snowdon (1,085 m), the highest mountain of Wales was already one of its top tourist attractions. English cleric and prolific amateur artist John Parker (1798–1860), who was well acquainted with the peak, confidently asserted that there was nowhere more public than the highest land of Snowdonia (Eryri) in summer. Be that as it may, the crowds during his lifetime were small compared to the 12,000 that opted to journey by rail, rather than walk, during the train's first full season in 1897. By today that figure has increased to about 120,000, not to mention the 500,000 or more walkers that annually head for the summit by following one of the five most popular paths and all doubtless harbouring the hope that they would not, at journey's end, be confronted by that which greeted Thomas Pennant (1726–98), namely 'A vast mist [that] enveloped the whole circuit of the mountain'.

On those infrequent days when the sky is blue and cloudless, the panorama is without equal. In contrast, the untidiness that characterizes the summit, the hub of severely eroded footpaths destined to suffer further degradation as a consequence of yet greater visitor numbers and stormier wetter winters of a perilously warmer world, is testimony to the sad fact that the wonders of this iconic National Nature Reserve, are a victim of its ever-increasing popularity. Many claim that Snowdon, the supposed resting place of the giant, Rhita Gawr, is at its most elegant and awesome-best when viewed from the vicinity of Cwm Dyli but the most dramatic prospect is that from Bwlch Glas, the meeting place of four paths situated between the summit and Carnedd Ugain (1,065 m). There, below the lip of the precipice, lies the craggy amphitheatre (cirque) of Glaslyn and Llyn Llydaw flanked to the north by the serrated arête of Crib y Ddysgl and Crib Goch (923 m), and the formidable cliffs of Y Lliwedd (898 m) to the south. The walk along the narrow, stony path from one end of the so-called Snowdon Horseshoe to the other is an experience only bettered perhaps on the Cuillin Ridge Traverse on Skye.

The Horseshoe and the entire Snowdonian massif is carved primarily from volcanic rocks and one of the outstanding achievements of Andrew Crombie Ramsay (1814–91), who was appointed Director-General of the Geological Survey in 1871, was to

Snowdon summit and the north-facing cliffs of Y Lliwedd

The cirque lakes of Glaslyn and Llyn Llydaw

unravel the broad details of its complex history. Most of the rocks – mainly thick layers of consolidated volcanic ash (ash-flow tuffs) and thinner lava flows – are the product of explosive eruptions that occurred on both volcanic islands and the sea floor about 450 million years ago. Some of the pale-coloured and well-bedded tuffs exposed on Snowdon's summit actually contain fossil sea shells, proof that the sea in which they lived was not only shallow, but also subject occasionally to an influx of ash from nearby terrestrial or submarine volcanoes that killed and buried the sea-floor creatures from time to time.

Ramsay's interest was not restricted to the nature and history of Snowdonia's hard rocks. On 20 July 1852 he married Louisa, daughter of the Reverend James Williams, rector of Llanfair-yng-Nghornwy (and great-grandfather of Kyffin Williams, widely regarded as Wales' defining twentieth-century artist), and his wife Frances. They spent their honeymoon in Switzerland, where the bridegroom fell in love with the Alpine glaciers and their associated landforms. His new-found love affair resulted in the publication of a small but classic account of *The Old Glaciers of Switzerland and North Wales* (1860). In it he insisted that 'Of all the valleys that lie in the heart of Snowdon, the largest and most magnificent is that of Llyn Llydaw ... [where] [t]he signs of a glacier are so evident ... that it is needless to describe all the details'. The most striking glacial landform is the serrated rim of the compound cirque on whose floor are the two deep rock-basin lakes of Glaslyn (39 metres) and Llyn Llydaw (58 metres). Beyond Llyn Llydaw, on the floor of Cwm Dyli, other glacial landforms abound, including bare rock surfaces smoothed and

scratched by the passage of the cirque glacier, and mounds of glacial debris.

Despite the magnificence of 'the most beautiful scene in North Wales', Ramsay was highly critical of environmental changes perpetrated by the owners of the copper mine situated high above Glaslyn's shore and served by the Miners' Track. He condemned the track's 'ugly causeway' across Llyn Llydaw and the brook 'sacrilegiously deepened to lower the [lake level]'. Equally unforgivable was the decision taken by the Snowdonia National Park Authority (Awdurdod Parc Cenedlaethol Eryri) to place slabs of grey granite from Portugal on the roof and floor of Hafod Eryri, the costly and obtrusive centre on Snowdon's summit, rather than local slate from Penrhyn Quarry (Chwarel y Penrhyn) or granite from Trefor.

018

Around Rhyd-ddu

(Ardal Rhyd-ddu) SH 569529

Wales possesses relatively few natural lakes beyond the confines of Snowdonia (Eryri) and of the 250 pools and lakes listed by Geraint Roberts in his book, *The Lakes of Eryri* (1995), most are small. Furthermore, rarely is it possible to see more than two or three together, except by looking westwards from the summit of Snowdon (Yr Wyddfa). Within the compass of that fine, expansive vista, the blue waters of seven lakes come into view, including three – Llyn Cwellyn, Llyn y Gadair and Llyn y Dywarchen – immortalized by poet and essayist T.H. Parry-Williams (1887–1975), Rhyd-ddu's most famous son, who prior to his retirement in 1952 was professor of Welsh at the University College of Wales, Aberystwyth.

Glacial erosion was responsible for not only gouging three of the lake basins, but also for breaching the area's watersheds, thereby disrupting its drainage pattern. The 37-metre-deep rock basin within

which lies Llyn Cwellyn was scooped out by the glacier that flowed north-westwards along Nant y Betws. Similarly, the glacier that sculpted Bwlch y Gylfin, the dramatic breach between the granite cliffs of Craig y Bera (c.620 m) and the volcanic rocks atop the summit of Y Garn (633 m) at the head of Dyffryn Nantlle, also gouged out the basins occupied by Llyn Nantlle Uchaf and Llyn Nantlle Isaf. However, the lower of the two lakes is no more, for it was drained and infilled with waste rock from the nearby Dorothea slate quarry.

Llyn y Dywarchen is also a rock-basin lake, fashioned largely from slaty rocks exposed beneath the shadow of Clogwynygarreg (336 m). The island, however, is a mass of hard igneous rock and its steep, rugged, north-facing slopes, as compared to its smoother and gentler south-facing slopes, indicate that it was moulded and

Llyn y Dywarchen, Bwlch y Gylfin, Llyn Nantlle Uchaf and the abandoned slate quarries of Dyffryn Nantlle

Cwm Clogwyn and Llyn Nadroedd (left) and Llyn Coch (right); Llyn y Gadair (left) and Llyn Cwellyn (right);
Llyn y Dywarchen (centre) and Dyffryn Nantlle beyond the breach of Bwlch y Gylfin

Spoil heaps of Glanyrafon slate quarry

streamlined by a northerly-flowing glacier.

Although the whole of Snowdonia, with the possible exception of some of the highest summits, lay buried beneath an ice sheet 20,000 years ago, the carbon dated organic material, which had accumulated in a small lake that once lay at the foot of the eastern slopes of Clogwynygarreg, indicated that the glaciers were in rapid retreat by 17,000 years ago. As a consequence, large quantities of glacial deposits accumulated on valley floors. The three small lakes – Llyn Nadroedd, Llyn Coch and Llyn Glas – on the floor of Cwm Clogwyn, at the foot of Snowdon, infill hollows amongst such deposits.

Despite its location, the shallow waters of Llyn y Gadair are not part of the catchment area of the river Colwyn that flows southwards to its confluence with the Glaslyn at Beddgelert. On leaving the lake, the river Gwyrfai turns north and crosses the former watershed in the vicinity of Rhyd-ddu, before continuing on its journey via Nant y Betws to the sea at Caernarfon.

Through the same breached watershed runs the A4085 and the Welsh Highland Railway, formerly the North Wales Narrow Gauge Railways [*sic*] that linked Dinas, near Caernarfon, and Rhyd-ddu. Opened in 1881, the railway's main function was to serve the Glanyrafon slate quarry, opposite Rhyd-ddu, and two small quarries on the shores of Llyn y Gadair. But by naming the terminus South Snowdon, rather than Rhyd-ddu, it's evident that the railway's promoters had one eye on the tourist trade. Indeed, in 1875, before the days of the Snowdon Mountain Railway, their sights were set on constructing a rack-and-pinion railway to Snowdon's summit. That overly ambitious dream was not fulfilled and their proposed plan to extend the line as far as Beddgelert, already a popular tourist destination, was also abandoned, as was the passenger-carrying service during the First World War. The financial viability of the railway was dealt a further blow following the closure of Glanyrafon quarry that produced blue-grey Ordovician slates, very different to the red and purple Cambrian slates of Dyffryn Nantlle.

Although the railway closed for a brief period in 1922, it was reopened in the July of that year by the Welsh Highland Railway company, who were responsible for extending the line through Beddgelert to Porthmadog, an undertaking completed in 1923. But the company was in financial difficulties and within the space of four years it was placed in the hands of the receiver. Regrettably, all attempts to solve its financial problems failed. As a result, the railway closed in 1937 and the railway lines themselves were lifted soon after the outbreak of the Second World War.

Since only the track-bed remained, Alun Llywelyn-Williams ventured to state categorically in his travel book, *Crwydro Arfon* [Wandering Arfon] (1959) that 'there's no hope of ever seeing again the little engine puffing its way through Aberglaslyn and Rhyd-ddu'. In hindsight it was a rash assertion. The first section of the Welsh Highland Railway (Rheilffordd Eryri) opened in October 1994. By August 2003 the *trên bach* – 'little engine' – could once more puff from Caernarfon to Rhyd-ddu, and all 40 kilometres to Porthmadog by February 2011.

Clogwyn Du'r Arddu

SH 601557

019

The excessively trodden path that leads to the summit of Yr Wyddfa (Snowdon) by following the track of the Snowdon Mountain Railway on the eastern slopes of Cwm Brwynog, has little to commend it. Although the attractive prospect of Foel Goch (605 m) and Moel Cynghorion (674 m) on the western side of the valley relieves the monotony, the only redeeming feature of the 7.5-kilometre trek is Clogwyn Du'r Arddu as seen from Clogwyn station, perched precariously atop the cliffs of Cwm Hetiau and Cwm Glas Bach. Though by no means the highest cliff in Wales, Clogwyn Du'r Arddu, which rises 300 metres above the shore of Llyn Du'r Arddu has, in the words of Jim Perrin, award-winning author and accomplished rock-climber, 'long since been celebrated by rock-climbers as the finest of British cliffs'. Its awesome sheer rock faces boast over 200 formidable climbs – some of extreme difficulty – that are an irresistible challenge and a compelling lure to those determined to conquer the steepest and most hold-less of walls.

Appropriately, it was the Reverend Peter Bailey Williams, a Welshman and rector of Llanberis, who undertook the first recorded climb of the 'black cliff'. According to William Bingley, an Englishman and a keen botanist eager to collect some of the mountain plants that Edward Llwyd (or Lhuyd) had found growing on the cliffs of Snowdon in the 1680s, it was Williams that 'started the wild idea of attempting to climb up the precipice', when both visited Cwm Du'r Arddu in 1798. 'After an hour from the commencement of our labour', wrote Bingley, 'we found ourselves on the brow of this dreadful precipice, and in possession of all the plants we expected to find.'

Without doubt, the precipice is one of Snowdonia's richest botanical sites and here, in 1639, botanist Thomas Johnson, recognised as the 'father of British field botany', discovered northern rock-cress (*Arabis petraea*), in addition to other arctic-alpine ferns and clubmosses on narrow shelves and in fissures, sheltered from

the sun's rays and beyond the reach of hungry sheep. The small, white flowers of northern rock-cress are inconspicuous compared to some of the other species that add splashes of colour to pockets of the 'black cliff' in spring and summer. More conspicuous are the pink flowers of moss campion (*Silene acaulis*), red-flowering purple saxifrage (*Saxifraga oppositifolia*), the clusters of small yellow flowers crowning the stems of roseroot (*Sedum rosea*), and the six-petalled, veined, white flowers of the Snowdon lily (*Gagea* [formerly *Lloydia*] *serotina*), first recorded by Edward Llwyd.

The rich variety of plants that characterize the cliff is largely attributable to the nature of the rocks. Calcareous conditions favour the growth of flowering plants such as moss campion and purple saxifrage, and ferns such as alpine woodsia (*Woodsia alpina*) and brittle bladder-fern (*Cystopteris fragilis*), but alpine clubmoss (*Diphasiastrum alpinum*) and fir clubmoss (*Huperzia selago*), two of the most common clubmosses, prefer thin, acidic soils.

With the exception of one layer of calcareous sandstone, Clogwyn Du'r Arddu is a thick pile of volcanic rocks, the product of

The ugly scar of the Llanberis Path near Clogwyn station

powerful and, at times, catastrophic submarine eruptions that shook the foundations of this part of 'Wales' during Ordovician times, about 450 million years ago. Dense, turbulent flows of hot volcanic ash gave rise to the oldest rocks that outcrop between the foot of the westernmost end of the cliff and the so-called Western Terrace, whose surface slopes steeply downwards towards the east and the centre of an enormous downfold or syncline. As it weathers, the volcanic ash (rhyolitic tuff) decomposes and forms patches of thin acidic soil. However, the grassy terrace marks the outcrop of a thinner layer of calcareous sandstone containing the fossilized remains of trilobites and shells that lived on the sea floor during intervals of relative quiet between successive violent volcanic eruptions.

Lying above the sandstone is a thick layer of rhyolite, a lava forced (intruded) into the older rocks of the area when it was in a molten state. Rhyolite is the foundation of the sheer cliffs (called the West Buttress by climbers) to the west of the syncline's axis but not to the east. Relative to the western half of Clogwyn Du'r Arddu, the eastern half (known as Clogwyn Coch) has been thrust upwards along a fault and, consequently, the rhyolite is restricted to the uppermost section of the cliff. Being a line of structural weakness, a mass of once molten rock (magma), almost black in appearance and clearly visible in the centre of the syncline, was later forced upwards along the line of the fault.

Whilst the nature and structure of the rocks have influenced the form of Clogwyn Du'r Arddu at the head of Cwm Brwynog, the wide open valley was moulded by a glacier prior to its disappearance, some 15,000 years ago. But the hummocky moraine damming Llyn Du'r Arddu, nestling under the shadow of the precipice, accumulated around the snout a small glacier that reoccupied the site between 13,000 and 11,500 years ago.

The Snowdon lily (© Gerallt Pennant)

Clogwyn Coch (right) and the syncline of Clogwyn Du'r Arddu

020

Moel Tryfan and Alexandra Slate Quarry

(Moel Tryfan a Chwarel Alexandra) SH 515562

Moel Tryfan (427 m), to the south-west of Caernarfon, overlooks Y Fron, Carmel and Rhosgadfan, three of the dispersed villages set amongst a patchwork of small fields typical of the agro-industrial settlements of the slate quarrying districts of northern Gwynedd that developed primarily during the nineteenth century. Between Moel Tryfan, and Nantlle and Tal-y-sarn on the floor of the Llynfi valley, are the remains of the greater part of the Dyffryn Nanlle slate quarrying area graphically described by Alun Llywelyn-Williams in his book *Crwydro Arfon* [Wandering Arfon] (1959) as 'one chaotic accumulation of tips and of dark, deep pools of water – dangerous too – which were once the chasms of quarries that have now closed'. Alexandra Quarry is the highest of those abandoned chasms and from its south-western extremity, below the summit of Moel

Tryfan, walkers are confronted by spectacular views of the coastal plain between Caernarfon and the summit of Yr Eifl, the coastal plateau of Anglesey (Ynys Môn) beyond the Menai Strait (Afon Menai), and the summits of the Nantlle Ridge (Crib Nantlle), between Craig Cwm Silyn (c.670 m) and Y Garn (633 m). But more noteworthy than the splendid vistas are the enigmatic deposits exposed here and there along the rim of the quarry and first described by Joshua Trimmer (1795–1857) in 1831.

Although born in Kent, Trimmer was brought up in Brentford, Middlesex, where his father, Joshua Kirkby Trimmer, a successful businessman, was the owner of a brick and tile works. Indeed, he invested a proportion of his wealth in the copper mines of Snowdonia (Eryri) – possibly those at the head of Dyffryn Nantlle –

Alexandra Slate Quarry: the quarry closed in the 1970s but in recent years Crown Slate Quarries Ltd are involved in the production of crushed slate waste

and in 1823 applied to the Crown for a lease to work quarries in Llanllechid, near Bethesda, a venture supervised by his 30-year-old son. By then, Joshua had developed an interest in geology and had settled for a while in the vicinity of Nantlle, and whilst exploring the summit of Moel Tryfan he chanced upon a thick sequence of stratified sand and gravel containing marine shells resting upon purple and green slate of Cambrian age. Although he did not realize it at the time, his discovery and interpretation of the marine deposits, which was the subject of a paper of his published in 1831, was a bone of contention amongst British geologists over a period of 50 years and more.

In accord with the accepted doctrine of the time, Trimmer attributed the deposits to the effects of the Noachian Flood, as recorded in Genesis: 'And the waters prevailed exceedingly upon the earth; and all the high hills … were covered'. Subsequently, 'the waters returned from off the earth continually' and as a consequence they deposited on the slopes of Moel Tryfan layers of sand and gravel containing the remains of over forty different species of sea shells.

However, in the opinion of the majority of geologists during the first half of the nineteenth century, the Noachian Flood was a fictional rather than a factual event. According to leading geologists of the period, such as Andrew Crombie Ramsay who was appointed Director of the Geological Survey of Wales, England and Scotland in 1845, the waters of the Flood did not cover the land, rather did the whole of Britain and western Europe sink beneath the waves. Ramsay maintained that, during the interval that witnessed the deposition of the shelly deposits of Moel Tryfan, only the highest

Yr Eifl, as seen from the Alexandra Slate Quarry

Marine sandy gravel beneath a thin layer of peat. When first discovered the sequence of stratified sand and gravel was about 11 metres thick.

mountaintops of Eryri appeared as islands above sea level. In time, argued Ramsay, the land regained its previous elevation but he never did offer an explanation of the process that might have been responsible for the wholesale depression and subsequent uplift of the land surface on a pan-European scale.

In the revised edition of his *magnum opus, The Geology of North Wales* (1881), Ramsay challenged those who were sceptical of his hypothesis. 'He would be a bold man', he said, 'who could see the ground and still maintain that these well bedded strata have all been shoved up 1,100 feet [335 m] out of the sea to the ground on which they lie'. One such 'bold man' was Thomas Belt, a shrewd geologist whose challenging hypothesis had appeared in a paper entitled 'The

Glacial Period', published in *Nature* in 1874. He proposed that a huge ice sheet, with its source in the mountains of north-west Scotland, the Lake District and north-east Ireland, was responsible for lifting the frozen deposits *en bloc* off the floor of the Irish Sea and transporting them upwards, before depositing them short of the summit of Moel Tryfan. Belt was right. The emplacement took place some 20,000 years ago, when the Last Glaciation was at its peak. Sadly, quarrying activity and the removal of sand and gravel by people have had a detrimental effect on what is a unique resource. Hopefully the designation of Moel Tryfan as a Site of Special Scientific Interest in 1990 will ensure the survival of what little remains.

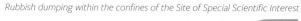

Rubbish dumping within the confines of the Site of Special Scientific Interest

Trefor and
Yr Eifl Granite Quarry

(Trefor a'r Gwaith) SH 372467

021

Abandoned following the departure of the last family in 1959, the former quarry village of Nant Gwrtheyrn, nestling at the foot of Mynydd y Garnfor or Mynydd Gwaith as it is known locally, now lives on as a Welsh-language learning and heritage centre. The three granite quarries – Cae'r Nant, Porth y Nant and Carreg y Llam – that sustained village life and were at their busiest during the late 1880s are long since disused and silent.

Shortly after quarrying began in earnest at Nant Gwrtheyrn in 1851, work also began on opening a new quarry on the northern slopes of Mynydd Gwaith (444 m), the westernmost of the three summits of Yr Eifl, sometimes mangled into English as 'The Rivals'. At the foot of Mynydd Gwaith the granite quarrying village of Trefor was established, named after Trefor Jones, foreman of the Welsh Granite Company, who was granted the honour of laying the village's foundation stone during a grand ceremony that took place on 12 April 1856. Alas, he died on 17 June 1860 and as a consequence was denied the opportunity to witness the development of the quarry – known locally as Y Gwaith (The Works) – which, by the 1880s, was

one of the largest in the world involved in the production of setts.

The quarry, which employed nigh on a thousand men at busy times, formed a staircase of ten galleries, the highest a mere 100 metres below the windswept summit of Mynydd Gwaith. On each gallery worked the quarrymen, whose task it was to secure enormous chunks of the blue-grey and pink granite destined to be fashioned into cube-shaped blocks by the settsmen in the shelter of their stone-built cabins. The setts were then loaded onto wagons that were transported down the twin-track, 850-metre-long incline, opened in 1867, and on as far as the quay, constructed in 1869. From thence, the setts were exported in their hundreds of thousands, paving blocks used to construct roads in cities, such as Liverpool, Manchester and London. Trefor granite was considered unequalled for the manufacture of such blocks on account of their resistance to wear and tear, which meant that they would not become slippery under the hooves of horses and the tyres of early motor vehicles. By the early years of the twentieth century, the quarry was not only exporting about 50,000 tonnes of setts annually, but also increasingly greater quantities of road-metal, its main output post the Second World War.

One need only walk the streets of Trefor in order to appreciate the attractive qualities of the local granite, which formed as magma (molten rock) cooled slowly and crystallized in enormous chambers deep within the Earth's crust, about 450 million years ago. At the time the area was part of a volcanic province that encompassed the Llŷn peninsula and Snowdonia (Eryri). But besides its use as a local building stone, the granite is encountered elsewhere in Wales for it has been used to fashion some of the country's most important memorials. The monument atop Ynys Galch, Porthmadog, commemorating those killed in both world wars, is most impressive. So, too, is the sculpture in Waunfawr commemorating John Evans (1770–99), who headed to North America in search of the 'Welsh Indians', members of the Mandan tribe, who lived in the upper reaches of the Missouri and were, according to tradition, descendents of Madog ab Owain Gwynedd, a legendary figure who, supposedly, discovered America three centuries before Christopher Columbus.

Curling stones

Of greater significance to all patriotic Welsh men and women are the three memorials that stand in Pencader, Corwen and Cilmeri, respectively. In 1952 a polished granite slab was unveiled in Pencader to commemorate the anonymous Hen Ŵr Pencader (The Old Man of Pencader) who, in words recorded by Gerald of Wales (Gerallt Gymro, c.1146–1223), expressed his faith in the future of the Welsh nation in defiance of Henry II's assertion to the contrary. In Corwen stands the splendid sculpture of Owain Glyndŵr set atop an eight-ton block of granite unveiled on 13 September 2007, three days prior to celebrating the anniversary of the day that Owain Glyndŵr was proclaimed Prince of Wales in Glyndyfrdwy on 16 September 1400. But by far the most impressive and poignant memorial is the 4.6-metre-high, undressed granite monolith erected atop a mound in 1956 besides the A483(T) at Cilmeri, near the place that Llywelyn ap Gruffudd (c.1225–82), the last native Prince of Wales, was slain in a skirmish by soldiers in the service of Edward I of England on 11 December 1282.

Although the quarry closed in the 1960s, its current owner, Trefor Davies, continues to extract blocks of Yr Eifl granite, which are fashioned into setts, curling stones and other decorative products in his village workshop. The curling stones are prepared exclusively on behalf of the Canada Curling Stone Company and used by Team Canada, whose men, women and wheelchair competitors won gold medals at the 2014 Sochi Olympic Games.

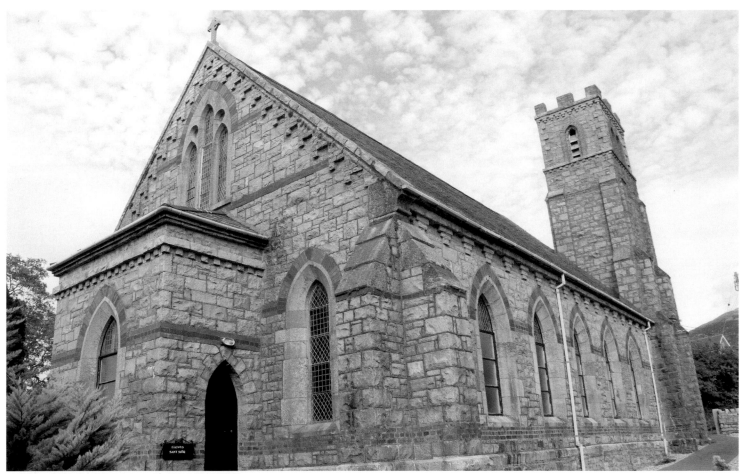

The church of Sant Siôr, Trefor, built of local granite, c.1880

022

Foel Gron, Mynytho

SH 301311

In his account of a year in Llŷn (*Blwyddyn yn Llŷn* [1990]) poet R.S. Thomas unforgettably describes the peninsula that stretches into the Irish Sea (Môr Iwerddon) south-west of Caernarfon as 'a branch of rock hanging between the sea and heaven, with the flower-like clouds wrapped around it'. Much of its spectacular coastline and conical hills, whose rocky summits stand proud of the gently undulating coastal plateau, was designated an Area of Outstanding Natural Beauty in 1956.

Amongst the hills, most prominent are the triple peaks of Yr Eifl (564 m), Garn Boduan (279 m), Garn Fadrun (371 m) and Mynydd

Rhiw (304 m), but no less impressive is Foel Gron (c.30 m), the hillock that overlooks the dispersed village of Mynytho. From its heather and gorse covered summit, which appears to have been enclosed with a roughly circular Bronze or Iron Age bank, walkers are greeted on a clear day by a panoramic view of the coast of Cardigan Bay (Bae Ceredigion) between Pwllheli and St David's Head (Penmaendewi), and that of Llŷn between Aber-soch and Hell's Mouth (Porth Neigwl). Today, this patch of common land, the habitat of larks and butterflies, is a place to relax but here, long ago, local commoners were faced with the wearisome task of gathering

Mynytho and the domed summit of Mynydd Tir Cwmwd as seen from the slopes of Foel Gron

enough heather to roof their mean cottages and collect firewood on the nearby heathland of Mynytho Common (Comin Mynytho). During dry summers such tasks were hampered by fires: 'Poor Foel Gron', records Thomas, 'cops it somehow or other every year, and [such fires] damage the heather which makes it so striking every summer'.

East of Foel Gron, the heathland crowning the domed summit of Mynydd Tir Cwmwd (133 m) that juts into the sea to the south of Llanbedrog is also enlivened by purple-flowering heathers. In fact, the headland supports an extensive area of species-poor lowland heath dominated by heather (*Calluna vulgaris*), bell heather (*Erica cinerea*) and western gorse (*Ulex gallii*), whilst occasional pockets of deeper peat on its southern slopes are characterized by cross-leaved heath (*Erica tetralix*) and deer-grass (*Trichophorum cespitosum*).

Igneous rock, a comparatively large body of fine-grained granite (microgranite), is the foundation of Mynydd Tir Cwmwd. It was formed when a large chamber of molten rock (magma), deep within the Earth's crust, was intruded into the midst of fossiliferous mudstones that had accumulated on the sea floor during the early Ordovician period, some 25 million years before the 450-million-year-old microgranite. The site is of special scientific interest to geologists because the rock, which contains large crystals in a groundmass of smaller ones, is comparatively rare within the history of the Ordovician in the British Isles. Up until 1949, three quarries established during the second half of the nineteenth century and situated along the south-east-facing cliffs of Mynydd Tir Cwmwd, were actively involved in the extraction of the unusual microgranite, used mainly in the production of setts for export.

Though much smaller than Mynydd Tir Cwmwd, Foel Gron is also a mass of microgranite and the former quarry floor is now a convenient parking ground alongside the B4413. Far more spectacular than the two microgranite intrusions is Garn Fadrun, a volcano-like landform carved from a body of hard igneous rock (microdiorite) that also cooled and crystallized in a subterranean magma chamber. This steep-sided hill, a short distance north of Foel Gron, is the highest and by far the most prominent of the volcanic hills south-west of Yr Eifl. Crowning its copiously rock-strewn and

Foel Gron's reddish microgranite

heather-clad summit are the ruins of walls and hut circles of an Iron Age hill fort. The defences, built about 2,300 years ago, were later strengthened and enlarged so that by 100 BC some 16 hectares had been enclosed. A further development took place during the early twelfth century for in his diary, penned in 1188 during his journey around Wales in the company of Archbishop Baldwin, Gerald of Wales (Gerallt Gymro) records that a stone castle '[belonging] to the sons of Owain' (namely Owain Gwynedd who died in 1170) and 'noted for having been a strong hold of the sons of *Owen Gwynedd*, *Roderick* and *Malgwn*', according to Thomas Pennant, author of *Tours in Wales* (1778 and 1781), stood atop Garn Fadrun.

Although familiar to Pwllheli-born poet Albert Evans-Jones (1895–1970) – better known by his bardic name, Cynan – Garn Fadrun's militaristic fortifications were of little or no appeal. As Wales' premier war poet of the First World War, Cynan's experiences of warfare whilst a member of the Royal Army Medical Corps serving in Salonika and France, first as an ambulance man and later as pastor, had a profound influence on his poetic works. He was greatly inspired by the peace and tranquillity of his native Llŷn and in his poem entitled 'Hwiangerddi' ['Lullabies'] he yearns longingly not for far-away Carn Fadrun but for its gentle breezes as he strives in vain to sleep to the deafening accompaniment of 'explosions on all sides'.

Garn Fadrun

Nant Gadwen and Mynydd y Rhiw

SH 212269

023

Old and defunct metal mines where metalliferous ores of lead, zinc, silver, copper, iron, gold or manganese, were extracted from subterranean lodes and brought to the surface, are to be found in all 13 of the old counties of Wales abolished and replaced by 22 unitary authorities in 1996. They are, nevertheless, most numerous in those parts of the country where the oldest rocks are encountered. There, mines noted for particular metalliferous ores are found, such as the lead–zinc–silver mines of north Ceredigion and west Montgomeryshire (Sir Drefaldwyn), the copper mines of Mynydd Parys and Snowdonia (Eryri) and the gold mines in the vicinity of Dolgellau. Less numerous and less well-known are the manganese mines of the Llŷn peninsula, in spite of the fact that most of the manganese ore produced in Britain during the twentieth century was the product of two mines near Aberdaron and, to a lesser extent, a number of smaller ventures in Y Rhinogydd, the mountains between Trawsfynydd and Barmouth (Abermo).

Near Llanfaelrhys, the remote church of Saint Maelrhys which stands on an exposed site near the cliffs and shores of Porth Ysgo, a public footpath follows the banks of Nant Gadwen as far as the point where it plunges into the sea at Porth Alwm. To walkers who choose to tread the path once trudged by miners destined to spend much of their working day underground in the Nant Gadwen

Spoil from the Nant Gadwen mine

manganese mine, signs of past industrial activity are evident on either bank of the stream: tunnels driven into the valley-side slopes for drainage and access to the concentrations of manganese ore; deep, open shafts on a level well above the stream; and a prominent waste tip on the valley floor.

Mining began on a small-scale in the 1850s but the mine experienced its most productive period during the early years of the twentieth century, following the construction of a pier at the foot of the cliffs at Porth Alwm in 1902–3 at a cost of £182. From thence the ore was exported to Ellesmere Port on the banks of the Manchester Ship Canal and from there to the steel furnaces of Brymbo, near Wrexham (Wrecsam), where it was used to harden and toughen the much sought after steel employed in the production of railway lines and the ship-building industry. Ore from the Benallt–Y Rhiw mine (known locally as *Gwaith y Rhiw*, 'the Rhiw works'), situated on the outskirts of Y Rhiw, a village some two kilometres north-east of Porth Alwm, was also transported to the pier for export.

Opencast pit of Gwaith y Rhiw

The Rhiw works was originally an opencast mine but deep shafts were later sunk in order to reach the manganese-bearing lodes to be found amongst the folded and broken layers of mudstone and associated igneous rocks formed about 475 million years ago. It appears that the ore accumulated around hydrothermal vents in the form of chimneys on the floor of the Ordovician sea, from which issued water, super-heated by contact with molten rock, rich in manganese-bearing minerals.

To reach Porth Alwm, the ore was transported in wagons down an incline as far as the upper terminus of a narrow-gauge mineral line. After a journey of 1.6 kilometres, the wagons were lowered down a second incline from the top of the hill overlooking the seaward end of Nant Gadwen and moved to the pier. The remains of the winding gear associated with the incline nearest the sea is to be seen to this day, reminding those walking that section of the Wales Coast Path between Hell's Mouth (Porth Neigwl) and Aberdaron of the industrial heritage of the Llŷn peninsula, oft perceived as an area that does not bear the imprint and scars of extractive industries.

The Nant Gadwen mine closed in 1927 and six years later the pier was dismantled, a decision which meant that ore raised at the Rhiw works would have to be transported by lorry as far as Pwllheli and thence by rail to Brymbo or Shotton steelworks. Even during the few years that preceded its closure in 1945, the mine near Y Rhiw, which was responsible for most of the 196,000 tonnes of manganese ore mined in the area between 1894 and 1945, employed about 150 men.

However, the windswept summit of Mynydd y Rhiw (304 m) was the focus of mining activity over 5,000 years before the exploitation of manganese ore. In 1958–9 archaeologists of the Royal Commission on the Ancient and Historical Monuments of Wales discovered traces of a Neolithic axe factory in the form of five quarry pits, 15 metres in diameter. Further possible quarry sites were identified following fieldwork undertaken in 2005 under the direction of the National Museum of Wales. Surprisingly, the stone used for axes was not a hard igneous rock but a narrow band of mudstone baked hard by the intense heat of molten rock injected into soft, Ordovician mudstones about 475 million years ago.

Old steam-engine boiler, Gwaith y Rhiw

024

Mynydd Mawr and Bardsey

(Mynydd Mawr ac Ynys Enlli) SH 140258

R.S. Thomas (1913–2000), one of the major English-language and European poets of the twentieth century, was not only noted for his nationalism, spirituality and deep dislike of the anglicization of Wales, but also his love of nature, the open air and the sea. There was, he said, no better seascape than the view towards Bardsey from Mynydd Mawr (c.150 m) at the westernmost tip of the Llŷn peninsula, especially during stormy weather when wind-whipped foam would be blown clear of the hill's summit. It was there on the steep, rocky slopes below the old Coastguard Lookout he would go to watch seabirds – a favourite pastime – to the accompaniment of waves breaking noisily at the foot of the cliffs, towering above Bardsey Sound (Swnt Enlli).

In 1953, some thirty years before the island was designated a National Nature Reserve, it was recognized as a Site of Special Scientific Interest. The same year witnessed the establishment of the Bardsey Bird and Field Observatory, one of only two accredited bird

Bardsey: its Norse name probably commemorates Bardr, a Viking leader

The cliffs of Trwyn Maen Melyn: huge boulders of white quartzite within the Gwna Mélange

observatories in Wales. Its main objective is to monitor and maintain a census of the breeding and migratory birds which use the island. In addition to being a permanent home for birds such as the raven, oystercatcher and chough, it's the seasonal nesting place of razorbills, guillemots, fulmars and many thousands of Manx shearwaters who lay their eggs in rabbit burrows. By so doing they are company for the 20,000 saints who, according to tradition, lie buried in the sacred turf of '*Enlli, Porth y Nef*', Bardsey, the Gateway to Heaven.

Ever since medieval times Bardsey has been a major centre of pilgrimage and three visits to the island were considered to be of equivalent benefit to the soul as one to Rome. Before crossing to the holy island, it is said that footsore, thirsty pilgrims would gather around the tidal inlet between the southern slopes of Mynydd Mawr and western slopes of Mynydd y Gwyddel (99 m) in order to partake of the crystal-clear waters of Ffynnon Fair (Mary's Well), exposed only at low tide. The crossing was preceded by a visit to the twelfth-century church of St Hywyn at Aberdaron, the sister church to St Mary's Augustinian Abbey situated on the island. In the safety of the mainland church at water's edge, pilgrims over the centuries would

79

pray for a safe passage to journey's end – Ynys Enlli, 'tide-race island' – across the notoriously troubled waters of Bardsey Sound, which over the centuries have claimed the lives of many souls, judging by the memorials in the cemetery at Aberdaron.

More often than not, the geology of each and every island, is a reflection of that of the nearby mainland, and it was at Aberdaron that R.S. Thomas became aware of 'how incredible and terribly old' were the rocks thereabouts. Furthermore, in his diary *Blwyddyn yn Llŷn* [A Year in Llŷn] (1990), he was at pains to stress that 'it's not possible to live in Llŷn without being mindful of the Earth's great age'. That said, it's the nature, rather than the age of Bardsey's rocks and those exposed along the northern coastline of the peninsula between the village of Morfa Nefyn and Mynydd Mawr, that has attracted the attention of geologists. Best seen in the cliffs of Trwyn Maen Melyn, south-west of Mynydd Mawr, the rocks are a so-called *mélange*, a French term used to describe a chaotic mixture of blocks

The source of Ffynnon Fair

and fragments of rocks of all shapes and sizes and many different origins set within a mass of finer-grained material. In the cliffs of Trwyn Maen Melyn, for example, the 3,000-metre-thick Gwna *Mélange* of Llŷn contains enormous boulders of white quartzite (a sandstone composed primarily of quartz grains) and whole and broken pillows of basaltic lava.

The Gwna *Mélange* is believed to be the product of a gigantic submarine landslide triggered by a catastrophic earthquake during a period of powerful earth movements hundreds of millions of years ago. As a matter of fact, the *mélange* was originally assigned to the Precambrian, the very earliest chapter in Earth's long history, an assignation that led R.S. Thomas to declare, 'Here I think of the centuries, / Six million of them, they say'. Indeed, the *mélange* does contain boulders of Coedana granite from central Anglesey (Ynys Môn), an igneous rock known to have crystallized deep within the Earth's crust 614 million years ago. Such evidence, however, indicates that the landslide that gave rise to the *mélange* must have occurred many millions of years after the formation of the granite. In addition to that, on Ynys Llanddwyn, the island near the southernmost tip of Anglesey, rocks believed to be of the same age as the Gwna *Mélange* contain microfossils of Cambrian age, a period that succeeded the Precambrian 540 million years ago. Though younger than once thought, the Gwna *Mélange* is one of the finest examples in the world of a remarkable and unusual rock type.

Broken pillows of basalt lava set within the mélange

Graig Ddu, Morfa Bychan

SH 522376

025

The rocky headland of Graig Ddu (50 m) juts seawards between two dissimilar beaches. In marked contrast to the pebbly beach of Rhiwfor Fawr, traceable westwards to Cricieth, a popular and attractive seaside town on the south-facing shores of Tremadog Bay (Bae Tremadog), Black Rock Sands (Traeth Morfa Bychan) is an extensive, three-kilometre stretch of hard, golden sands that offers unrestricted enjoyment to hordes of summer visitors. The beach extends as far as Ynys Cyngar, a sand-encroached rock outcrop on the shores of the Glaslyn estuary which was once a sheltered anchorage for slate-trading vessels in the late eighteenth and early nineteenth centuries, prior to the development of the nearby port of Porthmadog.

Graig Ddu – 'the black rock' – and the hilly land between it and Moel y Gest (262 m), the prominent eminence overlooking Porthmadog, are fashioned from mudstones and siltstones that accumulated in layers on the floor of a Cambrian sea, about 500 million years ago. However, the sedimentary strata forming the headland would not have survived the onslaught of waves had they not have been strengthened by the presence of dolerite, a hard igneous rock of Ordovician age, injected in the form of magma

Black Rock Sands and Y Rhinogydd, the mountains lying between the Glaslyn and Mawddach estuaries

(molten rock) amidst the softer mudstones and siltstones during a period of volcanic activity some 450 million years ago. Although dark grey dolerite protects the tip of the aptly-named headland and is the basis of the nearby prominent hillock of Carreg yr Eryr (53 m), a thin, slanting layer of the selfsame rock within a stone's throw of Graig Ddu has proved to be a line of weakness that has resulted in the creation of a wave-sculpted cave at beach level. Other smaller caves have been eroded along faults.

The headland on which Cricieth Castle stands defiantly is a mass of fine-grained, pink igneous rock of granitic composition that has also withstood the onslaught of waves. Built in the 1230s by Llywelyn Fawr (Llywelyn the Great) and extended by Llywelyn ap Gruffudd in the late 1250s, the fortress is one of the finest Welsh castles. Although conquered in 1283 by Edward I and repaired and strengthened in the fourteenth century during the reign of Edward II, the castle was surrendered to Owain Glynŵr in the first decade of

Columnar-jointed dolerite

The slanting layer of dolerite and associated sea cave

Thinly-layered Cambrian mudstones and siltstones

the fifteenth century, and destroyed. Despite its turbulent and bloody history, the ruin was memorably described by Jan Morris in her book, *The Matter of Wales* (1984), as 'the friendliest castle [in Wales] ... which stands on a sea promontory in the middle of the little resort as though it was put there for purely ornamental purposes'!

In addition to being used as building stone during the construction of the castle, water-worn pebbles and cobbles of the distinctive pink granitic rock are common in the pebble beach of Rhiwfor Fawr. They are largely derived from glacial deposits that were not only spread over much of the current land surface – such as the boulder-clay exposed in the cliffs of Morannedd at the eastern end of Cricieth promenade – but also beyond the present shoreline by a glacier flowing southwards off the Welsh mainland and across the floor of Tremadog Bay when the Last Glaciation was at its peak, 20,000 years ago. Rock fragments held firmly in the glacier's sole also left their indelible mark in the form of parallel scratches (striations) and grooves on bare, hard-rock surfaces, such as those plain to see on the ice-hewn tip of Graig Ddu.

As sea level rose at the end of the Last Glaciation, the stones within the off-shore glacial deposits were gradually washed ashore, forming a gravel dam across the mouth of the river Cedron, between Graig Ddu and the cliffs of Rhiwfor Fawr. The shallow-water lake – Llyn Ystumllyn – that accumulated behind the dam originally extended as far as Pentrefelin, a village on the main road between Porthmadog and Cricieth. Today, the former lake bed is a Site of Special Scientific Interest (SSSI), a freshwater marsh characterized by swamp and aquatic plants such as common reed (*Phragmites australis*), reed canary-grass (*Phalaris arundinacea*), soft-rush (*Juncus effusus*) and common marsh bedstraw (*Galium palustre*).

The SSSI also encompasses Rhiwfor Fawr beach, Morannedd cliffs and the Morfa Bychan beach and sand dune system, which includes pioneer dunes along the strandline, supporting sand couch (*Elytrigia juncea*) and prickly saltwort (*Salsola kali*), and active dunes further inland dominated by marram grass (*Ammophila arenaria*). The decision to designate both the dunes and beach a protected area is to be applauded, because several proposed developments and past ventures, such as motor cycle races, have threatened the very existence of such fragile habitats. But to this day car owners are allowed to access the beach and to drive across it, despite the fact that vehicles are visually intrusive, and a threat to the habitat of lugworms, shellfish and other burrowing creatures that live in the fine and coarse beach sand between high and low water mark.

Graig Ddu and Cricieth Castle

026

Traeth Mawr and afon Glaslyn

SH 580390

Anglican cleric, theologian and diarist John Wesley, who visited Wales on 35 occasions between 1737 and 1790, could not understand why the aid of a guide was necessary for those wishing to cross the Glaslyn estuary, known as Traeth Mawr: 'What need there is of guides over these sands I cannot conceive.' He recorded his ill-considered remark in his diary on 11 April 1749 after he had crossed the sands for the third time without the help of a local guide, but not on his own, for he was accompanied by a number of fellow-travellers between Dinas Mawddwy and Caernarfon. Furthermore, in March 1756, he gladly accepted the company of 'an honest Welshman [who] spoke no English' before he and his companions ventured to cross the perilous sands whilst *en route* to Caernarfon.

Though much shorter than following the circuitous path along the shores of the estuary through Llanfrothen, Aberglaslyn and Pren-teg, the journey between Minffordd and Penmorfa on opposite sides of the deceptively attractive sands of Traeth Mawr was fraught with danger. Over the years it claimed the lives of travellers and guides alike, until the greater part of the estuary was reclaimed from the sea by William Alexander Madocks' embankment – the Cob – across the mouth of the Glaslyn. Whilst few people would deny the long-term benefits of his bold scheme, it did disfigure the unspoilt character of what was once Wales' most magnificent estuary. In the opinion of J.A. Steers, author of *The Coastline of England and Wales* (1946), a masterpiece of careful erudition and lucid description, Madocks had only succeeded in adding 'a large area of not very valuable land to Caernarvonshire, but it hardly increased its natural beauty'! Be that as it may, two Glaslyn settlements – Porthmadog and Tremadog – commemorate Madocks and his environmentally-unfriendly project.

Traeth Mawr: the spire of St Mary's Church, Tremadog, is visible in the centre of the photograph

Traeth Mawr, the small wooded island of Ynys y Gwely and the western end of Hir Ynys

Little is known about the true nature and thickness of the deposits overlying the estuary's rock floor between the road bridge at Aberglaslyn and the confluence of the rivers Glaslyn and Dwyryd seaward of the Cob. That said, most are undoubtedly glacial in origin, dumped ahead of the rapidly retreating Glaslyn glacier, about 17,000 years ago. Sometime later, after the sea had risen to its present level, about 6,500–7,000 years ago, the glacial deposits were concealed under a few metres of alluvium – mainly sand and silt – distributed by the meandering river Glaslyn.

At low tide, 'Glaslyn's sparkling waters' assumed a complex braided pattern, its myriad channels flowing between ever-changing banks of sand and silt. Patches of salt-marsh developed here and there along the more sheltered shores. At high, spring tides, in particular, the prospect was totally different, as the estuary was transformed into a sea that extended inland as far as Aberglaslyn. Rising above the waters were a number of rocky islands, some small, such as Carreg y Gwartheg on which now stands St Mary's Church, Tremadog, and others very much larger, such as Ynys Hir, near Y Garreg, Llanfrothen. With the exception of Ynys Fawr near Pren-teg, the islands, headlands, such as Y Garth, Minffordd, and the spectacular cliffs overlooking Tremadog, were all fashioned from hard, igneous rocks attributable to the volcanism that characterized the Ordovician period, about 450 million years ago.

The fate of the former island-studded estuary was finally sealed following the opening of the Cob on 17 September 1811, a celebration later marred – much to the consternation of Madocks, who had purchased the Tan-yr-allt Estate near Tremadog in 1798 –

The river Glaslyn, Snowdon (left) and Y Cnicht (right)

Y Cnicht (left), Moelwyn Bach (right) and Minffordd quarry

when the embankment was breached during a storm in February 1812. On completion of the repairs, the work of draining Traeth Mawr began, depriving thousands of waterfowl and waders of a habitat that had for many a long year sustained their populations, especially during the winter.

Following the opening of the Cambrian Railway between Minffordd and Porthmadog in 1867, the pace of reclamation north of the railway embankment quickened leading to the creation of a vast area of flat, agricultural land. In contrast, the wetland between the railway and the Cob remains undrained, providing an invaluable refuge for birds and an attractive foreground to the much-photographed panorama of Eryri – the mountains of Snowdonia – best viewed from the footpath alongside the Ffestiniog Railway, which served to transport slate from Blaenau Ffestiniog to the harbour at Porthmadog between 1836 and 1946.

In spite of the far-reaching environmental changes that post-dated the building of the Cob, the area's transformation did not deter a pair of ospreys from nesting within the Glaslyn estuary. Ever since 2004 the nest site near Pren-teg has witnessed the annual arrival of new chicks, whilst the Pont Croesor Visitor Centre, opened in 2015 alongside the track of the Welsh Highland Railway, allows members of the public to view these still rare birds of prey catching fish and rearing their young in spring, before leaving Wales in late August–early September in order to spend winter months in west Africa.

Moelwyn Mawr, Moelwyn Bach and Tanygrisiau

SH 660440

027

As he headed for the summit of Moelwyn Mawr (770 m) in June 1962, naturalist William (Bill) Condry encountered little of botanical interest. Where there was any vegetation clothing the bare rocks 'it was mostly heather and bilberry, the "flora of poverty"' of acid soils. Near the high point, 'that keeps a watchful eye on the slate-quarry town of Blaenau Ffestiniog', his luck changed. Before him lay a patch of lime-loving plants: green spleenwort (*Asplenium viride*), brittle bladder fern (*Cystopteris fragilis*), mountain sorrel (*Oxyria digyna*) and northern rock-cress (*Arabis petraea*), an arctic-

alpine first discovered in Britain on Snowdon (Yr Wyddfa) in 1639 by English botanist Thomas Johnson. All owed their presence to the calcium within a small outcrop of dolerite, an igneous rock intruded into the mudstones – later transformed into slate – that are the foundation of Moelwyn Bach (710 m), Moelwyn Mawr and nearby Moel-yr-hydd (648 m).

Outcropping along the south-east-facing slopes of all three summits is a thick suite of igneous rocks. At first, volcanic ash (tuff) and lava, the product of submarine eruptions coeval with the

Moelwyn Bach, Moelwyn Mawr, Moel-yr-hydd and Cwmorthin

deposition of the mudstones, accumulated on the sea floor during Ordovician times, about 460 million years ago. Somewhat later, molten rock (magma) intruded into the tuffs, lava and mudstones, cooled and crystallized, forming thick layers of rhyolite, a fine-grained igneous rock. It's these hard rocks that form not only the rugged cliffs overlooking Llyn Stwlan, but also the nearby precipices of Clogwyn y Bustach, Clogwyn yr Oen, Craig yr Wrysgan and Craig Nyth y Gigfran, the latter two framing Cwmorthin, whose elongated floor hangs high above the former slate quarry village of Tanygrisiau.

Once a natural lake that filled a rock basin excavated by a glacier, Llyn Stwlan was enlarged by the Yale Electric Power Company in 1898–1900 and functioned as a reservoir supplying water to Dolwen hydro-electric power station built on the banks of the river Goedol, south of Tanygrisiau. The station generated electricity for the Votty and Bowydd slate quarries above Blaenau Ffestiniog, the first major electrification scheme for a Welsh slate quarry. Between 1957 and 1962, Llyn Stwlan (503 m) was further enlarged following the building

of a massive 36.6-metre high, 383-metre long, concrete dam wall, the most visible and scenically intrusive structure of the Tanygrisiau pumped-storage hydro-electric power scheme, the first of its kind in Britain. The power station stands on the shores of Llyn Tanygrisiau (c.190 m), the valley-bottom reservoir connected to Llyn Stwlan via underground pipelines. Opened in 1963, the project was the forerunner of a similar but far more ambitious enterprise at Dinorwig, near Llanberis, opened in 1984.

To follow the road to Llyn Stwlan, a climb of 368 metres, is a memorable experience. *En route* it heads past the amazing incline that linked Wrysgan slate quarry with the Ffestiniog Railway, utilized by the quarries of Blaenau Ffestinog to transport slates to the harbour at Porthmadog. In the veins of quartz within the dark-grey mudstones exposed on the uppermost side of the first of six hairpin bends, crystals of sphalerite (zinc ore) and galena (lead ore) are a reminder that metal mines were a feature of the slopes below the dam, as recently as the early years of the twentieth century.

Llyn Stwlan reservoir

Llyn Stwlan's dam wall

The incline serving Wrysgan slate quarry

With the exception of slate tips, little remains of the Moelwyn slate quarry, opened in the 1820s on the bleak, windswept cliffs above the shores of Llyn Stwlan. During the 1860s it developed underground and, at the end of a hard day's work, the quarrymen spent each night in the relative comfort of one of three barracks. The quarry, however, was an unsuccessful venture and it closed about 1900. Unfortunately, the upper section of the spectacular incline system that connected it to the Ffestiniog Railway was destroyed when Llyn Stwlan was enlarged.

In addition to transporting slates, the Ffestiniog Railway also carried setts and crushed rock from the former granite quarry, situated on the west-facing slopes of Moel Ystradau (296 m), opposite Tanygrisiau power station. Quarried for the last time during the 1930s, the fine-grained granite is the area's youngest rock. It formed as magma, filling an enormous chamber deep within the Earth's crust, cooled and crystallized, about 440 million years ago.

Due south of Moel Ystradau and clearly visible from Llyn Stwlan are the massive concrete buildings housing the two reactors of the now defunct Trawsfynydd nuclear power station, designed by Sir Basil Spence and hailed by some as a 'triumph of modernist architecture'. It generated electricity over a period of 26 years between 1965 and 1991. Decommissioning began in 1995, a process that will take a great number of years. 'But', wrote Bill Condry in 1966, 'the deliberate placing of a nuclear power-station in the heart of wild Wales and in the very centre of [the Snowdonia] National Park is [and was] surely a violent negation of everything a National Park stands for.'

028

Dinas Brân and Creigiau Eglwyseg

SJ 223431

Situated on the banks of the Dee (Dyfrdwy), Llangollen is best known as being the home of the International Musical Eisteddfod, held annually in the town ever since 1947. Established in order to try to heal some of the wounds caused by the Second World War, it has become a festival of music and dance renowned for its emphasis on national cultures and international cooperation. Other than the eisteddfod, the town has 'disappointingly little to offer in the way of urban charm or character', in the opinion of Edward Hubbard, author of *The Buildings of Wales: Clwyd* (1994). Furthermore, the character of the early sixteenth-century bridge

across the Dee, once hailed as one of the 'seven wonders of Wales', has been spoilt, for it was widened in 1873 and again in 1968–9 in order to cope with the demands of motorised transport.

Gone, too, have those summer days when it was possible for visitors with an eye to reaching the summit of Dinas Brân (320 m), the prominent castle-topped hill overlooking the much-admired Vale of Llangollen (Dyffryn Llangollen), to hire a donkey that would carry them up the steep, zigzag path of Allt y Mulod, 'the donkeys' hillside', also known as 'Donkey Hill'. A donkey was also called upon to convey vital goods destined for the summit snack bar, which was still in

valley floor. The aqueduct and canal between the Horseshoe Falls (Rhaeadr y Bedol), upstream of Llangollen, and Chirk Bank, downstream of Chirk (Y Waun), was designated a World Heritage Site in June 2009.

Despite its undeniable beauty, the Vale of Llangollen cannot compete with the grandeur of the west-facing escarpment of Creigiau Eglwyseg, formed of Carboniferous limestone; the remains of marine creatures that accumulated layer by layer on the floor of a warm, shallow, tropical sea, about 350 million years ago when 'Wales' lay athwart the equator. In contrast to the upper, bare-rock slopes, the escarpment's lower slopes are masked by scree, angular lumps of limestone frost-shattered during intensely cold periods, such as

The dilapidated walls of Dinas Brân Castle

existence in the 1930s. To reach the hilltop today involves a stiff climb of 250 metres from the river bridge but, at journey's end, visitors are rewarded by spectacular views of the Dee valley and uplands flanking the vale: the Berwyn mountains to the south-west and Creigiau Eglwyseg to the north.

To the east, the silvery-blue ribbon of the Llangollen Canal, designed by Thomas Telford and opened in 1808, leads the eye towards one of his masterpieces and one of the most splendid archaeological features of Britain's canal system. The Pontcysyllte aqueduct carries the canal across the Dee by way of a 310-metre-long and 3.6-metre-wide iron trough, some 39 metres above the

Creigiau Eglwyseg
Llangollen, home of the International Musical Eisteddfod

that between 13,000 and 11,500 years ago which marked the end of the Last Glaciation.

In the past, both the limestone cliffs and scree slopes were an important source of local building stone (the Old Armoury in Llangollen, now the headquarters of the International Eisteddfod, was built of limestone in the 1660s) and lime, used in the production of mortar and agricultural fertilizer. Several dilapidated limekilns are encountered on the scree slopes alongside the six-kilometre section of Offa's Dyke Path between Dinas Brân and World's End. The selfsame footpath also follows the line of a major fault separating rocks of very different ages, for the Carboniferous limestone is at least 60 million years younger than the grey-black Silurian mudstones and slates exposed at the foot of the scarp, and from which the hill of Dinas Brân was sculpted.

Although a building material of poor quality, the Silurian rocks outcropping on the summit of Dinas Brân were used not only to construct the defences of the univallate Iron Age hill fort crowning the hill, but also the rubble-stone walls of Dinas Brân Castle, the chief stronghold of Powys Fadog (a lordship centred upon the area between present-day Llangollen and Wrexham [Wrecsam]), whilst its spiritual centre was the Cistercian monastery of Valle Crucis (Glyn y Groes) situated about two kilometres north-west of the hill. The fortress was built in the north-west corner of the hill fort by Gruffudd ap Madog, probably during the 1260s, but Edward I's campaigning forces found it deserted and burnt down by 1277. By the time of the death of Llywelyn ap Gruffudd, Prince of Wales, in December 1282, most of Powys Fadog and the castle had been granted to John de Warenne, Earl of Surrey, who chose to abandon the property.

When John Leland (c.1506–52) saw Dinas Brân in about 1536, during his travels through Wales, it had already long been in ruins. George Borrow, who began the walk he described in *Wild Wales* (1862) at Llangollen, was suitably impressed by the picturesque and romantic ruin which, he claimed, 'bear[s] no slight resemblance to a crown'. In contrast, Jan Morris likened Dinas Brân, the most 'forlorn' of all Welsh castles, to 'a set of rotten teeth'!

Morfa Harlech and Morfa Dyffryn

SH 574295

029

Situated alongside the A496, a short distance south of Harlech, is Allt y Môr, a small gorse- and bracken-covered field owned by the National Trust and open to members of the public. It is one of the great viewpoints of Wales, for beyond the five-kilometre-long sandy beach, backed by an unbroken line of sand dunes terminating at the Dwyryd–Glaslyn estuary, stretches the great arc of the mountains of Snowdonia (Eryri), a panorama that embraces Y Cnicht, Snowdon (Yr Wyddfa), Moel Hebog and the hills of the Llŷn peninsula. Although the view to the south of the cliff-top vantage point cannot compete with that to the north, the dunes of Morfa Dyffryn National Nature Reserve are as important, if not more so than those of Morfa Harlech National Nature Reserve and both are part of an extensive dune system traceable from the Mawddach estuary in the south as far north as Morfa Bychan, between Porthmadog and Cricieth.

The importance of the dune system cannot be overemphasized for many of the dunes elsewhere in Wales are in poor condition. Rather than being dynamic, aeolian landforms subject to constant

Morfa Harlech: Snowdon (1,085 m) and Moel Hebog (782 m) are the two highest summits

change, most have been either spoilt or destroyed as a result of human interference, or fossilized under an unbroken cover of vegetation. Not that the Morfa Harlech and Morfa Dyffryn dunes, which have developed atop gravel spits, are undamaged. As farmers over the centuries have reclaimed extensive areas of salt-marsh between the spits and the abandoned sea cliffs – between Llandecwyn and Harlech in the case of Morfa Harlech, and between Llanfair and Llanaber in the case of Morfa Dyffryn – the dunes have diminished in area. Indeed, research work has indicated that the extent of bare, mobile sand has halved since the 1940s.

Despite being exposed to the full force of the prevailing south-westerly winds, the small, unstable embryo dunes strewn along the high water mark are the habitat of sea couch (*Elytrigia antherica*), whilst the fore-dunes are partially covered with marram (*Ammophila arenaria*). In the older dunes common centaury (*Centaurium erythraea*) and lady's bedstraw (*Galium verum*) are plentiful, whilst

carpets of dune helleborine (*Epipactis dunensis*) and creeping willow (*Salix repens*) grow in the damp dune hollows. But even the older, more stable dunes are also subject to the erosive power of the wind. One of the main features of the Morfa Dyffryn dunes are the large wind-eroded hollows that bear witness to the sand's mobility and of the coastline's changeable configuration.

In the past St Tanwg's Church, the old parish church of Harlech set within an ancient round churchyard, stood some distance from the sea and on several subsequent occasions blown sand has nearly overwhelmed the tiny medieval church, which now lies amongst the dunes. By 1853 the building was in poor condition but it was saved by the Society for the Protection of Ancient Buildings in 1884. Amongst the unearthed graves was that of the poet Siôn Phylip who drowned in Pwllheli in February 1620 while on his way home to Mochras, after spending time as a bard or minstrel in Anglesey (Ynys Môn).

Mochras, once an island at high tide, is a hillock of glacial debris

St Tanwg's Church, Llandanwg

Llandanwg sand dunes and Mochras

at the landward end of Sarn Badrig ('Patrick's Causeway'), a submarine ridge of boulder-clay capped with boulders, cobbles and gravel and traceable south-westwards, below the waters of Cardigan Bay (Bae Ceredigion) over a distance of about 20 kilometres. It's generally believed that the 'causeway', which is exposed at the ebb of spring tides, is probably a moraine that accumulated between the Glaslyn–Dwyryd glacier and the Mawddach glacier that flowed into the bay during the Last Glaciation.

Mochras was the focus of attention for geologists during the early 1970s following the publication of the results of a borehole sunk amidst the dunes, to a depth of 1,938 metres, between 1967 and 1969. Rocks of Cambrian age, formed about 500 million years ago, are the geological foundation of the Rhinogydd, the rugged mountains that overlook both Morfa Harlech and Morfa Dyffryn. But

much to the surprise of geologists, the oldest rocks encountered at the bottom of the borehole were Triassic in age, 300 million years younger than the Cambrian strata. It soon became evident that the old cliff line between Llandecwyn and Llanaber corresponds to an enormous north-south fault. The floor of the sedimentary basin to the west of the break has either been lowered thousands of metres – at least 3,750 metres according to one conservative estimate – in relation to the upland to the east, or that the high ground to the east of the fault has been uplifted by the same amount in relation to the territory west of the cliff line. Since the youngest rocks encountered in the borehole are about 25 million years old, the main movement along the fault probably took place about 20 million years ago, during the Alpine earth movements that resulted in the creation of the Alps.

030

Bwlch Tyddiad and Rhinog Fawr

SH 645314

Thirteen years after being appointed the first professor of Geology at the University of Cambridge in 1818, the Reverend Adam Sedgwick (1785–1873), one of the founders of modern geology and geological mentor of the young Charles Darwin, commenced his pioneering research work amongst some of Wales' oldest rocks. Following his investigations in north-west Wales, in particular, he identified a succession of rocks attributable to a geological period for which he coined the name Cambrian (after Cambria, the Latin name for Wales) in 1835. According to Sedgwick, Cambrian strata extended over the greater part of Gwynedd but their aerial extent was significantly reduced when rocks of supposed Upper Cambrian age were assigned to the succeeding Ordovician (named after the Ordovices, an Iron Age tribe located in present-day north Wales), a geological period whose existence was first recognized in 1879. Ever since then, the Harlech Dome, a huge, dome-shaped upfold centred to the south of Llyn Trawsfynydd, is the main outcrop of Cambrian rocks in north-west Wales. On the western flank of the fold rise the Rhinogydd, mountains whose craggy nature, profusion of scattered boulders, countless cliffs and shelves draped with scree, and clothed in places with heather and bilberry, render them far more difficult to walk – except for their herds of feral goats – than any other mountainous tract in Wales.

One of the Rhinogydd's other notable features is its numerous, small, remote lakes, most of which fill rock basins sculpted by 'ice age' glaciers. Author and ardent mountain lover Ioan Bowen Rees was in no doubt that Llyn Hywel, nestling at the foot of the south-facing cliffs of Rhinog Fach (712 m), was sheer perfection. Maybe so, but one of the most delightful and alluring of all is Llyn Cwmbychan, source of the river Artro which discharges into the sea near Llandanwg.

Although the minor road that heads inland from Llanbedr terminates near the head of the lake and Cwmbychan farmhouse, it's the start of a public footpath that climbs steadily to Bwlch Tyddiad, the col at the foot of the northern slopes of Rhinog Fawr (720 m). Above and beyond the oak and birch trees, where walkers are greeted with the birdsong of willow warbler, redstart and pied

Bwlch Tyddiad: the view east

Bare, ice-scoured Rhinog Grits

flycatcher in spring and summer, greenness is largely exchanged for naked rock on either side of a stone staircase, inappropriately known as the Roman Steps, for they were never trodden by legionnaires. The steps were probably constructed during the Middle Ages but it's not known by whom or for what purpose, although it has been suggested that they were part of a packhorse trading route.

The vista from Bwlch Tyddiad is spectacular. To the south-east, beyond the coniferous plantation of Coed-y-Brenin, is the summit of Rhobell Fawr (734 m), the eroded remains of a volcano that was active during early Ordovician times, about 480 million years ago. To the north-east, the skyline beyond Trawsfynydd's bleak moorlands, is dominated by Arennig Fawr (854 m), sculpted from hard igneous rocks, the product of volcanic activity that culminated about 470 million years ago.

When the Last Glaciation was at its peak, 20,000 years ago, the scene was very different. The entire area, including most of Wales, was covered by a vast ice sheet. South of Trawsfynydd the basal layers of ice flowed south along the valleys of the rivers Eden and Mawddach whilst the upper layers flowed west across the Rhinogydd. By so doing, the ice sheet's erosive power excavated the deep, narrow col of Bwlch Tyddiad, in addition to Bwlch Drws Ardudwy between Rhinog Fawr and Rhinog Fach. Furthermore, on

Llyn Cwmbychan

the bare, ice-scoured surfaces of the layered sandstones (Rhinog Grits) that are the very foundation of the Rhinogydd, scratches (striations) and grooves abound, incised by the abrasive action of stones frozen into the base of the westerly-flowing ice.

The survival of striations over the 15,000 years that have elapsed since the disappearance of the ice sheet is attributable to the hardness of the Rhinog Grits, a succession of grey-green sandstones deposited layer by layer on the sea floor, about 500 million years ago. Within each layer the size of the sand grains decreases progressively upwards. Such a pattern, known as graded bedding, develops when enormous quantities of coarse and fine sand are

washed into the sea from a nearby land surface and subsequently swept into deep ocean basins by powerful, turbulent currents. On reaching the ocean floor, deposition of coarse sand is followed progressively by finer and finer grains. It was this repetitive process that gave rise to the countless layers of sandstone seen piled high on top of one another on the north face of Rhinog Fawr. When confronted with the phenomenon, Andrew Crombie Ramsay, author of *The Geology of North Wales* (1881), was moved to proclaim that it's 'one of the grandest spectacles, both geologically and as a piece of rugged scenery, that North Wales affords'.

The north face of Rhinog Fawr

Gwynfynydd – the Dolgellau gold-field

(Gwynfynydd – Maes Aur Dolgellau) SH 735275

031

Gold: an attractive soft, shiny, malleable, ductile, sectile metal, yellow in colour, highly prized and much sought after since time immemorial. Over the centuries the lure of gold has persuaded prospectors in their droves to abandon home comforts, travel to the four corners of the Earth and suffer appalling hardships in their oft futile attempts to discover workable quantities of the precious metal. The practice of travelling to the ends of the Earth climaxed in the nineteenth century, a century of gold rushes when men, hearing the merest whisper of gold, were prepared to journey in their tens of thousands to outlandish gold-fields.

Above all else, it was the discovery of gold at Sutter's Mill, California, on 24 January 1848 that triggered the world's first major gold rush when, over a period of seven years, 300,000 people flocked to California to seek their fortune. However, five years before the name Sutter's Mill hit the headlines, Arthur Dean, an

engineer employed in the Cwm Heisian lead mine on the banks of the Mawddach, about 10 kilometres north of Dolgellau, discovered a tiny particle of gold in the mine's sieves. The discovery, which was the subject of a paper published in the Reports of the British Association for the Advancement of Science for 1844, caused great excitement but the first rich vein within the Dolgellau gold-field – by far the most prosperous in Britain – was not found until 1859. It was discovered in the Clogau mine, situated about a kilometre north of Bont-ddu on the banks of the Mawddach west of Dolgellau, and over a period of 10 years, between 1860 and 1869, it produced 13,900 ounces (1 troy ounce = 31.1 g) of gold valued at about £53,000 (£4.4 million in 2017).

Gwynfynydd's 'golden age' dawned on 11 July 1887. The gold-bearing lode, discovered in the mine situated close to the Cwm Heisian mine (sold as a 'gold-mine' for the princely sum of £14,000

Ruined buildings of the Gwynfynydd gold mine

in 1862!), was exceedingly rich and within the space of two years it yielded 12,000 ounces of gold. With the exception of relatively few unproductive and unprofitable years, the 'golden age' lasted until 1915 by which time the mine had produced almost 41,000 ounces of gold, with a value of about £130,000 (£9.4 million in 2017)

But the good years between 1887 and 1915 came at a price. In order to extract the gold it was necessary to crush 95,000 tonnes of hard, valueless quartz in the large mill near the confluence of the rivers Mawddach and Cain and between the two waterfalls, Rhaeadr Mawddach and Pistyll Cain. At best, it proved impossible to win more than a couple of ounces of gold for every ton of crushed quartz, the principal mineral forming the veins containing grains, thin threads

and an occasional nugget of the valuable metal, in addition to pyrite ('fool's gold'), sphalerite (zinc ore) and galena (lead ore). Furthermore, the sinking of shafts and the creation of tunnels in order to access the lodes deep underground necessitated the excavation of hundreds and thousands of tonnes of the local country rock – mainly mudstone but also hard igneous rocks. The black mudstones, which host most of the mineral veins, accumulated on the sea floor during Cambrian times, about 500 million years ago, but the lodes themselves are of Ordovicin age. They were formed when hot fluids, originating from the active volcanic centre of Rhobell Fawr, deposited their mineral treasures in fractures in the Cambrian rocks some 480 million years ago.

Ruins of Cwm Heisian lead mine

River Mawddach

Rhaeadr Mawddach and part of the remains of the Gwynfynydd mill

Post-1915 Gwynfynydd's story is one of declining fortunes. The welcome increase in the price of gold during the 1930s was offset by a disastrous fire which in February 1935 destroyed the renovated mill whose turbines were powered by water drawn from the river near Rhaeadr Mawddach. The exploitation of a promising lode discovered in 1983 proved uneconomical. The attempt to develop Gwynfynydd as a tourist attraction in the 1990s also failed and all underground mining operations ended at the site in 1998. For a time, one of the former Gwynfynydd miners reworked some of the waste tips in order to recover the little gold that remained within them but that venture too ended in 2007. It now remains to be seen whether the Welsh jewellery firm Clogau Gold, who purchased the Gwynfynydd mine and surrounding land in 2013 and have subsequently submitted an application to the Crown Estate with a view to restart mining on a small scale, realize their dreams. In the meantime, the unsightly but historically important dilapidated buildings, associated ruins and ugly waste tips are a stain on one small part of the Snowdonia National Park (Parc Cenedlaethol Eryri).

But the search for elusive nuggets of Welsh gold, prized on account of its origin and scarcity, goes on amongst those fortune seekers armed with pan and spade. They too dream that their patient quest for gold by panning Mawddach's sand and gravel will bear fruit someday.

032

Llyn Tegid, Y Bala

SH 905330

There are in Wales numerous lakes of sparkling charm but 'no Maggiore, no Annecy is livelier than the spectacle of Llyn Tegid, Bala Lake to the English, on a bright summer afternoon'. So said Jan Morris in her book *The Matter of Wales* (1984), a bold claim that would have been dismissed by Ioan Pedr (1833–77), author of a Welsh-language essay entitled 'Llyn Tegid a Daeareg' (Llyn Tegid and Geology [1876]), for he insisted that the lake, the largest natural body of water in Wales, was 'the most beautiful in the world'. However, it was neither the lake's beauty nor its geology that prompted its designation as a Site of Special Scientific Interest. The 'fine expanse of water', 5.75 kilometres long, is of 'special interest' on account of its wildlife: its aquatic plants; one particular species of snail; and the fish that thrive in the lake's relatively nutrient deficient waters which reach a maximum depth of c.42 metres.

In places, between the open water and the drier shores, grows a profusion of canary-grass (*Phalaris canariensis*), bottle sedge (*Carex rostrata*) and bladder-sedge (*Carex vesicaria*). And in summer the white flowers of common marsh bedstraw (*Galium palustre*), the yellow of marsh-marigold (*Caltha palustris*) and the pink of ragged-robin (*Lychnis flos-cuculi*) enliven the smaller clusters of bladder sedge.

Much rarer than the rarest of the shallow-water plants is the glutinous snail, one of the rarest freshwater snails in Europe that was first recorded in Llyn Tegid in the 1850s. A century later, the once abundant creature was nowhere to be found, despite further searches in the 1960s and in 1989. It was presumed extinct until the snail, for which there is no record of it in any other lake in Britain, was rediscovered in September 1998.

The river Llafar delta projecting into the lake near Glan-llyn, one of two, Welsh-language, outdoor activity centres run by Urdd Gobaith Cymru, founded in 1922.
The annual Urdd Eisteddfod is the largest youth festival in Europe.

The most notable fish in the lake is the *gwyniad*, a uniquely Welsh whitefish that has no English name. Prior to the warm, post-glacial period that succeeded the disappearance of the last vestiges of ice from the mountains of Wales 11,500 years ago, the fish would migrate out to sea via the Dee (Dyfrdwy). Intolerant of increasingly warmer river water, the *gwyniad* became confined to the cooler lake waters, where it has evolved to form a genetically distinct population that is unique to Llyn Tegid. There, in the deep, cold-water basin, it feeds mainly on microscopic animals and, as a consequence, it appears that it seldom shows any interest in anglers' lures; but it can be netted.

The rock basin, now occupied by Llyn Tegid, was gouged out by the erosive power of a glacier, although the valley's slopes between Llanuwchllyn and Y Bala are much gentler than the steep-sided, craggy glacial troughs of Snowdonia (Eryri), such as Nant Peris.

Over-deepening of the valley floor was facilitated by the presence of a fault, a major line of structural weakness whose onshore path runs from the coast at Tywyn, through the middle of Llyn Tegid, past Corwen and on towards the Welsh border south-west of Chester, a distance of 95 kilometres. *En route* the fault has disturbed rocks of different age, indicating that the tear has been periodically active over a period of 500 million years. As a result, its path is characterized by a narrow belt of broken rocks, a line of weakness that is at its weakest where the rocks themselves, such as the mudstones outcropping on either side of the lake, are inherently weak. By bulldozing a pathway through the shattered and broken rock, the Dee glacier excavated the Llyn Tegid rock basin that is considerably larger than the dimensions of the current lake.

Since the disappearance of the ice, rivers have been sweeping considerable quantities of sand and gravel, including some large boulders, into the lake. Ioan Pedr reported that in June 1781 a major flood occurred in Llanuwchllyn that caused the river Twrch, a tributary of the Dee, to seek an alternative course after its channel was choked with debris and boulders that had been swept down by a torrent. The fluvial deposits that have accumulated at the upper end of the lake as a result of the action of the rivers Dee and Twrch, and at the lower end by the river Tryweryn, indicate that Llyn Tegid was, at one time, at least three kilometres longer than its current length. Furthermore, its width between the deltas of the rivers Llafar and Glyn on the north-west and south-east shores, respectively, is half that near St Beuno's Church, Llanycil, that stands on a small, stony delta at Abercelyn.

The church is now the centre of Byd Mary Jones World, a state-of-the-art visitor and educational centre that tells the story of 15-year-old Mary Jones, who, in 1800, walked 42 kilometres along stony tracks from Llanfihangel y Pennant to Y Bala in order to get a Bible from the Reverend Thomas Charles (1755–1814). Four years later, Charles, who is buried in St Beuno's churchyard, played a part in establishing the British and Foreign Bible Society.

The Nant Pant-y-march delta. Glan-llyn is situated on the opposite shore.

Pistyll Rhaeadr

SJ 074295

033

By claiming that all but one – Snowdon (Yr Wyddfa) – of 'The Seven Wonders of Wales' are located in the north-east of the country, the anonymous rhymester responsible for the doggerel verse, composed in the late eighteenth or early nineteenth century, evidently had little or no knowledge of Wales' undisputed wonders:

> Pistyll Rhaeadr and Wrexham steeple,
> Snowdon's mountain without its people,
> Overton yew trees, St Winefride's well,
> Llangollen's bridge and Gresford bells.

That said, Pistyll Rhaeadr, a wondrous waterfall situated six kilometres up-valley of Llanrhaeadr-ym-Mochnant, is deserving of the appellation. Indeed, its geological and geomorphological significance was officially recognised when the fall was designated a Site of Special Scientific Interest, the 1,000th such site in Wales on the day that the slate plaque was unveiled in May 2000.

Pistyll Rhaeadr is the highest waterfall in Wales. It marks the point where the appropriately named afon Disgynfa, 'the descending river', whose source lies at the foot of the south-east-facing ridge of the Berwyn mountains (Y Berwyn), plunges 75 metres into the head of Cwm Blowty. But it's not one unbroken descent. After falling 50 metres into a plunge pool, the river flows under a natural arch and falls a further 25 metres into a deeper rock basin, before following a rocky channel under Tan-y-pistyll bridge, on which visitors can stand and admire the grand spectacle. 'There are many remarkable cataracts in Britain', wrote George Borrow, author of *Wild Wales* (1862), 'but this Rhyadr [*sic*], the grand cataract of North Wales, far exceeds them all in altitude and beauty'.

Although the natural wonder made a lasting impression on Borrow on the occasion of his visit in the summer of 1854, he reminded his readers that 'even this cataract has its blemish'. He

The black natural arch between the two falls

disliked intensely the 'ugly black bridge or semicircle of rock, about two feet [0.6 m] in diameter and about twenty feet [6 m] high' which, in his opinion, 'intercepts the sight, and prevents [onlookers] from taking in the whole fall at once'. In point of fact, he expressed the hope that 'nature in one of her floods' would sweep the 'unsightly object' away. Furthermore, he was informed by the Welshwoman, who lived in the nearby Swiss-like cottage and had guided him to the natural arch, where both 'were almost blinded by the spray', that the waterfall was a terrifying sight in winter, 'for it is then like a sea, and roars like thunder or a mad bull'.

The eminent naturalist and antiquary, Thomas Pennant (1726–98), author of *Tours in Wales* (1778 and 1781), visited 'the celebrated cataract *Pistill Rhaiadr*' in the early to mid 1770s. Unlike Borrow, he was impressed by the 'noble arch' but not so by the treeless prospect: 'The defect of this noble fall', said he, 'is the want of wood.' Borrow, on the other hand, was greeted by wooded slopes and 'groves of pine', a young woodland that today includes mature beech, oak, ash and sycamore trees, some of which had been planted well over 150 years ago. In addition to the trees, outcropping rocks under the shade of the wooded slopes support a lush and profuse growth of mosses, ferns, lichens and liverworts that thrive in the damp microclimate at the head of Cwm Blowty.

Geographically, Pistyll Rhaeadr denotes the boundary between two valleys of very different character. Afon Disgynfa, above the lip of the waterfall, follows a steep course via a channel full of boulders. But beyond the foot of the fall and its confluence with Nant y Llyn, which drains Llyn Lluncaws, a lake occupying a cirque basin nestling under the shadow of Moel Sych (827 m), the river Rhaeadr (as it is known beyond the place where the two rivers meet) meanders across the floor of a steep-sided glacial trough.

The cliff over which the river Disgynfa plunges is a 15-metre layer of hard volcanic ash (ignimbrite), the product of a short-lived, explosive eruption that took place towards the end of Ordovician times, some 450 million years ago. As the hot ash-flow cooled, columnar cracks (joints) developed at right angles to its surface, near vertical joints that remain evident in the face of the cliff. Beneath the layer of ignimbrite lies a succession of Ordovician slates that accumulated originally as layers of mud on an ancient sea floor. Being less able than the volcanic rock to withstand the erosive power of cascading water, the river Disgynfa succeeded in fashioning the rock arch, which was such an eyesore in Borrow's hypercritical opinion. Either side of the river channel, beyond the foot of the fall, the steep, lower valley-side slopes are coated with scree, frost-

shattered fragments of slate that probably accumulated during the intensely cold period, between 13,000 and 11,500 years ago, at the very end of the Last Glaciation. Whilst freeze-thaw action was shattering the slates, small glaciers reoccupied pre-existing cirque basins in the Berwyn mountains, such as that within which lies Llyn Lluncaws.

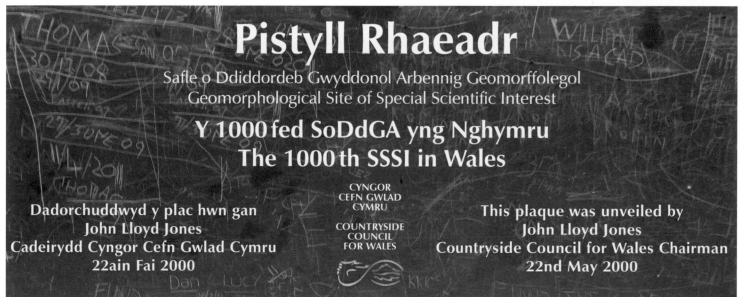

034

Bwlch y Groes, Aran Fawddwy and Aran Benllyn

SH 913232

Ioan Bowen Rees, an ardent mountain lover and author of four Welsh-language books on the subject, maintained that the twin summits of Aran Fawddwy (905 m) and Aran Benllyn (885 m) that dominate the watershed between the rivers Dee (Dyfrdwy) and Dyfi have two contrasting aspects. When viewed from the west – from the A494 between Dolgellau and Y Bala – he insisted that their slopes are 'smooth, grassy and uninteresting'. But when observed from the east, from the vicinity of Bwlch y Groes, the remote col through which passes the narrow mountain road between Llanuwchllyn and Llanymawddwy, they 'bear the rocky stamp of Eryri's giants'. Two of those giants – Arennig Fawr (854 m), east of Trawsfynydd, and Yr Wyddfa (Snowdon; 1,085 m) itself – are visible

from the col and in the case of both, together with the majestic east-facing cliffs of Aran Fawddwy and Aran Benllyn, their austere rugged grandeur can be attributed to the Ordovician volcanic rocks from which they have been fashioned.

During a period of powerful volcanic eruptions that occurred about 460 million years ago, the cooling and crystallization of repeated dense flows of red-hot volcanic ash resulted in the formation of hard, unyielding ash-flow tuffs. The conspicuous boundary between the tuffs and the sequence of later mudstones, that are the foundation of the lower ground at the foot of the escarpment, is evident below the two high summits. On account of their solidity, the dark volcanic cliffs below which nestles the small

At the foot of Aran Fawddwy lies the glacially-sculpted rock basin of Creiglyn Dyfi

lake of Creiglyn Dyfi are ideally suited for novice climbers. So claimed Owen Glynne Jones, a young Welshman who, according to Ioan Bowen Rees, was one of the leading pioneers of rock climbing before his untimely death, following a horrendous accident in the Alps, in 1899.

In the opinion of eighteenth-century naturalist Thomas Pennant, Aran Fawddwy and Aran Benllyn rank as the Alps of Wales and, like those imposing peaks, the imprint of the glaciers that sculpted them are plain to see. In particular, the landforms bear witness to the natural climatic changes that characterized the concluding millennia of the Last Glaciation that finally came to an end about 11,500 years ago. The immense erosive power of glaciers that formed under the shadow of the escarpment not only excavated the two cirques at the head of Cwm Llaethnant and Cwm Croes, but also the two smaller, rock-walled amphitheatres whose rock basins impound the waters of Creiglyn Dyfi and Llyn Lliwbran. Glacier flow also transformed the two valleys either side of the watershed between tributaries of the rivers Dee and Dyfi into steep-sided glacial troughs. Furthermore, Cwm Llaethnant is a fine example of a hanging valley, for between the cliffs of Ogof Ddu and Graig Tŷ-nant the turbulent Llaethnant plunges over a 120-metre-high rock step to the meadow-lined floor of the Dyfi valley, itself deepened by a glacier mightier than that which occupied Cwm Llaethnant 20,000 years ago.

Although climatic warming triggered the disappearance of the area's last small glaciers 11,500 years ago, arctic-alpine plants such as starry saxifrage (*Saxifraga stellaris*), mossy saxifrage (*Saxifraga hypnoides*), reflexed stonecrop (*Sedum rupestre*) and fir clubmoss (*Huperzia selago*), discovered by Edward Llwyd (Keeper of the Ashmolean, Oxford) on the cliffs above Llyn Lliwbran in April 1682, are a reminder of past glacial conditions.

Climate change has also been a feature of post-glacial times and the wetter, milder conditions that characterized upland Wales about 6,000 years ago led to the development of blanket bogs such as the thick, waterlogged blanket of dark-brown peat that once extended unbroken across the foothills of Clipiau Duon and Llechwedd Du, between Cwm Llaethnant and Bwlch y Groes. Thomas Pennant noted that the bog which gave 'shelter to multitudes of red grouse, and a few black [grouse]' was also an invaluable source of domestic

Aran Fawddwy's rock buttresses and crags

Hags of dried, eroded peat resulting from the dissection of blanket bog

109

fuel 'to all the inhabitants' in their valley-bottom homes. However, winning the fuel proved problematic on account of the remoteness of the peat beds and the difficulty of transporting the cut peat, for 'the roads from the brows of the mountains, in general, are too steep even for a horse'.

The abandoned turbaries, once the habitat of *sphagnum* mosses and plants such as heather (*Calluna vulgaris*), common cottongrass (*Eriophorum angustifolium*) and tussocky purple moor-grass (*Molinia caerulea*) capable of withstanding the acidic conditions, remain boggy but much eroded. Peat cutting and land drainage in order to create sheep pastures has, in places, greatly damaged the blanket bog, as is testified by the eroded hags of dried peat. The aforementioned practices are also environmentally damaging. Intact peatbogs act as sponges, storing water and releasing it slowly, thereby reducing the risk of flash-floods downstream. Furthermore, the peatland ecosystem is the most efficient carbon sink on planet Earth but as peat dries and oxidizes it releases into the atmosphere carbon dioxide, the most important of the greenhouse gases responsible for triggering anthropogenic global warming, one of the greatest challenges facing humankind today.

Dyfi meadows below the cliffs of Ogof Ddu

The roadside cross near the summit of Bwlch y Groes, 'the pass of the cross', recalls a pilgrimage that took place in September 1989

Cwm Cywarch

SH 855183

035

Situated either side of Cwm Cerist are two sequestered valleys whose existence, tranquillity and beauty is beyond the ken of the vast majority of drivers hurrying along the busy A470 – the main arterial road linking north and south Wales – in the vicinity of Dinas Mawddwy. The smaller of the two valleys, Cwm Maesglasau, described as 'a small valley far from the merriment of mankind', was the subject of Angharad Price's *O! Tyn y Gorchudd* (2002), an award-winning evocation of twentieth-century rural mid Wales, subsequently published in English under the title of *The Life of Rebecca Jones* (2010). Like the Cerist, augmented by the waters of

Nant Maesglasau, the Cywarch too is a tributary of the Dyfi and from its confluence it's a journey of about three and a half kilometres along a narrow country lane to reach the small, valley-head Snowdonia National Park (Parc Cenedlaethol Eryri) car park at the foot of Craig Cywarch.

The stark dissimilarity between the dark, craggy cliffs and scree slopes of Craig Cywarch and the valley's smooth, verdant, over-steepened slopes is attributable to Cwm Cywarch's contrasting rock types and their differing response to the erosive power of 'ice age' glaciers. Craig Cywarch (c.700 m) and nearby Creigiau Camddwr's

Craig Cywarch and the peaty surface of Fawnog Fawr, 'the great peatbog'

hard rocks are the product of powerful volcanic eruptions and the resultant flows of once red-hot ash (ash-flow tuffs). Following the cessation of Ordovician volcanic activity some 455 million years ago, a thick sequence of mudstones accumulated on the floor of an ancient sea, softer rocks from which was sculpted the deep, trough-shaped valley by the combined power of two glaciers whose source lay under the shadow of Craig Cywarch and Pen Main (680 m) at the head of Hengwm. The two joined forces at the upper end of Cwm Cywarch near the former site of the Cowarch [*sic*] lead mine and a conspicuous ice-moulded outcrop of ash-low tuffs.

On the deserted summit between Glasgwm (774 m), above Craig Cywarch, and the peak of Aran Fawddwy (905 m), are several old shafts and levels dug in the forlorn hope of discovering a rich vein or two of lead within the volcanic rocks. The search proved fruitless. The only mine worthy of the name was Cowarch, situated near the foot of Creigiau Camddwr, although few remains have survived the passage of time. Some work took place prior to 1770 and several shafts and levels were excavated during 1840s but to no avail, according to the testimony of one anonymous miner. Reopening the mine under a new name – Great Cowarch – in the early 1850s also proved to be a largely unsuccessful venture. After a further period of inactivity, Cowarch reopened under the name Penyrallt, for which there is little or no record after 1862 when it produced a mere 21 tonnes of lead ore. Whilst surveying the valley in 1887, Ordnance Survey officers recorded the remains of the mine that had long-since ceased working

Despite the demise of mining, the opening of two small places of worship – Bethlehem (1876), a Welsh Congregationalist chapel, and Tarsus (1877), a Calvinistic Methodist cause – suggests that Cwm Cywarch's population peaked in the 1870s. However, neither cause survived to celebrate its centenary. Both closed in the second half of the twentieth century, a period that witnessed the construction of Bryn Hafod, in 1960, by The Mountain Club, Stafford, on the site of an old derelict lead mine building. The property testifies to the popularity of the buttresses and crags of Craig Cywarch in particular amongst the rock climbing fraternity. During the 1950s the first of many routes were described and graded as to the severity of the climb and, in accordance with the practice of climbers heedless of

the Welsh language and culture, given English names. Although the hard, volcanic rock provides good holds, its wetness, according to the authors of website summitpost.org/glasgwm-craig-cywarch, is a nuisance, for climbers are faced with the 'thankless task' of 'constantly having to clear soggy vegetation from a route, particularly if you are seconding and have to endure a constant shower of wet moss and lichen', which is, of course, 'easily brushed off with [a] wire brush'. Apparently, many other routes 'require excessive gardening'!

Despite the fact that the Cwm Cywarch cliffs, which rise 560 metres above the flat surface of Fawnog Fawr, have not been designated a Site of Special Scientific Interest, such activity is irresponsible, unacceptable and reprehensible. The presence of small quantities of lime in the ash-flow tuffs sustains a profusion of notable mountain plants including green spleenwort (*Asplenium viride*), mountain sorrel (*Oxyria digyna*), lesser meadow-rue (*Thalictrum minus*), roseroot (*Sedum rosea*), globeflower (*Trollius europaeus*) and mossy saxifrage (*Saxifraga hypnoides*), in addition to bryophytes, a large group of seedless green plants that include the mosses, liverworts and hornworts. It would be a tragedy if any one of these floral treasures were to be lost as a consequence of the activities of some uncaring and inconsiderate members of rock climbing clubs.

An ice-moulded, whaleback outcrop (*roche moutonée*) of ash-flow tuff amongst bracken. The small cliff at its leading edge faces in the direction of ice movement.

Craig Cywarch (left), Creigiau Camddwr (right), Bryn Hafod and spoil heap of Cowarch lead mine

036

Dyffryn Mawddach and Precipice Walk

(Dyffryn Mawddach a Llwybr Cynwch) SH 739211

Ioan Bowen Rees (1929–99), author of four Welsh books on the subject of mountains, was quick to learn on Foel Faner (290 m) and Foel Cynwch (c.320 m), two somewhat insignificant hills three kilometres north of Dolgellau, that there is no better a vantage point than a low summit in the vicinity of high summits. A sound observation, for at the southernmost end of Precipice Walk, high above the meadows of Dyffryn Mawddach and some 50 metres below the old hill fort crowning Foel Faner, walkers are confronted by a magnificent view of the north-facing escarpment of Cadair Idris, a panorama described by Rees as being 'worthy of the Alps'. Charles Darwin, who often stayed near Barmouth (Abermo), was equally impressed. In a letter dated 22 June 1869 to his close friend, Sir Joseph Dalton Hooker, one of the greatest British botanists of the nineteenth century, he wrote: 'Old Cader [sic] is a grand fellow, and shows himself off superbly with every changing light.'

The centrepiece of the escarpment, traceable from Gau Graig in the east to Tyrrau Mawr in the west, is Pen y Gadair (893 m) which overlooks the imposing cirque on whose floor nestles Llyn y Gadair. It was from this cirque basin, and four other craggy amphitheatres between it and Gau Graig, that small glaciers flowed to augment the powerful Mawddach glacier on its relentless journey towards Cardigan Bay (Bae Ceredigion). As it did so, it widened and deepened '[t]he fjord-like Mawddach ... perhaps the loveliest of all Gwynedd's fine estuaries', in the words of Sophia Acland, author of *Wales from the Air* (1990).

The radiocarbon age of the oldest organic deposits that lie on

Llyn Cynwch and Pen y Gadair

the floor of Llyn Gwernan, some two kilometres north of Llyn y Gadair, indicates that the glacier which had occupied Dyffryn Mawddach at the peak of the Last Glaciation, 20,000 years ago, had disappeared by 16,500 years ago. During its retreat it left a legacy of glacial deposits on the valley floor, which were later topped by a thick sequence of post-glacial estuarine and marine sands and clays as the sea level rose following the melting of the world's continental ice sheets. A minimum of 48 metres of post-glacial deposits were recorded in a borehole sunk in the estuary, south of Barmouth.

Such deposits also contain grains of gold, which over the centuries have been swept downstream by the Mawddach and its tributaries from the gold-bearing rocks of the Dolgellau gold-field, once the location of notable gold mines such as Gwynfynydd and Clogau. Although rare, Mawddach's estuarine gold reserves were the focus of attention of the multinational mining corporation Rio Tinto Zinc (RTZ, now Rio Tinto) during the early 1970s. River-bed deposits were examined by the company's geologists and seismic surveys took place in the estuary in April and May 1970. Apparently, the company intended to excavate and sieve the valley-floor deposits between Barmouth railway bridge and Penmaenpool (Penmaen-pŵl), work which would have destroyed the natural beauty of the estuary. Much to the relief of those who campaigned vigorously against the proposed environmentally damaging scheme, RTZ abandoned its plans in March 1972.

Dyffryn Mawddach and estuary

The cirque of Llyn y Gadair below the summit of Cadair Idris

disseminated within 500-million-year-old Cambrian rocks. The only economically viable means of exploiting such an ore body would necessitate the excavation of a vast opencast pit.

The scale of such a venture, within the Snowdonia National Park (Parc Cenedlaethol Eryri), was totally unacceptable not only in the opinion of many individuals but also several environmental organizations, such as the Campaign for the Protection of Rural Wales (Ymgyrch Diogelu Cymru Wledig), Friends of the Earth (Cyfeillion y Ddaear) and the Snowdonia Society (Cymdeithas Eryri). Others, such as members of the Dolgellau Rural District Council, were in favour of the enterprise, believing that the mine would employ about 500 workers. However, Riofinex abandoned its proposed venture in the late 1970s, primarily as a result of the fall in the price of copper.

In a Welsh policy document published in 2016, the Snowdonia National Park Authority stated that 'it's difficult to foresee any circumstances in the future when it would be considered acceptable to extract from the large opencast pit which would be necessary to mine [the body of copper ore] discovered'. Difficult, perhaps, but it's equally difficult to believe that a large, multinational mining company would not wish to look towards Capel Hermon once again if the price of copper was right.

In the meantime, Riofinex Ltd (a mining company now dissolved), which had submitted a planning application to search for copper ore in the vicinity of Capel Hermon, a mere five kilometres to the north of Foel Cynwch, were granted permission by the then Welsh Office (now the Welsh Assembly Government) in July 1971 to undertake geological investigations in the area. A core-drilling programme proved the existence of an extensive ore zone containing up to 200 million tonnes of a low-grade copper ore (0.3 per cent copper)

The river Mawddach at the foot of Foel Cynwch

Castell y Bere
and Craig y Deryn

SH 668085

037

'Even in a land where castles occupy so many dramatic positions,' wrote the authors of *The Buildings of Wales: Gwynedd* (2009), 'few can match this site, with the castle on an island of rock in the Dysynni valley, in the foothills of Cadair Idris'. Moreover, Castell y Bere occupies a special place in the hearts and minds of all patriotic Welsh men and women. It was built by Llywelyn ap Iorwerth (Llywelyn Fawr) in the 1220s, not only as a sign of his determination to assume authority over Meirionnydd, but also as a military stronghold in what Gerald of Wales (Gerallt Gymro) considered to be 'the rudest and roughest of all the Welsh districts' in 1188.

Because Castell y Bere was the stronghold of the war against English oppression in 1282–3, Edward I decided to send a strong army to the Dysynni valley to lay siege to the castle, which lasted for ten days. The Welsh were compelled to yield on 25 April 1283. Ironically, the fortress, the last Welsh stronghold to fall in the war of 1282–3, was destroyed by the Welsh during the revolt of Madog ap Llywelyn in 1294 and, despite a desire amongst the English to recapture the castle, it was left to decay and assume its current ruinous state.

The elongated ridge on which the ruined walls and towers stand is, in effect, a small island of volcanic rocks shaped by the passage of a glacier that has left its mark in the form of scratches on the ice-polished surfaces of hard volcanic ash outcropping at the entrance to the site. To an enemy approaching the castle from the mountains to the north-east or the sea to the south-west, it looked deceptively unimpressive, for the building, constructed of rough blocks of local stone, was nowhere wider than 40 metres. But between the north and south towers it was 128 metres in length. Furthermore, and apart from the two deep ditches excavated to protect the stronghold's entranceway, the steep, rocky slopes that rise dramatically from the flat floor of the Dysynni valley were an effective, natural, defensive barrier. So too was the Dysynni

floodplain which, at the time, would have been a tract of boggy ground through which the river Cadair meandered as far as its confluence with the Dysynni near Pont Ystumanner. If an enemy were to attack the fortress from the south-west, there atop the towering crag of Craig y Deryn ('Bird Rock'; 233 m), according to tradition, stood Tyrrau'r Gwylwyr ('the Watchmen's Towers'), whose occupants could warn their compatriots in the castle of an impending assault.

Crowning the summit of Craig y Deryn is Gaer Wen, a small hill fort dating, in all probability, from the Iron Age. But owing to the hill's craggy cliffs, only its eastern slope is defended by two lines of earth and stone ramparts. Little else is known about the fort except for the fact that its occupants were not alone, for Craig y Deryn has long since been the haunt of cormorants, which nest on its highest ledges. Nowhere else in Britain do these large, dark, long-necked sea birds nest so far from the sea, and during the breeding season, between April and May, some 60 pairs are commonly to be seen heading back to their roosts and nests at dusk. It's possible that the

Craig y Deryn

nesting place dates back to the time when the sea extended inland as far as the foot of the rock, before river-borne deposits choked the valley floor.

No less remarkable than a cormorant colony situated nine kilometres from the sea is Craig y Deryn itself. This diverse habitat, an amalgam of rock outcrops, grassland, heathland and bracken, is an important nesting place of choughs, and on the north-west-facing cliff numerous mosses and liverworts – some of which are rare – have been recorded. Of particular interest are some of the very rare mosses to be found growing on the surface of large boulders amongst the scree, appositely described by Thomas Pennant (1726–98) as 'a prodigious stream of stones, which extend some hundreds of yards from the bottom of the rock, and is formed by the continual lapse of fragments from it'.

In reality, Craig y Deryn is a combination of three summits, the highest of which (258 m) lies between the most conspicuous pinnacle (233 m) and the lowest (231 m). It has been carved from the same hard volcanic rock that forms not only the foundation of the ridge upon which Castell y Bere was built, but is also responsible for the relative narrowness of the valley between the two prominent landmarks. The rock is the product of highly explosive volcanic eruptions that occurred during the Ordovician period, some 450 million years ago, and the outcrop of the resultant pile of once red-hot volcanic ash is traceable through the softer mudstones of the area as far as Llyn Cau, at the foot of Cadair Idris.

The view down-valley from Castell y Bere

The view towards Llanfihangel y Pennant, up-valley of the castle (facing page)

038

Cadair Idris and Llyn Cau

SH 711130

'*Kader Idris* is probably one of the highest mountains in Britain' – so said Edmund Gibson about the 'chair' of the legendary giant, Idris, in his revised version of William Camden's *Britannia* (1722) – adding that 'it affords some variety of Alpine plants'. Of that there is no doubt, although Cadair Idris cannot be ranked amongst the giants, for there are in Britain over 300 Munros, mountains whose summits exceed 3,000 feet (914.4 m), whilst that of Pen y Gadair (893 m) is 21.4 metres short of the qualifying height.

One of the first naturalists to list some of the mountain's upland plants was Edward Llwyd (or Lhuyd), who contributed valuable additions to the revised versions of *Britannia*, published by Gibson in 1695 and also in 1722. In May 1682, for example, he recorded two species of flowering plants typical of high rock ledges, namely lesser meadow-rue (*Thalictrum minus*) and roseroot (*Sedum rosea*). But in the nooks and crannies of mainly north-facing cliffs, beyond the reach of sheep, arctic-alpine species abound, such as moss campion (*Silene acaulis*), starry saxifrage (*Saxifraga stellaris*) and the early flowering purple saxifrage (*Saxifraga oppositifolia*), the most

beautiful of all the arctic-alpine plants in the opinion of William (Bill) Condry, who during the twentieth century was the pre-eminent writer on the natural history of Wales, his adopted country.

Notwithstanding its rich arctic-alpine and mountain flora, Cadair Idris is renowned as the location of one of the finest assemblages of glacial and periglacial landforms in Wales. By far the most impressive is the majestic, armchair-shaped amphitheatre of Cwm Cau, considered by W.V. Lewis (1907–61), the pioneering glacial geomorphologist born in Pontypridd, to be the finest example of a cirque in Britain. Gouged by the erosive power of an 'ice age' glacier, the rock basin at the foot of the steep, head and side walls, now occupied by Llyn Cau, is about 50 metres deep.

A closer look indicates that the cirque's form mirrors the nature of the rocks: the lake basin and the lower cliffs below Craig Gau – the saddle between the summits of Pen y Gadair and Craig Cwm Amarch (791 m) – correspond to the outcrop of relatively soft and easily eroded mudstones, whereas the highest cliffs, below the two summits, are fashioned out of harder and more resistant volcanic

An ice-moulded, whaleback rock

Glacial deposits (till), a mixture of stones large and small set in a clayey matrix, forming the Llyn Cau moraine

rocks, the product of eruptions that took place during the Ordovician period, about 450 million years ago. Successive flows of red-hot volcanic ash gave rise to the thick sequence of pyroclastic rocks that are the foundation of the cliffs which overlook the southern shores of Llyn Cau. Piled high on the opposite shore is a succession of equally ancient basaltic lava flows and, since those on the summit of Pen y Gadair assume the form of ill-shaped pillows, it's evident that the lava issued from volcanic fissures on the sea floor. During the early years of the nineteenth century, many people were of the opinion that Llyn Cau itself occupied an ancient volcanic crater. However, although Richard Wilson's painting entitled *Llyn-y-Cau, Cader Idris* (c.1765–6) – one of the Welsh artist's most celebrated works – bears a striking resemblance to a crater lake, Charles Kingsley, author of *Town Geology* (1877), was at pains to

Llyn Cau and Craig Cwm Amarch

stress that 'Any one acquainted with recent [volcanic] craters would see at once that [Llyn Cau] is not an ancient one'.

In addition to the cirque of Llyn Cau, Cwm Cau also bears the indelible stamp of glacial processes active not only during the Last Glaciation but also during earlier glacial episodes of the Great Ice Age, the latest 2.6-million-year-long chapter of Earth history characterized by a series of very cold periods separated by times when the climate was as warm or warmer than it is today. On the floor of Cwm Cau – deepened and straightened by a glacier whose base was armed with large and small stones – polished, scratched and grooved ice-moulded rock surfaces abound. But because the Cwm Cau glacier was less powerful than the larger, neighbouring Cwm Dysynni glacier, its valley floor hangs about 270 metres above the Minffordd meadows. Cwm Cau therefore ranks as a fine example

of a hanging valley, reoccupied by Nant Cadair following the disappearance of all the glaciers of Wales, some 15,000 years ago.

During the brief glacial interval between 13,000 and 11,500 years ago, small glaciers did reform in most of the cirques of Wales, including that at the head of Cwm Cau. A moraine accumulated around its snout, obscuring the threshold of the rock basin, later to be filled by Llyn Cau. In contrast, periglacial conditions – intensely cold ice-free areas in the vicinity of glaciers – characterized the high summits, where much of the ground is covered by blockfields, accumulations of angular boulders the product of frost-shattered bedrock. The sight prompted diarist Francis Kilvert (1840–79), who climbed Cadair Idris in June 1871, to declare that it 'is the stoniest, dreariest, most desolate mountain I was ever on'!

Pen y Gadair (left) and Mynydd Moel (863 m; right), from the vicinity of Corris Uchaf

Llyn Myngul, Tal-y-llyn

SH 718100

039

The journey downhill from Bwlch Llyn Bach (285 m), under the shadow of Mynydd Gwerngraig and Cefn y Clawdd in the upper reaches of Cwm Rhwyddfor, offers careful drivers unrivalled views down a valley as straight as a ramrod. From the site of the former small lake, after which the pass was named, the A487 hurries downhill before reaching the flat meadows at a height of 85 metres above sea level, lying between Minffordd, the starting point of one of the well-trodden paths leading to the summit of Cadair Idris, and the head of Llyn Myngul. That's a drop of 200 metres in less than four kilometres along a valley originally the product of the erosive work of the river Dysynni that carved its way through the shattered rocks denoting the line of a major fault, a tear traceable from the sea at Tywyn, through Y Bala and on towards the Welsh border.

Furthermore, the more keen-eyed driver cannot fail to spot the unmistakeable signs that testify to the inherent instability of the steep, valley-side slopes above and below the main road, under the

Llyn Myngul and the natural dam, bathed in sunshine

dark shadows of Craig y Llam and opposite the impressive scree slopes at the foot of the cliff-bound amphitheatre (cirque) of Craig Cwm Rhwyddfor. On several occasions, the Highways Department of Gwynedd County Council has had to undertake extensive and expensive work to repair and strengthen the road's retaining wall, thereby preventing sections from giving way and slipping headlong to the floor of Cwm Rhwyddfor. Above the A487, it has also been necessary to erect fences and metal barriers in the hope of preventing large boulders from falling and landing on the road. Although troublesome, the rockfalls and landslips that have befallen Cwm Rhwyddfor in the recent past pale into insignificance when compared to the Graig Goch landslide that resulted in the creation of Llyn Myngul.

As regards its shape and as its name suggests, Llyn Myngul (narrow-necked lake) is an example of a ribbon lake, one of the characteristic features of glacial valleys gouged deeper, wider and straighter by 'ice age' glaciers. But rather than filling a rock basin on the valley floor, the waters of Llyn Myngul were impounded by a gigantic landslide (or possibly a combination of two slips), whose accumulated debris, rising about eight metres above the lake surface and the site of the Ty'n y Cornel Hotel, is clearly to be seen at the foot of Graig Goch (586 m).

By taking full advantage of the structurally weak rocks along the line of the Tal-y-llyn–Y Bala Fault, the Dysynni glacier that occupied the valley during the height of the Last Glaciation, 20,000 years ago, not only over-deepened it, but also acted as a buttress supporting its steep slopes, at their highest below Graig Goch and the opposite summit of Foel Ddu (448 m). But some time following the recession and disappearance of the glacier, between 17,000 and 15,000 years ago, there occurred a landslide like no other the length and breadth of Britain. Without a mass of ice to support them, the unstable slopes below Graig Goch, the higher of the two summits, collapsed and within a matter of seconds about 40 million cubic metres of rock – mainly mudstone – hurtled downslope at an estimated speed of 50 metres a second, choking the valley floor and climbing part way up the lower slopes of Foel Ddu. High above the hummocky surface of the accumulated rock debris, traceable over a distance of a kilometre between the Ty'n y Cornel Hotel and Maesypandy farm,

the outline of the landslide's uppermost scar is, to this day, clearly evident immediately below the summit of Graig Goch.

The lake, impounded by the colossal landslide, was at its longest and deepest some time before the accumulating water overtopped its natural dam. After that, the level lowered as the river Dysynni breached the dam and excavated a meandering gorge, up to 20 metres deep, through the jumbled heaps of shattered rock. At one and the same time, streams deposited their load of sand and mud on the lake floor. That process continues to this day below the hanging valley of Cwm Amarch, where the convex curve of the delta shoreline on which stands Pentre farm edges forward inexorably towards the centre of the lake. The flat, green meadows traceable from the head of the lake, near Dolffanog, to Minffordd, were also once part of a much longer lake.

Llyn Myngul, currently no deeper that about three metres, will eventually cease to exist as a consequence of the slow accumulation of sediments on its floor. Since that day is not destined to dawn in the near future, the lake will remain as one beloved by anglers. Indeed, ever since Colonel Vaughan of Hengwrt, near Dolgellau, the library of which was a treasure house of ancient Welsh manuscripts, built the Ty'n y Cornel Hotel in 1844, the 89-hectare lake has been a mecca for fly fishermen.

The ice-gouged cirque of Cwm Rhwyddfor

Llyn Myngul, Cwm Rhwyddfor, and Bwlch Llyn Bach in the distance

040

The Breidden Hills

(Y Breiddin a'r bryniau cyfagos) SJ 295144

In the opinion of T.I. Ellis (1899–1970), author of several books on Welsh themes, the very sight of the Breidden Hills was sufficient to raise the spirits of Welsh men and women when travelling westwards towards Wales 'after many miles in the midst of lowland England'! Breidden Hill (365 m) itself is easily recognized from a distance, not only on account of its height above the extensive, flat floodplain of the river Severn (afon Hafren), but also because Rodney's Pillar stands atop its summit. Erected yn 1781 in memory of the English admiral Sir George Brydges Rodney, not on the occasion

of one of his important naval battles nor his death on 24 May 1792, but because the petty gentry of Montgomeryshire (sir Drefaldwyn) wished it to be known that the oak timber used to construct his naval vessels was the product of their land.

Less prominent but far more interesting than the obtrusive pillar are the remains of the banks and ditches of one of the largest hill forts of the Welsh border country, although parts of the 28-hectare stronghold have been destroyed as the large Criggion (Crugion) Quarry bit ever deeper into the steep, north-west-facing slopes of

Buithy Hill (290 m) and Middletown Hill (367 m)

Breidden Hill. The rocky hilltop site has a long history. Although used sporadically in the later Neolithic and Early Bronze Age, the earliest defensive banks were built during the Bronze Age, about 3,000 years ago, and some 2,700 years before an Iron Age hill fort, incorporating numerous roundhouses, was superimposed upon the earlier signs of occupation. Whilst it is unclear whether the Iron Age occupation continued beyond about 100 BC, the third- and fourth-century pottery discovered by archaeologists indicates that the site was also used during the later Roman period.

The summit of Breidden Hill is not the only defensive site amongst the cluster of nearby hills. South-east of the hilltop is the univallate hill fort of Middletown Hill (Cefn y Castell, 367 m). A smaller fort, noted for its strong defences, also crowns the summit of Bausley Hill (c.190 m), north-east of Middletown Hill.

But it was 'that great mass of rocky mountains, distinguished by the names of *Freiddin*, *Moel y Gollfa*, and *Cevn y Castell*', rather than the area's hill forts, that made a lasting impression upon naturalist and antiquary Thomas Pennant, author of *Tours in Wales* (1778 and 1781). His response was echoed by geologist Roderick Impey Murchison, author of *The Silurian System* (1839), his *magnum opus* published 16 years before he was appointed Director-General of the Geological Survey. In his opinion, the Breidden Hills were 'justly admired for their picturesque forms when viewed from the surrounding region', adding that Moel y Golfa, when 'viewed from the south-west, appears like Vesuvius'.

In reality, only the three highest hills – Breidden Hill, Moel y Golfa and Middletown Hill–Bausley Hill – are fashioned either wholly or largely of hard volcanic rocks, whilst the intervening lower ground is carved from less resistant mudstones and sandstones. Although all the volcanic rocks were formed during Ordovician times, about 450 million years ago, the oldest, forming the foundation of the 1.5-kilometre-long Middletown Hill–Bausley Hill ridge, are mainly volcanic ashes (tuffs), the product of violent eruptions that occurred beneath the sea and on volcanic islands. Mudstones found in association with the tuffs contain the fossilized remains of corals that thrived in the warm waters surrounding the islands during periods when the volcanoes were temporarily dormant.

The substantial mass of andesitic lava (named after the South American Andes) that forms the foundation of Moel y Golfa is somewhat younger than the tuffs and mudstones of Middletown Hill–Baudsley Hill. In all probability, the lava was the basis of a volcanic island around which accumulated layer upon layer of sand, pebbles, cobbles and boulders that ultimately gave rise to an andesitic conglomerate. A similar conglomerate forms the ridge upon which stands the castle that overlooks Montgomery (Trefaldwyn). It's therefore possible that the raw material of that particular rock is also the product of the Moel y Golfa volcanic centre.

In contrast to the volcanic rocks of Moel y Golfa and Middletown Hill–Bausley Hill, Breidden Hill is sculpted from a huge mass of dolerite, a dark-coloured igneous rock, formed following the slow crystallization of magma (molten rock), intruded into the midst of mudstones, deep within the Earth's crust. The dolerite has been actively quarried at Criggion ever since 1866, when the stone was used to cobble the streets of Manchester and other English cities. The land abutting Criggion Quarry, in the vicinity of Rodney's Pillar, is a Site of Special Scientific Interest on account of its rich variety of uncommon plants. It was here that naturalist Edward Llwyd (1660–1709) recorded for the very first time spiked speedwell (*Veronica spicata*), a lime-loving, blue-flowering plant that thrives on the minute quantity of calcium within the dolerite.

Criggion Quarry: the stone is mainly used in the road-construction industry

Powis Castle, Welshpool

041

(Y Castell Coch, Y Trallwng) SJ 216065

Powis Castle, aptly known as Y Castell Coch (the red castle) in Welsh, was built during the thirteenth century by Gruffudd ap Gwenwynwyn, Lord of Powys Wenwynwyn, a Welsh territory which later became the core of Montgomeryshire (sir Drefaldwyn). Because Gruffudd chose to support the English, his fortress was destroyed by Llywelyn ap Gruffudd in 1274. However, within the space of three years, Gruffudd regained his lordship, again with the aid of the English, and began the task of rebuilding the castle, work which was destined to continue until the eighteenth century, although much was accomplished during the 1530s. It was then that Edward Grey, 3rd Baron Grey of Powis, initiated a major rebuilding programme that began the process of transforming Powis Castle into a luxurious country residence. Following the death of the last of the Lords of Powys, both the castle and the estate were purchased by Sir Edward Herbert in 1587. It was he and members of his family who were responsible for the Entrance Hall, the Grand Staircase and the magnificent Long Gallery inside the palatial mansion, whose main entrance is sited between two, medieval drum towers. Unsurprisingly, Powis was dubbed the 'most comfortable castle [in Wales]' by Jan Morris.

Established in the seventeenth century, further developed during the eighteenth century and restored to their former glory in the twentieth century, the terraces, and formal and informal gardens, located below the rocky ridge upon which the castle was built, are in the opinion of many the prime attraction of Powis Castle. They are, without doubt, amongst the finest in Wales, although not all their features met with the approval of Thomas Pennant, on the occasion of his visit during the second half of the eighteenth century. He disapproved of the 'laborious series of flight of steps' between successive terraces and was highly critical of 'The gardens [that] were filled with waterworks: the whole in imitation of the wretched taste of *St. Germains en Laye*, which the late family had a most unfortunate opportunity of copying'! Saint-Germain-en-Laye was the court near Paris where James II and the family of William Herbert, son of Sir Edward Herbert, spent a period in exile. The family returned home in 1703, two years after the king's death.

Somewhat surprisingly Pennant had nothing to say regarding the castle's most notable attribute: the red rock used by stone masons throughout the castle's long history. The first geological description of the stone used to build the castle walls is to be found in *The Silurian System* (1839), Roderick Impey Murchison's masterpiece published with the support of 350 subscribers, including Lady Lucy Clive and Viscount Clive, M.P., both members of the family who inherited Powis Castle and the estate in 1801.

Murchison confidently and correctly asserted that 'The rock beneath the castle is a red grit, in parts so calcareous and highly charged with portions of encrinital stems as to constitute an impure limestone.' The 'red grit', mainly a mixture of sand and tiny pebbles, not only forms the ridge upon which stands the castle, but also a near parallel ridge on the far side of the car park at the rear of the building. Small quarries on both ridges were the source of the castle's building stone, a rock now known as the Powis Castle Conglomerate that originated as a beach and shallow-water deposit along the eastern shores of a sea that extended across most of 'Wales' during Silurian times, about 440 million years ago. The 'encrinital stems' recorded by Murchison are the broken, fossilized stems of crinoids, marine creatures, often misleadingly called 'sea lilies'.

Small, round, cross sections of crinoid stems in the calcareous Powis Castle Conglomerate

Orangey-red (above) and buff-coloured (right) Triassic sandstone

However, the conglomerate's red colour is a later feature. During the Permian period, about 260 million years ago, when 'Wales' baked under a hot desert sun, groundwater oxidised iron-bearing minerals within the older conglomerate, causing it to acquire a rusty-red colour.

Although ideally suited for the construction of walls, the conglomerate is not a freestone, a stone homogeneous enough and of sufficiently fine grain that can be cut 'freely' in any direction either with a saw or mallet and chisel. As a consequence, it could not be cut and dressed to provide stonework suitable to form frames within which to set windows and doors, nor could it be used to construct decorative pillars. The chosen freestone, an orangey-red and buff-coloured Triassic sandstone, known to have been used to build the Roman city of Viroconium Cornoviorum (Wroxeter) besides the river Severn (afon Hafren) near Shrewsbury (Amwythig), came from the famous Grinshill quarries, about 12 kilometres north of Shrewsbury.

It's not known how the blocks of Grinshill sandstone were transported to Powis Castle but the Severn provided a possible link. Despite its length, a boat journey along the meandering course of the river between Shrewsbury and Welshpool would have been an easier and less laborious mode of transport than dragging heavily laden carts along rough tracks across country.

042

Montgomery and its castle

(Trefaldwyn a'i chastell) SO 222968

In appearance, the elegant little Welsh border town of Montgomery (Trefaldwyn) is very English and predominantly Georgian, a place considered by historian John Davies, author of *The Making of Wales* (1996), to be 'one of the most delightful Georgian architectural feasts in Wales'. It was built on the summit and flanks of a hillock, and at the foot of a wooded ridge on which stands the ruins of Montgomery Castle, whose Welsh name, Castell Baldwyn, and that of the town (Trefaldwyn; Baldwin's settlement),

commemorates the twelfth-century Marcher Lord Baldwyn de Bollers. Approached from Welshpool (Y Trallwng) and Forden (Ffordun), the road and the course of Offa's Dyke crosses the floodplain of the Camlad, a tributary of the Severn (Hafren), which flows, somewhat unusually, into Wales from its source in England.

It was on the rolling lowland tract between the river and the castle that one of the major battles of the Civil War in Wales was fought on 17 September 1644. Allegedly, the Royalists were defeated

The lowland between Camlad's meadows and the castle. Beyond lie the wooded hills north of Forden.

in the space of an hour, leaving the castle, begun by Henry III in 1223, in the possession of the Parliamentarians. Five years later, the castle was destroyed by order of Parliament, an act that brought to an end over 400 years of the fortress' turbulent history.

Only by climbing the steep path that leads from the centre of town to the castle ruins is it possible to appreciate fully its excellent defensive and strategic position. Since the north–south ridge upon which the thirteenth-century castle was built rises to a height of about 220 metres, those living within its walls were blessed with uninterrupted views of the countryside towards the north and east. However, Ffridd Faldwyn (248 m), a prominent hilltop crowned by an Iron Age hill fort, prevented the castle's residents from seeing Hen Domen, the eleventh-century motte and bailey castle predating Montgomery Castle, which overlooked the Severn's floodplain, near Rhydwhyman (Rhyd Chwima) ford. There, in September 1267, rather than within the stronger stone-built walls of Montgomery Castle, the Treaty of Montgomery was concluded, an agreement that not only recognized Llywelyn ap Gruffudd as Prince of Wales, but also

heralded, at least for a time, a stable relationship between the English Crown and the new Principality of Wales.

The stone used to build the castle walls was obtained from two, deep trenches, the outermost spanned by a one-time drawbridge that gave access to the middle ward, and the innermost spanned by a drawbridge between the middle and inner ward. The rock is a conglomerate, a mass of pebbles, cobbles and boulders of andesitic lava set within a matrix of sand, which originally accumulated on the sea floor following volcanic eruptions that took place during the Ordovician period, about 450 million years ago, either in the vicinity of Moel y Golfa, 18 kilometres to the north-north-east or Corndon Hill (513 m), 7.6 kilometres to the east.

Although the locally derived volcanic conglomerate, which is the foundation of the rocky ridge overlooking the town, proved eminently suitable for the construction of rubble walls, it did not satisfy all of the demands of the stonemasons employed to build the castle. In order to fashion jambs and lintels, such as those framing the door leading into one of the inner gatehouses, it was necessary

Dressed blocks of sandstone framing the inner gatehouse doorway

to acquire a supply of freestones that could be neatly dressed and carved. The stone selected was a reddish-brown and purplish sandstone, a rock nowhere to be found amongst the sandstones and mudstones outcropping around the 'island' of hard volcanic conglomerate.

Occasional blocks of reddish-brown sandstone are also to be seen in the walls of St Nicholas' Church that stands in the town, atop a mound of glacial deposits. Like the castle, the nave was built of rubble-stone during the 1220s but the windows are framed with dressed blocks of orangey-red or rust-coloured Triassic sandstone derived, in all probability, from the ancient Grinshill quarries situated about 35 kilometres, as the crow flies, north-east of Montgomery. Triassic sandstone from the same quarries was also used to fashion the window and door frames of Powis Castle (Y Castell Coch) on the outskirts of the nearby town of Welshpool (Y Trallwng).

However, the Permian–Triassic sandstones of the Welsh border country vary greatly in colour: some are red, orangey or cream coloured, whilst others are reddish-brown or maroon, such as Shrewsbury sandstone, dressed blocks of which are encountered in some of the older buildings of the one-time county of Montgomeryshire. It's therefore possible that the stonemasons who built Montgomery Castle acquired their stock of freestone, not from Grinshill but somewhere in the vicinity of Shrewsbury (Amwythig). Hitherto, the freestone's exact provenance remains a geological mystery for which there is no satisfactory answer. But once the puzzle is solved, it will be possible to learn a great deal more about at least one of the important medieval trade routes.

Talerddig

SH 930000

043

Eight months before Countess Vane cut the first sod of the Newtown and Machynlleth Railway during a grand ceremony that took place in Machynlleth on 27 November 1857, local draper and rhymester Richard Jones composed 'Cân y Rheilffordd' (The Railway's Song), 25 verses extolling the many perceived benefits of the proposed venture. As a shopkeeper, he not only dreamt of shops full to overflowing of 'lovely ladies from faraway England purchasing local goods', but urged all and sundry to support the long-awaited railway.

The two contractors entrusted with the task of creating the railway that would provide a link between towns and villages of the mid Wales borderland and the west coast were David Davies (1818–90), a native of Llandinam, and Thomas Savin (1826–89), born near Oswestry (Croesoswallt), Shropshire. However, working relations between the two men were not good and Davies dissolved the partnership in October 1860, a little over two years before the grand opening of the Newtown and Machynlleth Railway in January 1863. Two years later an irritable Davies, mindful of past disagreements, was moved to remark before a Parliamentary Committee that 'Mr Savin is only a half Welshman, I am a whole one'!

After the split, the entire venture was Davies' responsibility and to his credit he did his best to employ local workmen and make use of local resources as he sought to achieve his goal. The construction of the railway was no mean feat. Between Machynlleth, some 15 metres above sea level, and Newtown (Y Drenewydd) at a height of 122 metres, the single-line track climbs 197 metres over a distance of 21 kilometres as far as Talerddig summit (c.212 m), the watershed between east- and west-flowing rivers, before descending 75 metres over a distance of 22 kilometres.

Besides the steep 1 in 52 gradient between Cemmaes Road and Talerddig stations, a climb that not all steam trains were able to negotiate without the aid of an additional locomotive, Davies'

'The Arch', a splendid example of an anticline

greatest achievement was the creation of a 37-metre-deep defile through Talerddig's rocks, the deepest rock cutting in the world at the time of its completion. Despite its depth, it's only about 200 metres long and, as a consequence, few passengers aboard today's faster travelling diesel trains are neither aware of its existence nor of the prodigious feat of Davies' labour force.

Formed initially of alternating layers of sand and mud that accumulated on the sea floor during Silurian times, about 440 million years ago, the sandstones and mudstones of Talerddig were, some 40 million years later, deformed during a period of earth movements. One notable feature that testifies to the power of those movements is 'The Arch', an upfold alongside the A470 on the outskirts of Talerddig village visible to all keen-eyed road and rail passengers.

Prior to creating the defile through Talerddig's rocks, Davies had to oversee the drainage of a troublesome tract of marshy land south of the proposed breach. His typically audacious plan involved diverting the river Carno in a northerly direction so that it became part of the Dyfi catchment, rather than a tributary of the river Severn (Hafren) to the south. On completion of that task, the hard, wearisome, pick-and-shovel work of excavating the cutting began in June 1859, a job completed by the 200–300-strong workforce in September 1861. A by-product of their toil was an enormous quantity of valuable building stone (and allegedly the occasional grain of gold!), blocks of sandstone used to construct the many bridges and embankments, in addition to station buildings, between Talerddig and Machynlleth.

Davies had promised that the Newtown and Machynlleth Railway would be completed by 1 May 1862. And so it was. On that day the first steam locomotive – aptly named *Llandinam* – travelled to the new station at Machynlleth, built on the firm foundations of Craig-y-bwch overlooking the Dyfi floodplain. Eight months later, on

Saturday, 3 January 1863, the railway line was officially opened. At 9:00 a.m. two steam locomotives – *Talerddig* and *Countess Vane* – departed Machynlleth and laboriously hauled 22 carriages with 1,500 passengers aboard over Talerddig summit and on to Newtown. Dubbed 'a monstrous train' by Davies, it was scheduled to reach its destination within the space of one and three-quarter hours but it took almost three hours! Apparently, it was touch and go as to whether the heavily-laden train would successfully ascend the steepest, five-kilometre-long section between Llanbryn-mair and Talerddig, where all could marvel at the cutting, Davies' *pièce de résistance*. But succeed it did.

Gazing into the cutting after its completion, Davies is reported to have said: 'I often feared this was going to be the rock of my destruction, but with hard work and Heaven's blessings it has proved to be the rock of my salvation.' Davies went on from Talerddig to become one of Wales' greatest industrial entrepreneurs. His Ocean Coal Company, founded in 1887, came to dominate coalmining in the Rhondda and Ogmore (Ogwr) valleys.

Llanbryn-mair railway bridge built of sandstone blocks obtained, in all probability, from the Talerddig cutting

044

Foel Fadian and Foel Esgair-y-llyn

SN 828954

On a clear day, the panorama that awaits walkers who venture to the top of Foel Fadian (564 m), the highest summit in the former county of Montgomeryshire (Sir Drefaldwyn, now absorbed into Powys), is truly spectacular. For accomplished author, journalist, radio and television broadcaster, and traveller Wynford Vaughan-Thomas, who had served as president and chairman of the Campaign for the Protection of Rural Wales (Ymgyrch Diogelu Cymru Wledig) between 1968 and 1975, it ranked as one of his cherished viewpoints. Indeed, following his death in 1987, members of the campaign raised money in order to erect a monument – in the form of a toposcope – in his memory at the foot of Foel Fadian and alongside the mountain road between Machynlleth and Dylife. From the viewing platform it's claimed that it is possible to see thirteen of Wales' highest summits, some of which exceed 914 metres (3,000 feet), peaks classified as Munros in Scotland.

Historically the area north-west and south-west of Foel Fadian is

Foel Fadian and the gorge-like valley below the cliffs of Esgairfochnant Clipyn Du and the upper reaches of Cwm Dulas (right)

Owain Glyndŵr country and, according to tradition, it was on the summit of Pumlumon Fawr (752 m), eight kilometres south-west of Foel Fadian, that he raised his banner after his famous victory at Hyddgen in 1401, a battle that was part of the Welsh revolt against English rule. In an area where so many stories about Glyndŵr and his soldiers have survived the passage of time, it's fitting that one small section of the 217-kilometre-long Glyndŵr's Way (Llwybr Glyndŵr) between Machynlleth and Llanidloes, cuts across the slopes above Nant Fadian as far as Bwlch y Graig and Creigiau Esgairfochnant, before heading on towards Dylife.

The terrifying gorge-like valley below the cliffs of Esgairfochnant is the location of one of the most remote and inaccessible metal mines in the whole of Wales. The Foel Fadian mine, situated on a foundation of layered Silurian mudstones that underlie the steep, bare, unstable slopes of the ravine, opened in the 1870s. However, despite their best efforts and unremitting hard labour, the miners failed to find lodes of any real value and consequently the venture closed after succeeding to produce a mere 25 tonnes of copper ore. The neighbouring Glaslyn mine, established on the eastern slopes of Cwm Dulas, under the shadow of Foel Esgair-y-llyn (505 m), fared no better. By today, the levels and shafts driven into the hillside during the 1850s and 1870s in order to reach the veins of lead and copper ore are largely hidden beneath a carpet of heather. Concealed too are the remains of the floors where the valuable ore was separated from minerals of no commercial value, such as quartz, and the host rock.

On the banks of the Dulas at the foot of Foel Esgair-y-llyn, once stood Esgair Llyn. Little or nothing remains of the homestead and the community is no more, but Esgair Llyn lives on in the memory of Welsh patriot, former president of Plaid Cymru, businessman and folk singer Dafydd Iwan and his many followers. In response to the impassioned plea of former Welsh rugby international Ray Gravell,

he composed an evocative ballad, sung to the tune of the popular Irish folk song, 'The Fields of Athenry', recalling his childhood days in Esgair Llyn, a place which has now achieved a degree of immortality.

The Dulas, one of many tributaries of the Dyfi, occupies a valley whose beauty and enchantment increases towards its remote and deserted upper reaches, under the shadow of Tarren Bwlch-gwyn (c.500 m) and Clipyn Du (c.550 m), two towering cliffs which bear the imprint of the glacier that sculpted Cwm Dulas when the Last Glaciation was at its peak, 20,000 years ago.

Another feature of the incomparable beauty of the open access land between Tarren Bwlch-gwyn and Foel Fadian is Glaslyn, the shallow lake which is the centrepiece of the largest (230 hectares) and wildest nature reserve owned and managed by the Montgomeryshire Wildlife Trust (Ymddiriedolaeth Natur Maldwyn). The reserve's largest habitat, equivalent to five per cent of the area of the Pumlumon Site of Special Scientific Interest, is heather moorland, interlaced with bilberry and crowberry. Because much of this once extensive upland habitat in Wales has been given over to sheep grazing and forestry plantations, it's now comparatively scarce. The Trust is therefore involved in returning part of the agriculturally 'improved' grassland to heather moor once again, an ideal habitat for breeding red grouse, skylark and wheatear. Of importance too are boggy areas where insect-eating plants such as round-leaved sundew (*Drosera rotundifolia*) and common butterwort (*Pinguicula vulgaris*) flourish alongside *sphagnum* mosses, rushes, sedges and common cotton grass (*Eriophorum angustifolium*).

Although the attractiveness of Glaslyn is evident to all who choose to follow the clearly defined footpath around its shores, it's poor in wildlife because of the very low nutrient supply in its waters. Such a habitat, which is also comparatively scarce, supports quillwort (*Isoetes lacustris*), an unusual aquatic which here grows at the southernmost limit of its territory.

Dylife and Ffrwd Fawr

SN 861941

045

Remote, bleak and virtually devoid of life: precious little remains of the great mining settlement of Dylife where once hundreds were employed in one of the foremost lead mines of Wales. Although it's possible that lead ore (galena) was worked by the Romans, who had established a fortlet on the hill summit of Penycrocbren (469 m) overlooking the site of what was destined to become the centre of lead mining activity, it was the discovery of the rich Llechwedd Du vein and subsequent lodes that induced the rapid development of Dylife in that all-too-brief period of prosperity between 1850 and 1880. In 1851 the mine that employed about 300 men, women and children produced over 1,000 tonnes of lead ore. Twelve years later its output had increased to over 2,500 tonnes, a total not achieved by any other lead mine in Wales until the Fan mine, near Llanidloes, produced over 4,400 tonnes in 1870.

The Dylife mine could boast the largest waterwheel ever in action in Wales. Known as 'y Rhod Goch' (red wheel) or 'Martha [of] Dylife' its diameter measured 19.2 metres. Dylife was also regarded to be the best mechanically equipped metal mine in Britain, on account of the cages that transported miners to and from the bottom of the shafts and raised ore to the surface. By the early 1870s, one of its shafts ranked as the deepest amongst all the metal mines of central Wales, for it plunged to a depth of 305 metres.

By the late 1860s–early 1870s, Dylife was home to a thousand inhabitants served by two Nonconformist chapels; St David's Church; the Dylife Mining Company Cottages, built specifically to house male and female miners; three inns; a school and post office. But after the boom years, bust. With the cessation of mining during the early 1890s, the establishments, founded to serve the needs of the miners and their families, closed one by one and, as a result, the village died as the men and women sought a livelihood elsewhere. Cultural

The Star Inn and an ugly grey spread of mine spoil

The cemetery adjoining the ruinous walls of St David's Church

activities, such as the annual Eisteddfod and meetings of *Y Gymdeithas Lenyddol* (Literary Society) also came to an end.

The Star Inn survives, together with a few cottages and the two converted chapels – the Calvinistic Methodist and Baptist places of worship built in 1842 and 1852, respectively. St David's Church, opened in August 1856, was demolished in 1962. Somewhat surprisingly, visible signs of the once flourishing industry, such as shafts, horse-whim platforms, leats, waterwheel pits and engine houses, are also few and far between, although the area still attracts industrial archaeologists and historians eager to learn more about a remarkable mining venture which, during its lifetime, produced over 37,000 tonnes of lead ore, about 1,560 tonnes of copper ore and almost 400 tonnes of zinc ore.

Apart from its industrial past, Dylife is unsurprisingly renowned for its waterfall, Ffrwd Fawr, because the place-name Dylife (*dylif*[*au*], torrent[s]) signifies a place of torrents. On the outskirts of the 'lost' village the river Twymyn, which flows alongside the minor road linking Llanidloes and Machynlleth, is augmented by the waters of Nant Bryn-moel, before plunging to the floor of a narrow, craggy gorge some 50 metres below the lip of the precipice composed of hard, Silurian sandstone. For about 150 metres beyond the fall the river is confined to a rocky channel, before heading

Ffrwd Fawr

The river Twymyn and its narrow V-shaped and broader U-shaped valley north of the waterfall

northwards along the floor of a V-shaped valley that suddenly broadens into one of the loveliest valleys imaginable through which the Twymyn flows north in the direction of Llanbryn-mair.

The course of the Twymyn north of Ffrwd Fawr is in striking contrast to its easterly course above the fall. For the greater part of their course, its tributaries too head south-eastwards in the general direction of the gap in the hills through which passes the minor road from Dylife to Staylittle (Penffordd-las). Such a pattern clearly indicates that the Twymyn and its south-easterly flowing tributaries originally joined forces and headed through the gap to become part of the headwaters of the southerly-flowing Clywedog. The dramatic change in the direction of flow of the Twymyn in the vicinity of Ffrwd Fawr is a classic example of river capture.

Although it's not altogether clear as to what caused the capture, it was probably triggered by the erosive power of an 'ice age' glacier which widened and deepened the Twymyn valley north of the current location of the waterfall and V-shaped valley. Following the disappearance of the glacier, the greatly deepened valley revitalized the erosional ability of the river's headwaters. In time, one such headwater stream not only excavated the deep V-shaped valley but also intercepted and captured that part of the Twymyn that originally flowed eastwards and became part of the Clywedog's catchment area. The capture also augmented the discharge of the northerly-flowing Twymyn, thereby increasing its ability to deepen further the V-shaped valley downstream of Ffrwd Fawr, one of the highest and most graceful of Welsh waterfalls.

Y Borth–Ynys-las and Cors Fochno

SN 608890

046

Only at close of day, when the flat, calm sea and foamless waves lazily lapped the shore, was it possible for the residents of Aberdyfi to hear the sweet notes of the church bells of Cantre'r Gwaelod. But ever since the summer of 2011, when a bell was hung beneath the seaside town's landing stage as part of the Time and Tide Bell Project, its melodious chime, triggered by the movement of the waves at high tide, is a constant reminder of the mythical lowland kingdom of Cantre'r Gwaelod and its 16 fine cities. Due to the negligence of Seithennin who, in a drunken stupor, forgot to close the sluices in the embankments that prevented the sea from gaining access to the once fertile lowland, Cantre'r Gwaelod was drowned beneath the waters of Cardigan Bay (Bae Ceredigion). Despite his inexcusable behaviour, Seithennin has been made a scapegoat for a disaster that was, after all, a consequence of the post-glacial worldwide rise in sea level.

During the peak of the Last Glaciation, some 20,000 years ago, when north-west Europe and the northern half of North America lay buried beneath enormous ice sheets, worldwide sea level was about 130 metres below its present level. As the climate warmed, those huge ice sheets were relatively slow to release their grip on the land,

Cors Fochno dominated by a tapestry of russet- and brown-coloured sphagnum mosses

but not so the ice cap that covered the greater part of Wales and, as consequence, the lowland that lay beyond the country's present coastline was colonised by woodland. The stumps of pine, oak, alder, hazel and birch trees, rooted in the peaty soil in which they grew, are still to be seen occasionally between high and low water mark between Y Borth and Ynys-las, especially in the wake of ferocious winter storms. During the time that the so-called buried forests flourished, the tale of 'Branwen ferch [daughter of] Llŷr' in The Mabinogion records that 'the sea was not wide' between Wales and Ireland and as a result the giant, 'Bendigeidfran waded across ... Later the sea spread out when it flooded the kingdoms'.

By carbon dating some of the wood from the buried forest, the evidence that gave rise to the legend of Cantre'r Gwaelod, it's evident that the sea 'flooded the kingdoms' about 7,000–6,500 years ago, a marine incursion that not only killed the trees, but also undermined and eroded the high ground south of Y Borth. Under the influence of the prevailing south-westerly winds, the accumulated wave-eroded debris at the foot of the cliffs was swept continuously northwards across part of the once forested lowland, a movement that led to the formation of a spit, a shingle ridge extending from Y Borth as far as the sand dunes of Ynys-las.

Landward of the protective barrier, the great peatbog of Cors Fochno (also known as Borth Bog) developed, one of two of Wales' largest raised bogs (Cors Caron is the other), both of which are rich repositories of information enabling Earth scientists to chart past climatic and environmental changes.

The pollen record indicates that reed swamp, the first vegetation to take advantage of the more stable, sheltered conditions behind the spit was succeeded by alder-carr, birch scrub and eventually by forest trees. By about 6,000 years ago, however, the forest was overwhelmed by *Sphagnum* peatbog – four to five metres deep – during a period of increased rainfall. As emphasised by naturalist William Condry, 'Many have been the attempts to drain this great morass, but although agriculture has nibbled around its margins, its centre, raised like the crown on a bowling green, remains inviolate.' It is, undoubtedly, a highly protected landscape, for it forms a component part of the Dyfi National Nature Reserve, which includes the Ynys-las dunes and Dyfi estuary, and has been designated a UNESCO biosphere reserve. But such designations are no protection against the far-reaching environmental changes expected as a result of the continued rise in sea level during the present and future centuries.

145

Situated largely on the lee side of the pebble bank, the holiday resort of Y Borth, home to little more than 1,500 inhabitants, is already the beneficiary of a two-stage £18 million coastal protection scheme which has involved the construction of three near-shore rock breakwaters and two rock groynes. Ceredigion County Council anticipate that the entire scheme, officially opened in September 2015, will provide 'defence against a 1 in 100-year event [but] reducing with sea level rise'. The scheme's efficacy will therefore be much reduced by the end of the century when sea level, the consequence of anthropomorphically triggered global warming, is predicted to be a metre higher than at present.

In the meantime, as sea level continues to rise, the Aberdyfi Time and Tide Bell, one of five located around the shores of Britain by project artist Marcus Vergette, will toll evermore frequently; a recurrent reminder to all global warming deniers of one of the greatest challenges facing humankind.

Ynys-las buried forest and layers of peat exposed following the severe winter storms of 2013–14

Cwm y Maes-mawr and Carn Owen

SN 723880

047

Today the upper reaches of Cwm y Maes-mawr, midway between Tal-y-bont and Pumlumon, and east of the confluence of the rivers Cyneiniog and Cwmere, lie off the beaten track. But things were very different during the late nineteenth century, as testified by the ruins of the Bwlch-glas lead mine at the far end of the potholed country lane, and the remains of the earthworks of a double-tracked rope-worked incline. It rises steeply from the head of the valley, at a height of about 290 metres, to the floor of the col, at a height of 420 metres, at the foot of the southern slopes of Carn Owen (482 m). Except for one shaft, all obvious traces of Henfwlch mine, which stood on the floor of the col and produced lead ore and a lesser quantity of copper ore during the second half of the nineteenth century, have long since disappeared. Few, too, are the remains of the Hafan lead, copper and zinc mine situated about halfway up the incline and worked in conjunction with Henfwlch, although the underground workings were independent of one another.

However, the spectacular valley-head incline had little or nothing to do with the Henfwlch and Hafan mines. That engineering masterpiece was part of the Plynlimon [sic; Pumlumon] and Hafan Tramway, the brainchild of two men, Thomas Molyneux, a wealthy Lancastrian entrepreneur, and his local agent, Captain John Davies of Tal-y-bont, who developed the tramway with the intention that it should serve the Bryn-glas mine and the Havan [sic] Sett Quarry on the northern slopes of Carn Owen. Molyneux was aware that Aberystwyth Town Council had made some use of the coarse sandstone for street crossings, but he knew full well that it would be impossible to develop the quarry and employ 'in a short time five hundred men' without establishing a tramway linking the quarry with the Cambrian Railway at Llanfihangel Genau'r-glyn, seven kilometres north of Aberystwyth.

On 11 January 1896 a large crowd gathered in Tal-y-bont to witness Sir Pryse Pryse of Gogerddan, the area's leading landowner, cutting the tramway's first sod, before retiring to the White Lion Hotel where, according to the report in *The Aberystwyth Observer*, 'a well-served tea, with ham and eggs, was provided'. By spring 1897, the c.11.5-kilometre-long Plynlimon and Hafan Tramway was complete as far as the foot of the incline. So too was the incline itself and the 2.5-kilometre-long extension to the Hafan quarry, which

Part of the ruins and waste tips of Bryn-glas mine

Carn Owen quarry and the small incline (right) up the hill's southern slopes

necessitated the creation of a small incline up the southern slopes of Carn Owen and a contour hugging tramway as far as the quarry. In the same year, the venture took delivery of the first of three steam engines and a carriage for transporting sightseeing passengers.

Following the first trial run to the foot of the incline on 19 August 1897, the 30 passengers were led up the incline and on to the Hafan quarry. The successful trial convinced the *Cambrian News* reporter that the tramway, which had not received the authorisation of the Board of Trade to operate such a service, would be a great attraction and would 'afford visitors to Aberystwyth an opportunity

of investigating the comparatively unknown but truly beautiful scenery in the neighbourhood'. The special excursions to the foot of the incline did prove popular throughout the summer months, but the passenger service was losing money and consequently it ceased operating in August 1898 and closed entirely in the following year.

Hafan quarry fared no better. According to E.A. Wade, author of *The Plynlimon & Hafan Tramway* (1997), 'The setts proved to be of little use for the paving of streets as they were too hard and did not grit, and horses tended to slip on them'. An insufficient demand for the product, 'coupled with the steadily increasing costs of

Cwm y Maes-mawr from the top of the great incline

transhipment at Llanfihangel [Genau'r-glyn] and Aberystwyth', rendered the quarry unprofitable, so it too closed in 1899 and by the end of the year most of the tramway's rails had been lifted.

Contrary to the original scheme, the tramway did not service the Bryn-glas mine, despite the fact that the track-bed passed between its main buildings. The mine itself, opened in the late 1880s, was worked intermittently until its closure in 1923. During its short life the mineral veins within the local Silurian mudstones yielded about 1,250 tonnes of lead, over 6,300 ounces (1 troy ounce = 31.1 g) of silver and a small quantity of zinc ore.

However, the mine's closure did not signal the end of Cwm y Maes-mawr's chequered industrial history. Between 1956 and 1961 McAlpine and Co. opened the large Carn Owen quarry, situated on the floor of the col at the head of the old incline. The 445 million year old Ordovician rocks, a chaotic mass of light-grey sandstones embedded within dark-grey mudstones, were eminently suitable for the construction of the nearby Nant-y-moch reservoir dam, part of the Cwm Rheidol hydro-electric power scheme opened in July 1964.

048

Pumlumon and Nant-y-moch

SN 790870

Pumlumon frightened London-born Benjamin Heath Malkin, author of *The Scenery, Antiquities, and Biography of South Wales* (1804). He considered that it was the most dangerous mountain in Wales on account of its innumerable squelchy peatbogs. Although George Borrow offers a more appreciative description of the upland in *Wild Wales* (1862) he too was of the opinion that the scene from the summit of Pumlumon Fawr (752 m) 'would have been cheerless in the extreme had not a bright sun lighted up the landscape'. About him, 'A mountain wilderness extended on every side, a waste of russet-coloured hills, with here and there a black, craggy summit. No signs of life or cultivation, and the eye might search in vain for a grove of even a single tree'. In contrast, in the eyes of naturalist William Condry (1918–98), who

with his wife Penny spent a few years of their married life in a primitive cottage on the south-western flank of Pumlumon, the mountain's wild loneliness was neither cheerless nor dreary for it offered unrivalled 'views across Wales; the untrammelled, undulating miles of the high plateau; the mountain silence; [and] the coolness of the uplands after the airless, hot valleys'.

Whereas Condry enjoyed Pumlumon and oft paid his respects 'to the sources of the rivers of which Plynlimon [*sic*] is the famous mother', it's doubtful whether Borrow would have made for the highest summits of the Elenydd mountains – thought to be the highest in the world by his shepherd companion! – had he not set his sights on visiting the sources of the rivers Rheidol, Wye (Gwy) and Severn (Hafren) and partaking of their sparkling waters. The

Llyn Nant-y-cagl and the summit of Pumlumon Fawr

Confluence of the rivers Llechwedd-mawr and Hyddgen

source of the westerly-flowing Rheidol is the small, beautiful lake at the head of Cwm Llygad Rheidol nestling below Pumlumon Fawr. But both the Wye and Severn, whose source was described by Borrow as being 'rather shabby … for so noble a stream', flow south-east, the former rising east of Pumlumon Fawr and the latter near the summit of Pumlumon Cwmbiga (612 m).

Geologically, the upland was carved from a thick succession of Ordovician mudstones and sandstones that outcrop in the core of a complex upfold or dome surrounded by younger Silurian rocks, mainly mudstones that weather a rusty-brown colour. Although rivers have been primarily responsible for excavating the area's valleys, the landscape also bears the undeniable stamp of glacial processes. The rock basin within which lies Llyn Llygad Rheidol at the foot of the encircling craggy cliffs of Graig Las owes its origin to the erosive power of a glacier. Glaciers, too, armed with rock fragments, have left scratches and grooves on glacially-polished and smoothed rock surfaces, and greatly deepened certain valley

reaches, which in recent times have proved to be ideal locations for the creation of reservoirs.

The Rheidol valley is at its deepest at the confluence of two glacial troughs, the chosen site for the construction of the dam wall of Nant-y-moch reservoir, one vital element of a hydro-electric power scheme which has been generating renewable electrical energy ever since 1964. Some would argue that the Nant-y-moch reservoir has made fair part of Pumlumon's desolate landscape. Others lament the fact that the waters of Nant-y-moch have not only drowned two beautiful valleys but have also destroyed a Welsh way of life.

In 1957 the old Nant-y-moch farmhouse, then the highest inhabited farm in the valley and the home of the brothers John and James James, was demolished. So, too, was Blaenrheidol Calvinistic Methodist chapel, built in 1895. After the two aged shepherds had departed their home for the last time, the remote valleys of the rivers Rheidol, Llechwedd-mawr, Hengwm and Hyddgen were left devoid of human habitation. By today, traces of past human activity are all that remain. Bronze Age cairns crown some of the summits, including Pumlumon Fawr, whilst the valleys are littered with more recent evidence dating from the late Middle Ages to the turn of the twentieth century, such as the ruins of a summer dwelling (*hafod*) or a temporary shepherd's dwelling (*lluest*), a sheepfold or peat pit, the source of the fuel burnt to heat the scattered abodes.

Here too the memory of Owain Glyndŵr (Owen Glendower of the English), who instigated a fierce and long-running revolt against the English rule of Wales, lives on. Less than a year after he was proclaimed Prince of Wales by a close circle of friends and family in Glyndyfrdwy (beween Llangollen and Corwen) on 16 September 1400, he defeated a numerically superior English force at Hyddgen. To this day, at the foot of Banc Llechwedd-mawr and near the banks of the river Hyddgen, two kilometres north-west of Llyn Llygad Rheidol, stand Cerrig Cyfamod Glyndŵr (Glyndŵr's Covenant Stones), two boulders of white quartz, some 20 metres apart, which purport to mark the site of Glyndŵr's success. A roadside memorial commemorating his victory stands near the dam wall of Nant-y-moch reservoir.

Nant-y-moch reservoir   *Battle of Hyddgen memorial*

Cwmystwyth

SN 805746

049

Through the heart of Wales run innumerable centuries-old tracks once trodden by drovers and their livestock bound for the markets of London. Part of one such track heads eastwards through Cwmystwyth before continuing in a south-easterly direction, via the upper reaches of Cwm Elan, to Rhayader (Rhaeadr Gwy). It was a route familiar to English poet and antiquary John Leland who, whilst journeying on horseback westwards through Cwmystwyth sometime between 1534 and 1543, was confronted by a desolate scene, an industrially polluted landscape that predates the golden age of the lead mining industry of Cardiganshire (Ceredigion) by over 300 years. Here, he recorded in his *Itinerary*, there 'hathe beene great digging for leade the smelting whereof hathe destroyed the wooddes that grew plentifully thereabout'. Although a great but idle digging at the time of Leland's visit, the Cwmystwyth mine, destined

to become one of the largest and most successful enterprises amongst the 73 lead mines in operation in 'rural' Cardiganshire in 1850, was by no means the earliest metal mining venture in the upper reaches of the Ystwyth valley.

On the slopes of Bryn Copa, high above the banks of the Ystwyth and to the east of the main Cwmystwyth mine workings, lie one of the earliest and most important metal mining sites in Europe. Here archaeologists discovered implements such as hammer stones and antler picks utilized by Bronze Age miners, some 4,000 years ago, to extract copper ore from mineral veins, a metal required for the production of bronze tools. The lodes containing the ores of copper (chalcopyrite), lead (galena) and zinc (sphalerite) are amongst 50 or more mineralized veins found in association with dozens of near-parallel faults, fractures traceable from the south-south-west to the

north-north-east through the sedimentary Ordovician and Silurian rocks of mid Wales.

Far more environmentally damaging than the work of Bronze Age miners was hushing (water-scouring), the technique employed from the mid fifteenth century to the last quarter of the eighteenth century to expose workable lodes of silvery-grey galena. Hushing involves the sudden release of water from large storage tanks or ponds at high level. As the water rushes downslope it washes away all traces of soil and loose rock fragments, leaving the mineral veins open to view on bare rock surfaces. Radiocarbon dates confirm that the oldest hushing leats (channels) in the vicinity of the opencast workings of Graig Fawr that scar the upper, south-facing slopes of the Cwmystwyth mine, date from about 1460. Nowhere in Britain are there finer examples of this particular mining technique and the opencast workings at the foot of the Graig Fawr cliffs are the most impressive in Wales.

The site of the main mine, designated a Scheduled Ancient Monument, is an industrial archaeologist's paradise, a site noteworthy for its network of contour hugging leats; tramways; ruined buildings, including the foundation of the former huge ore-dressing mill, offices and barracks; deep shafts; adits that drained water from the underground workings; waterwheel pits, and waste tips, largely devoid of plants except for species such as sea campion (*Silene uniflora*) and forked spleenwort (*Asplenium septentrionale*) which seem to thrive in the polluted ground.

For the greater part of the nineteenth century the prosperous Cwmystwyth mine was a hive of activity. Following the discovery of one exceedingly rich lode, the mine succeeded to produce over 13,000 tonnes of lead ore between November 1826 and March 1827. More typical, however, was the annual average output of well over 1,000 tonnes maintained between 1850 and 1868. During the mine's long life, that finally came to an end in 1921, it produced at least

Ruins of Cwmystwyth mine's main buildings

254,000 tonnes of lead ore, in addition to over 9,300 kilograms of silver (galena contains a small amount of silver) and about 193,000 tonnes of sphalerite.

But success came at a price. Those who sought a living in lead mines almost inevitably suffered ill health. The inhaling of silica-laden dust, in particular, coupled with the wet conditions, led to chronic lung diseases, leaving miners easy prey to tubercular infection and an early death, as testified by the gravestones in local chapel and church cemeteries. In addition, the poisonous waste has been responsible for polluting both the rivers and nearby farmland of the ore field.

'By the 1870s', wrote W.J. Lewis, author of *Lead Mining in Wales* (1967) and *An Illustrated History of Cardiganshire* (1970), 'the best veins [in the mines of north Ceredigion] were becoming worked out, and this at a time when there was increasing competition from cheap ores from Spain, North America and Australia ... By 1931 all mines were closed'. Their story and that of the lead mining industry of Wales was once told at the former Llywernog silver-lead mine museum, near Ponterwyd, now called The Silver Mountain Experience, 'a place where magic, history, fear and fun clash'! Regrettably, it does less than justice to an industry that has left its imprint on the landscape of every county in Wales.

A vein of galena

Polluted water emerging via an adit from the underground workings

050

Cwm-hir Abbey

(Abaty Cwm-hir) SO 057711

The 13 medieval religious houses built in Wales by the Cistercians have two notable features in common: their remote locations and scenically beautiful settings. Most isolated of all is Cwm-hir Abbey – 'abbey of the long valley' – visited and succinctly described by John Leland in the 1530s, at a time when time itself, the weather and, most of all, the destructive activities of man had already reduced the once magnificent monastic church and attendant buildings to a partial ruin: 'Comehere an abbay of White Monkes stondith betwixt ii great hills [the slopes of Great Park (439 m) to the north and Llywy (466 m) to the south] in Melennith [Maelienydd] in a bottom wher rennith a litle brooke [Clywedog Brook].'

The abbey, a daughter of Whitland Abbey (Abaty Hendy-gwyn) some 20 kilometres west of Carmarthen (Caerfyrddin), was established in 1176 under the patronage of Cadwallon ap Madog, Lord of Maelienydd, killed by followers of Roger Mortimer, the greatest of the Lords of the March, in 1179. However, in all probability it was during the early years of the thirteenth century, when the area was under the control of Llywelyn ab Iorwerth (Llywelyn the Great) that the monks of Cwm-hir embarked upon the ambitious task of constructing the Cistercian monastery. The 78-metre-long and 24.5-metre-wide nave of the resplendent church – longer than that of Westminster Abbey and amongst the longest monastic and

cathedral naves in Britain – prompted Leland to remark that 'No chirch in Wales is seene of such length as the fundation of walles there begun doth show'; 'there begun' because the church was never completed.

Regrettably, the abbey was partly destroyed by Owain Glyndŵr's men in 1402 because the property was once more under the control of the Mortimer family. Following the dissolution of the monasteries, during the years between 1536 and 1543, the building deteriorated

and was soon plundered for its stone. As a result, little survives of the original edifice except for the dilapidated external walls of the north and south aisle and the moulded bases of three piers out of a total of 14 columns. Nothing remains of the west wall, but parts of the south and north transept walls have survived.

Hard, coarse-grained, grey sandstone of Ordovician age, incapable of being fashioned into well-proportioned building blocks, not to mention slender columns, was used for the construction of

Ruined south wall and transept (above) and base of nave pier (below)

The column is fashioned from buff-coloured freestone of unknown provenance

the rubble-stone walling. It was derived from a series of quarries on the flanks of Great Park, a hill beset with conifers. One of the most prominent quarries amongst the trees is Fowler's Cave, which readily yielded squarish blocks of sandstone, in addition to irregular lumps, that satisfied the demands of the stonemasons.

However, slender pillars, door and window jambs and other dressings could only be fashioned from a freestone, an easily cut, fine-grained stone. Extensive use was made of a buff- or cream-coloured sandstone, very different in texture and colour to the local rock and hence pieces of the dressed, plundered stone are readily identified in the walls of churches, farms, houses and gardens within a radius of about 20 kilometres of the ruined abbey. For example, the splendid thirteenth-century, finely-carved arcade in St Idloes' Church, Llanidloes, some 17 kilometres north-west of Cwm-hir, is part of the 14-bay aisled nave of the Cistercian church of Cwm-hir Abbey that was removed to its present location in 1540–2. Llanddewi Hall, the sixteenth-century mansion house six kilometres east of Cwm-hir, is almost entirely built of dressed stones acquired from the abbey. Two kilometres down-valley of Cwm-hir Abbey stands Tŷ

Fowler's Cave Quarry

Faenor, a seventeenth-century mansion. That too is faced with blocks of dressed, buff-coloured sandstone, and numerous pieces of the freestone excavated from around the house are to be seen in the garden. One of the finest but much weathered examples of the use made of the freestone lies in the private garden of Cwm-hir Home Farm, near the information centre that traces the abbey's history. The tympanum, a copy of which is set above the door of nearby St Mary's Church, depicts the Ascension.

For many years it was thought that the freestone used by the stonemasons of Cwm-hir Abbey was acquired from the famous Grinshill quarries, the source of Grinshill sandstone, about 12 kilometres north of Shrewsbury. Although very similar in appearance to Grinshill sandstone of Triassic age, a recent analysis of the composition of the two rock types has shown that the abbey freestone did not come from Grinshill. Hitherto its source remains a mystery.

Notwithstanding its impressive dimensions, its delightful setting and its location on that part of Glyndŵr's Way (Llwybr Glyndŵr) between Llanbadarn Fynydd and Llanidloes, the abbey in the minds of Welsh patriots is a place of pilgrimage, for within the church the monks buried the beheaded body of Llywelyn Ein Llyw Olaf ('Our Last Leader'), Prince of Wales, killed by the English in a skirmish at Cilmeri on 11 December 1282.

Foel Valve Tower and Nant-gwyllt church (right)

Cwm Elan

SN 925645

051

Many years before the construction of the four Elan dams, 'divine' was the word that the poet Shelley chose to describe the scenery of Cwm Elan, where he had lived for a time. Since his days the area has been transformed into what the *Shell Guide to Mid Wales* (1960) calls 'a new lake district', an inappropriate choice of words considering that the lakes of the English Lake District are natural phenomena. That said, it's a view shared by the thousands who annually visit the valley to admire the 'glorious lakeland', according to the authors of *Discovering Britain* (1982), 'with the reflections of trees, crags and sky mirrored in the shining water'. Yet though spectacular it's not a scene admired by all.

'I see no real beauty in any man-drowned valley however essential they are to industrialisation and to cities far away', wrote naturalist William Condry in his biographical book, *Wildlife, My Life* (1995). 'Nor have I ever loved those waters', he added, 'under which the City of Birmingham drowned the beautiful Elan valley.'

The natural beauty of the remote Elan valley was destroyed following the construction of four reservoirs – Caban-coch, Carreg-ddu, Penygarreg and Craig Goch – by Birmingham Corporation between 1893 and 1904. Its fate was sealed during the 1860s. At the time, James Mansergh, a renowned civil and water engineer, was involved in the construction of the mid Wales railway and, during the course of his work, he identified Cwm Elan as a possible location for the construction of reservoirs: an area of high rainfall; deep, narrow valleys; and impermeable rocks. In 1890, after having been approached by Birmingham City Water Committee to prepare a detailed report on the suitability of Cwm Elan for reservoir construction, Mansergh concluded that there was no better location, a recommendation accepted by the committee. Despite local opposition, an Act of Parliament passed in 1892 granted Birmingham Corporation the right to purchase compulsorily 18,400 hectares of 'gathering grounds'. The work of building the four dams and the 117-kilometre-long pipeline, that could deliver water to Birmingham via gravity rather than expensive pumping, began in 1893 under the supervision of Mansergh.

Geological factors determined the location of the Caban-coch dam, the lower of the four reservoirs. There the valley is at its narrowest, a feature attributable to the hardness of the Caban-coch Conglomerate whose outcrop can be traced from one side of the valley to the other. This remarkable rock is composed of layers of conglomerate (rounded and semi-rounded pebbles and cobbles in a matrix of sand) and coarse-grained sandstone; originally a mixture of stones and sand that had accumulated on an ancient continental shelf, about 440 million years ago, before being dislodged and deposited layer upon layer on the deep sea floor.

Rough blocks of Caban-coch Conglomerate obtained from the two quarries – Chwarel y Gigfran and Chwarel Craig Cnwch – situated on the valley-side slopes either side of the Caban-coch dam

Penygarreg reservoir

wall, formed the core of all four dams. However, it was incapable of being readily fashioned into regular-shaped blocks and hence loads of Pennant sandstone from Craig yr Hesg quarry, Pontypridd, and both Newmead sandstone and dolerite from quarries at Llanelwedd, Builth Wells (Llanfair-ym-Muallt) were acquired to produce the facing stones on the exterior walls of the dams, designed in such a way as to allow water, when the reservoirs were full to overflowing, to cascade unhindered to river level. At such times, declared Mansergh, the water overflowing the 37-metre-high Caban-coch dam wall would rank as the finest waterfall in Wales!

Construction of the four reservoirs, in addition to a temporary 50-kilometre-long railway laid solely to serve the building sites, was undoubtedly one of the civil engineering masterpieces of nineteenth-century Britain, an undertaking once reported as being the 'eighth wonder of the world'. Mansergh's stupendous feat of engineering deserves recognition, so too the remarkable character of its architecture called, of all things, 'Birmingham baroque'! It's seen at its best in the form of the Foel Valve Tower, with its copper dome, that stands on the shores of the Carreg-ddu reservoir. On the opposite shore, beyond the viaduct built on a submerged dam wall which separates the Caban-coch reservoir from the Carreg-ddu reservoir, stands Nant-gwyllt church built in 1898–1900 in place of the 1770s church that was demolished. A number of farms and cottages, a mill, chapel and school, and two mansions – Cwm Elan

and Nant-gwyllt House, each a residence of Shelley – were also flooded. Wealthy landowners received financial compensation but not tenant farmers. Smallholders had to abandon their cottages. Servants lost their jobs. In all, the homes of over 100 residents were destroyed. Ffransis George Payne, author of *Crwydro Sir Faesyfed* (1966, 1968), a delightful two-volume account of his wanderings through his native Radnorshire, poignantly reminds his readers that it was not simply a valley that lay submerged, Cwm Elan's Welsh rural culture was also drowned and irretrievably lost.

Chwarel y Gigfran

Caban-coch Conglomerate

052

Llynnoedd Teifi and Elenydd Mountains

(Llynnoedd Teifi a'r Elenydd) SN 784676

After spending a day in Lampeter (Llanbedr Pont Steffan) and following a restful night's sleep in Strata Florida Abbey (Abaty Ystrad-fflur) in April 1188, Gerald of Wales (Gerallt Gymro) and his companions continued on their journey, 'leaving on our right the lofty mountains of Moruge, called Elenydd in Welsh', without delay. Not so the English antiquary John Leland (c.1506–52), who journeyed through Wales and England between 1534 and 1543, for it was his task to visit religious establishments such as Strata Florida Abbey in order to record their treasures on behalf of Henry VIII.

Whilst at Strata Florida, Leland ventured as far as Llynnoedd Teifi

(Teifi Pools, an English misnomer), thereby providing readers of his *Itinerary* (1710) with a none too flattering description of the desolate beauty of one small portion of the Elenydd mountains. After completing the four-kilometre 'craggi and stoni' journey from the abbey to Llyn Teifi, he travelled a further three kilometres northwards to the summit of Carreg Naw Llyn (562 m), some 6.5 kilometres north-east of the abbey as the crow flies. From his vantage point Leland 'saw in no place within sight no woodd but al hilly pastures', although, to his relief, 'The hilles bytwyxt Linne Tyue [Llyn Teifi] and Cragnaugllin [Carreg Naw Llyn] were not in sight so

Llyn Teifi reservoir and peatbog at the foot of Pen y Bryn

stony as the hilles bytwyxt Stratfler [Ystrad-fflur] and Llin Tyue'. Nevertheless, to him 'The ground al about [Llyn] Tyue and a great mile toward Stratfler is horrible with the sighte of bare stones'.

Despite Leland's pronouncement, Elenydd's wildness and solitude possesses an undeniable beauty, although its beauty is not wholly natural by any means. The pollen record from the peatbog of Bryniau Pica, south-east of Llyn Egnant, shows that the oak and alder trees that once clothed the now bare hill summits was being rapidly cleared by Bronze Age shepherds. Areas where trees once thrived witnessed the spread of plants of open ground such as ribwort plantain (*Plantago lanceolata*), greater plantain (*Plantago major*), broad-leaved dock (*Rumex obtusifolius*) and braken (*Pteridium aquilinum*). By 2,000 years ago the upland looked much as it does today. Some woodland survived on the slopes of the upper Teifi valley but, following the foundation of the Cistercian abbey of Strata Florida in 1164, their days were also numbered. Sheep-raising resulted in the clearance of much of the land in their possession. Many of the trees not felled by the monks were destroyed during the reign of Edward I (1239–1307) who, during his campaign to conquer the Welsh principality of Llywelyn ap Gruffudd, was eager to deny the Welsh the use of hideaways where they could lie in ambush.

Clearly, the landscape described by Leland was one that had been deliberately deforested. He also knew full well that trees could not re-establish themselves as long as the goats that he encountered were allowed to wander the area and devour seedlings and young trees. An additional unnatural element in the landscape was a portion of the Monks' Trod, linking Strata Florida with its sister abbey in Cwm-hir, established in 1176. The 40-kilometre-long pathway, which in part heads across the bleak peat moorland and rocky hillocks of Elenydd, is considered to be one of the best surviving medieval trackways in Britain. Unfortunately, however, sections of the trod between Llynnoedd Teifi and Cwm Elan have suffered as a result of the use made of it by drivers of off-road vehicles, before such activity was banned.

Not all of the six lakes, known as Llynnoedd Teifi, can claim to be entirely natural either. In the early years of the twentieth century, Llyn Teifi was enlarged by building a dam wall at the outflow of the Teifi. Furthermore, the waters of Nant Lluest were dammed immediately west of the 'bottomless' Llyn Teifi, thereby creating a small reservoir on the site of a peatbog lying between two rock ridges, Cnwc (438 m) and Pen y Bryn (439 m). In 1966 a dam was built across the lower end of Llyn Egnant. Beyond the lake, Nant Egnant becomes a tributary of the river Mwyro, which in turn feeds the Teifi near Strata Florida Abbey.

The three wholly natural lakes – Llyn Hir, Llyn y Gorlan and Llyn Bach – lie between Llyn Teifi and Llyn Egnant. During the Middle Ages it is said that all the lakes, with the exception of the small, man-made reservoir, were stocked with fish by the Cistercian monks and were renowned for the trout and eels that thrived in their peaty waters. Leland refers specifically to the 'plentiful trouttes and elys' in Llyn Hir and the 'trouttes as red as salmon' in Llyn Egnant.

Besides the ice-sculpted ridges and hollow, the most natural elements within the landscape are the acidic peatbogs and marshes, characterized by various species of *sphagnum* moss, sedges and reeds, together with flowering plants such as common cottongrass (*Eriophorum angustifolium*), bogbean (*Menyanthes trifoliata*), common butterwort (*Pinguicula vulgaris*) and round-leaved sundew (*Drosera rotundifolia*).

Round-leaved sundew

Common butterwort

Tregaron Bog

(Cors Caron) SN 690635

053

For an unforgettable, evocative word portrait of Tregaron Bog, there is none better than that in 'Plu'r Gweunydd' (Cottongrass), one of a collection of Welsh-language essays in *Yn y Wlad* (1921), written by Sir Owen M. Edwards (1858–1920), an immensely gifted Welsh scholar, author and educator. One winter's day, as he gazed from the window of the train that trundled across the wetland, between Strata Florida (the station was situated in Ystradmeurig) and Tregaron, what greeted him was 'a cold, dead bog', 'an ugly bog', an expanse of 'untrodden wetland, cold muddy pools, an occasional shapeless, languishing tree, devoid of flowers and life'. Then, on the occasion of a later summertime journey, the bog that he had likened to 'the valley of the shadow of death' had been transformed under the warm rays of the sun. The transformation was the work of *plu'r gweunydd*: 'They were there in their thousands, in groves of gentle, wavy, alive, sunny whiteness. It was they that bestowed on the old ugly black bog its white splendour.' Its Welsh name is Cors Caron, although it's also known as Cors Goch Glan Teifi ('the Red Bog of Teifi's shore'), a reference to the dark red-coloured, winter stems of cottongrass, through which the river meanders.

Besides cottongrass, the 800-hectare bog is replete with wetland plants and mosses, 'for whom', wrote William Condry, 'the sour soils of peatbogs are the sweetest of all environments'. About

Past evidence of peat-cutting

170 different species of birds – especially wetland birds – have also been recorded here and amongst them about 40 are known to breed on site. Among the birds of prey, red kites are a common sight and were, for many years, fed on winter afternoons near Pont Einon, where the Teifi bids farewell to the bog and continues on its southward journey towards Lampeter (Llanbedr Pont Steffan). In recognition of its rich wildlife and the fact that it is one of only two large raised mires in Wales and one of the best examples of a raised bog in Britain, Tregaron Bog has been designated a National Nature Reserve. It is also a wetland of international importance.

In reality, Tregaron Bog is a combination of three dome-shaped, raised bogs. The largest is situated west of the river channel, whilst the other two lie close to its eastern shore. All three developed slowly after the glacier that occupied the Teifi valley during the Last Glaciation had retreated north, but not before a hummocky ridge of glacial deposits had built up in front of the glacier's snout when that had stood stationary for a while in the vicinity of present-day Tregaron. Behind the moraine dam, a shallow lake formed and on its floor a layer of inorganic, blue-grey clay accumulated during the cold period before plants had begun to clothe the valley sides and hills. The lake diminished in size, not only as the Teifi and its tributaries deposited layers of silt on its floor, but also as aquatic plants

West door of Strata Florida Abbey

colonized its shores. With the disappearance of open water, *sphagnum* mosses grew in abundance and their partially decomposed remains led to the build-up of deep layers of dark-brown peat that have taken around 12,000 years to form. By today, the summits of the three peat domes are several metres higher than the surrounding ground and, as a consequence, the raised bog vegetation is wholly rain-fed.

Because of its acidic nature, tree pollen and that of other plants has been preserved in each and every layer of peat. As a result, the bog incorporates an invaluable and dateable record of environmental and climatic changes over the centuries. Beyond the bog, trees clothed the landscape until late in the Bronze Age but they were replaced, to a large extent, by open grassland in the succeeding Iron Age. It appears that livestock farming was the order of the day until the Cistercians, founders of nearby Strata Florida

Abbey (Abaty Ystrad-fflur) in 1164, also introduced arable farming, a practice recorded by the presence of pollen characteristic of agricultural land in the upper peat layers of Tregaron Bog.

In all probability, the practice of cutting bog peat for fuel was also introduced by the monks of Strata Florida. Dafydd ap Gwilym (*fl.* 1340–70), the greatest of medieval Welsh poets, is believed to have been buried in the abbey, and in his poem 'Y Pwll Mawn' ('The Peat Pit') he recalls falling off his horse and into such a pit one evening, whilst on his way to meet one of his many lovers! However, the evidence suggests that peat-cutting was at its peak in the early twentieth century, and did not end until the 1960s. Evidence of past activity is to be seen either side of the boardwalk that leads as far as the Observation Building on the banks of the Teifi at the centre of the wetland. To appreciate fully the splendour of Cors Caron, a visit to the building is essential.

167

054

Stanner–Hanter Rocks

(Creigiau Stanner–Hanter) SO 262583

The summit of Hergest Ridge (426 m) to the west of Kington (Ceintun), reached by following that section of Offa's Dyke Path to the north-east of Gladestry (Llanfair Llythynwg), is a splendid vantage point from which to see and appreciate the form of a line of three remarkable hills whose south-east-facing slopes overlook the Welsh–English border. The three – Hanter Hill (414 m), Worsell Wood (c.300 m) and Stanner Rocks (c.330 m) – represent 'islands' of hard igneous rocks bounded by a sequence of softer and much younger mudstones, which accumulated on the sea floor during Silurian times, some 420 million years ago. In contrast, the molten rock (magma) that gave rise to the dark-grey igneous rocks (mainly dolerite and gabbro), crystallized deep within the Earth's crust during a period of volcanic activity about 710 million years ago, an age determined by radiometrically dating zircon grains, a mineral noted for its indestructibility and consequent longevity. Indeed, one of the six, dated zircon grains extracted from a rock sample obtained on Hanter Hill yielded an age of 1,035 million years! That grain is thought to have been derived from a pre-existing rock and was subsequently recycled and incorporated into the 710-million-year-old magma. All six age determinations confirm that the Stanner–

Hanter rocks are the oldest so far found in Wales and England, and form the foundation upon which all other later rocks lie.

There is no better place to examine the ancient rocks than in the old quarry, situated at the southern end of Stanner Rocks hill and alongside the A44, part way between Kington and New Radnor (Maesyfed). But because the site has been designated a National Nature Reserve and Site of Special Scientific Interest on account of its botanical treasures rather that its geological interest, visitors are urged not to venture further than the quarry floor so as to ensure that the plants are neither disturbed nor damaged. Foremost amongst its botanical treasures is the early star-of-Bethlehem (*Gagea bohemica*) – often known as the Radnor Lily – for Stanner Rocks is the only place in Britain where it can be found. Following the collection of a shrivelled specimen in 1965 and another in 1974, the two long-past-their-best plants were incorrectly identified as the Snowdon lily (*Gagea serotina*), despite the fact that Stanner Rocks were known to lie well to the south of the territory of that well-known arctic-alpine plant, first discovered in the mountains of Snowdonia by Edward Llwyd (1660–1709). The Radnor Lily's true identity was finally confirmed in 1978 following the discovery in

The slopes of Hanter Hill and the wooded hills of Worsell Wood and Stanner Rocks

January 1975 of a fresh specimen, complete with its cluster of bright yellow petals. The plant owes its presence, at least in part, to the rocks, for the lime within them and the site's thin soils, rich in humus, nourish its growth. Furthermore, the thin, quick-drying soils suppress and discourage the spread of species likely to take possession of its restricted habitat.

According to Ffrancis Payne (1900–92), a Welsh-speaking native of Kington and former head of the department of material culture at the Welsh Folk Museum (now the National History Museum), the area's old folk would refer to Stanner Rocks as 'The Devil's Garden', a wholly inappropriate description of a natural, paradisiacal, rock garden noted for its rare and unusual plants. Because the rock face is south-facing, the thin calcareous soils are quick to respond to the warmth of spring sunshine, thereby ensuring the survival of not only wildflowers characteristic of warmer climes, but also rare species of bryophytes with mainly Mediterranean distributions, all of which thrive on the south-facing, sun-baked, igneous rock outcrop.

Compared to the drab backdrop of the dark-grey rock, the various flowers form small, cheerful oases of colour: purple-crimson flowers of bloody crane's-bill (*Geranium sanguineum*); bright yellow blooms of common rock-rose (*Helianthemum nummularium*); blue flowering stalks of spiked speedwell (*Veronica spicata*); red petals of sticky catchfly (*Lychnis viscaria*); small white flowers of English stonecrop (*Sedum anglicum*); and tufted, blue-green heads atop the branches of rock stonecrop (*Sedum forsterianum*). Needless to say the rich array of wildflowers also attract a host of insects and as many as 27 species of butterfly have been recorded on site, including the silver-washed fritillary (*Argynnis paphia*) and wall brown (*Lasiommata megera*).

Many of the plant species that thrive on Stanner Rocks are rare in Britain and need to be conserved. Furthermore, because of the fragility of their habitat, those wishing to study them more closely are required to contact Natural Resources Wales prior to their visit in order to ensure that a member of staff is available to accompany them on site. Natural Resources Wales, who own and manage the nature reserve, is the Government sponsored body charged with the task of ensuring that 'the environmental and natural resources of Wales are sustainably maintained, sustainably enhanced and sustainably used, now and in the future'.

Early star-of-Bethlehem (© Margaret Roberts)

Hergest Ridge

(Cefn Hergest) SO 255562

055

To students of early Welsh literature, Hergest is a name inseparable from one of the most treasured of medieval Welsh manuscripts, The Red Book of Hergest, now in the safe keeping of the Bodleian Library, Oxford, was once possessed by the Vaughan family of Hergest Court, landowners and generous patrons of Welsh literature. The much altered manor house, reputed to have been build c.1430 for Thomas Vaughan, stands at the foot of the south-east-facing slopes of Hergest Ridge, which today lies for the most part in Herefordshire. To reach its summit from Wales, walkers must first head for Gladestry (Llanfair Llythynwg, 'St Mary's church in [the realm of] Dyfnog's tribe'), in order to join that section of Offa's Dyke Path that traverses the ridge. Although no vestige of the late eighth-century, monumental earthwork – built as a frontier line between Mercia, the powerful kingdom of middle England and the smaller Welsh kingdoms to the west – is encountered *en route*, the path is clearly demarcated. At first, relatively steep and stony, the Silurian

Hergest Ridge and Black Mountains escarpment

mudstones and siltstones underfoot that are the foundation stones of Hergest Ridge soon disappear from sight beneath a grassy path set between swathes of bracken.

Between Prestatyn in the north and Chepstow (Cas-gwent) in the south, the 290-kilometre-long, long-distance trail crosses the Wales–England border 20 times. Wales must be bid farewell in order to reach the highest point of Hergest Ridge (426 m), a summit three metres higher than the height of the nearby defunct, concrete triangulation pillar (423 m) that stands beside a pile of stones. Several similar stone mounds top the ridge, some of which may be prehistoric cairns, whilst others probably date from the early years of the twentieth century and the Second World War, when parts of the common land were cleared prior to ploughing.

However, the predominantly cobble- and boulder-sized stones are not derived from the underlying Silurian rocks. Rather, they are erratics, fragments of 'foreign' rocks scattered across the area as the ice sheet that overrode Wales and adjoining parts of England, some 20,000 years ago, melted. Notable amongst the glacial erratics are blocks of gabbro, a hard igneous rock that crystallized deep within the Earth's crust over 700 million years ago. Measuring two cubic metres, the Whet Stone that rests upon the ridge's most northerly summit, is by far the largest gabbro erratic and, according to tradition, local farmers used to place food for the consumption of local folk around its base during the Black Death. The gabbro outcrops on the nearby slopes of Hanter Hill, and through the breach between the hill and Hergest Ridge runs the Welsh–English boundary.

Because of the height of Hergest Ridge in relation to the surrounding territory, the panoramic views that greet those walking Offa's Dyke Path are breathtaking. To the north-west stands the prominent, 660-metre-high upland of Radnor Forest (Fforest Clud), a dome of Silurian rock bounded by steep slopes. No less

Hanter Hill, source of the gabbro glacial erratics

The old triangulation pillar and cairn

conspicuous to the south of Radnor Forest are the summits of Gwaunceste Hill (542 m) and Glasgwm Hill (522 m), the source of the upper tributaries of the Arrow (afon Arwy), that skirts the foot of Hergest Ridge in the vicinity of Hergest Court.

In marked contrast to the hills west of Hergest Ridge is the scene far to the east-south-east. Nowhere does the land within the territory of the Old Red Sandstone rise much higher than 260 metres, so there is little to detract from the impressive prospect of the Malvern Hills, whose highest summit, Worcestershire Beacon (425 m), is one metre short of the maximum height of Hergest Ridge. Malvern, a name Celtic in origin, is derived from the Welsh words *moel* (bare) and *bryn(iau)* (hill[s]), hence Y Moelfryniau in Welsh, a 13-kilometre-long, narrow ridge of Precambrian igneous and metamorphic rocks, some 675 million years old. Like the Stanner–Hanter hills adjoining Hergest Ridge, the Malvern Hills are also carved from hard rocks, which have resisted erosion far better than the sedimentary rocks of the surrounding area.

But by far the most imposing panorama is that to the south and south-west. To the south, beyond the Wye valley (dyffryn Gwy), rise the Black Mountains (Y Mynydd Du) escarpment that overlooks Hay-on-Wye (Y Gelli Gandryll), which hosts the annual Hay Festival of Literature & Arts. Further west, beyond the breach in the Old Red Sandstone escarpment through which flows the river Usk (afon

Wysg), the twin summits – Pen y Fan (886 m) and Corn Du (873 m) – of the Brecon Beacons (Bannau Brycheiniog) come into view. These, the highest mountains of Wales south of Cadair Idris (893 m), are formed primarily of red sandstones and mudstones deposited by rivers on an ancient landmass during Devonian times, some 20 million years after the older, Silurian rocks of Hergest Ridge had accumulated on a sea floor, about 420 million years ago.

Two erratics: a large block of conglomerate, of unknown provenance, and a smaller lump of gabbro

173

056

The Carneddau, Llanelwedd

SO 066540

In the minds of the farming community and those members of the public with an interest in the kaleidoscopic range of rural activities on show, Llanelwedd and nearby Builth Wells (Llanfair-ym-Muallt) are synonymous with the Royal Welsh Show, held annually on the floodplain of the river Wye (afon Gwy). In contrast, the agricultural show is of lesser interest to both geologists and archaeologists, than the allure of the Carneddau, uplands that were the subject of numerous watercolour paintings executed by artist Thomas Jones (1742–1803), who hailed from Pencerrig, Llanelwedd. Examples of his work are housed in the National Library of Wales.

Unlike their namesake in Snowdonia, the Carneddau are hills rather than mountains, since not one of a cluster of summits exceeds 445 metres above sea level. Nevertheless, Ffransis Payne (1870–1949), author of two Welsh-language books chronicling his journeys around the old county of Radnorshire, was correct to declare that the hills were 'mountainous in appearance and of

interesting form'. Here, he added, 'the vistas are simply a reflection of the area's geology dressed in a beautiful skin'. Geologists would argue that that assertion is true of almost every part of Wales, whilst some local residents and visitors alike might question the appropriateness of the adjective 'beautiful' to describe an area scarred by the conspicuous galleries of Llanelwedd quarry.

Even in the early 1960s when Payne was busily writing the first of his two books, the quarry 'bit deeply into the southern slopes of the Carneddau'. Today, the much deeper bite prompted archaeologists of the Clwyd–Powys Archaeological Trust to excavate two burial cairns situated perilously close to the lip of the uppermost gallery. The excavation, undertaken in October–November 2007–8, confirmed that the cairns were constructed during the Bronze Age, about 4,000 years ago, by members of some of the earliest communities to establish themselves in this part of central Wales. Moreover, it appears that both burial mounds were located at a

point that offered uninterrupted views of that portion of the Wye valley, extending from the Elenydd mountains to the west of Rhayader (Rhaeadr Gwy) towards the north, as far as the Black Mountains (Y Mynydd Du) towards the south.

Although quarrying inevitably results in the destruction of geological evidence, it also serves to bring to light hitherto undisclosed information about the rocks of the Carneddau and the processes that led to their formation. Most are volcanic in origin, the product of submarine eruptions that took place during Ordovician times, some 470 million years ago. But overlying and underlying the thick accumulations of volcanic ash (ash-flow tuffs) and lava, are layers of black, fossiliferous mudstones deposited on the floor of a shallow sea before and after the explosive eruptions. Following the cessation of volcanicity, that part of the rock pile above sea level was pounded and eroded by the waves, a process that led to the deposition of offshore sand, the raw material of Newmead sandstone exposed in a series of old quarries alongside the footpath that heads north from the nearby entrance to Llanelwedd quarry.

The buildings of Builth Wells, a town which developed during the nineteenth century when visitors would flock to its wells to partake of the local spring water, bear witness to the importance of both Newmead sandstone and stone from Llanelwedd quarry as a source of valuable building stones, utilized locally and further afield. Dressed stones of both, together with Pennant sandstone from the Craig yr Hesg Quarry at Pontypridd, were used to face the dam walls of the Cwm Elan reservoirs, built in mid Wales by Birmingham Corporation between 1893 and 1904.

Newmead sandstone was also used to construct the first monument erected alongside the A483(T) at Cilmeri in 1902 in memory of Llywelyn ap Gruffudd, the last native Prince of Wales. The benefactor who decided to build the obelisk at his own expense was landowner and author Stanley Price Morgan Bligh (1870–1949), born in Brecon (Aberhonddu) and educated at Eton and Oxford University. The tapering, 3.6-metre-high pillar was constructed of eight dressed blocks of Newmead sandstone and set to stand in a field close to the spot where Llywelyn was slain by soldiers in the service of Edward I of England. Unimaginative and unimposing in appearance, Bligh's obelisk was replaced in 1956 by the current

Llanelwedd quarry galleries

Former Newmead sandstone quarry

memorial, a large, impressive, rough-hewn block of granite, acquired from the quarry at Trefor, on the northern flanks of Yr Eifl, south-west of Caernarfon. However, either side of the entrance to the Cilmeri monolith, which stands atop a prominent grassy mound, are sad reminders of Bligh's patriotic act. Partially obscured by weeds and half buried besides two polished slabs of Trefor granite, one bearing the inscription in Welsh and the other in English informing visitors that it was 'Near this spot was killed our Prince Llywelyn 1282', are cubes of Newmead sandstone, the remains of the original obelisk.

A cube of Newmead sandstone below the inscribed slab of Trefor granite

The Presbyterian chapel, Builth Wells, built of Newmead sandstone

Llanwrtyd and the area's healing wells

057

(Llanwrtyd a bro'r ffynhonnau iachusol) SN 960475

Ever since the establishment of the Artillery Range in the early 1940s, Mynydd Epynt and its imposing north-facing escarpment, extending almost unbroken from Tirabad in the west to Builth (Llanfair-ym-Muallt) in the east, has been out of bounds to members of the public. Although walkers and motorists are permitted at times to stop at the viewpoint and picnic site alongside the high point of the B4519 linking Garth and Upper Chapel (Capel Uchaf) – the only road that crosses the upland – nowhere is it possible to access safely the crest of the escarpment. Fortuitously, at a point where the road enters the range, a narrow strip of open access land includes the summit of Pennau (393 m), a vantage point that offers panoramic views second to none of the southern and eastern extremity of the Elenydd mountains of central Wales. Therein lies the source of the Irfon, a river that departs its narrow, upland, valley tract near Llanwrtyd. Beyond the town, that claims to be the smallest in Britain, it threads its way through hill country as far as Llangamarch, a village situated at the foot of the escarpment and at the confluence of the rivers Irfon and Camarch.

The conifer plantations in the centre background mark the point where the Irfon departs its upland, valley tract. St Cadmarch's Church, Llangamarch, is visible above the tree-lined Irfon valley in the centre of the photograph.

Dôl-y-coed's mighty sulphur well

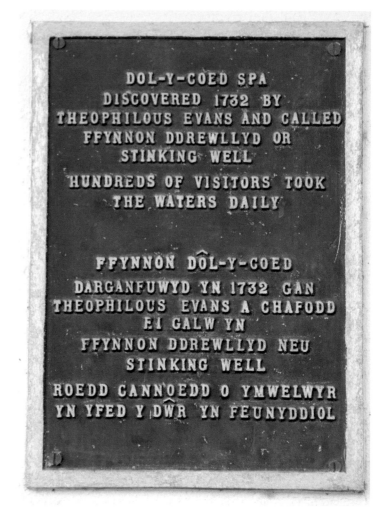

Llangamarch's most prominent landmark is the tower of St Cadmarch's Church and in its cemetery lies the grave of Theophilus Evans (1693–1767), cleric and historian who, in 1738 was given the living of Llangamarch, which was later joined with Llanwrtyd and Abergwesyn. As a historian, he's remembered for his *Drych y Prif Oesoedd* (1716, 1740), a biased account of the early history of Wales, but in and around his home village and Llanwrtyd he's remembered as the discoverer of the 'stinking well' (*y ffynnon ddrewllyd*) in 1732, one of the allegedly healing wells of Pont-rhyd-y-fferau, the settlement that became the focus of Llanwrtyd in the second half of the nineteenth century. According to Evans, the waters of the stinking well in the grounds of Dôl-y-coed had 'much the same gusto as a newly discharged gun' and after he had partaken of them it appears that he was cured of scurvy. The waters of Dôl-y-coed actually stink of hydrogen sulphide – of rotten eggs – which here derives from the decomposition of pyrite or 'fool's gold' (iron sulphide), a mineral common in the area's Ordovician mudstones.

A century later, the Reverend J. Kilsby Jones (1813–89), who is buried in the parish churchyard at Llanwrtyd, was also firmly of the

opinion that the mineral waters had medicinal properties: 'This, dear reader,' he wrote in Welsh, 'will strengthen your nerves ... and will quicken the flow of your blood and will give you the strength of a giant in place of weakness'!

Even before the opening of the railway through central Wales in 1868, wealthy members of society from all quarters of Britain flocked to the four hotels in Pont-rhyd-y-fferau in order to drink their daily measure of malodorous and unsavoury sulphurous spring water. Following the opening of Llanwrtyd Wells railway station, the majority of visitors came from south and south-west Wales, Welsh speakers in the main who set about organizing eisteddfodau, concerts and summer schools in the small town.

The Dôl-y-coed spa buildings were erected by the owner of 'Dolecoed [sic] Hotel & Spa', a first-class hotel that boasted, amongst other things, 40 bedrooms, several lounges, indoor sulphur baths, a billiard room and garage accommodation for 14 cars. Furthermore, it was argued that the spring was as good as the ancient, world-famous sulphurous hot springs of Aix-les-Bains in south-east France! In 1897, the year that Queen Victoria celebrated her diamond jubilee, Victoria Wells were opened, a rival establishment to Dôl-y-coed. Six years later the Abernant Lake Hotel (now an activity centre for youngsters), built on the site of Abernant farmhouse, opened its doors. It was, without doubt, Llanwrtyd's grandest hotel that possessed its own sulphurous spring. In 1922, Henfron Well was the last to open, an additional 'fountain of health' and in its 'spacious pump room' visitors were able to sip medicinal waters 'specially recommended for Neurasthenia, Anaemia, and Skin Diseases'.

Not to be outdone by the allegedly curative powers of Llanwrtyd's springs, the owner of the Lake Hotel, Llangamarch, insisted that his 'spacious pump-room' was the only one in Britain serving drinkable barium water, beneficial to those suffering heart disease, gout and rheumatism.

After the Second World War and following the establishment of the National Health Service in 1948, the custom of drinking medicinal well-water came to an end and, as a consequence, the once busy pump houses and associated well buildings fell into disuse. Although the Dôl-y-coed spa buildings have been restored, valetudinarians no longer seek health there. In the meantime Llanwrtyd, though still calling itself 'Wells', has developed as a tourist centre, frequented by walkers, anglers and pony trekkers. It also stages 'man versus horse' races and has the dubious distinction of staging the annual World Bog Snorkelling Championship!

The former Dolecoed [sic] Hotel

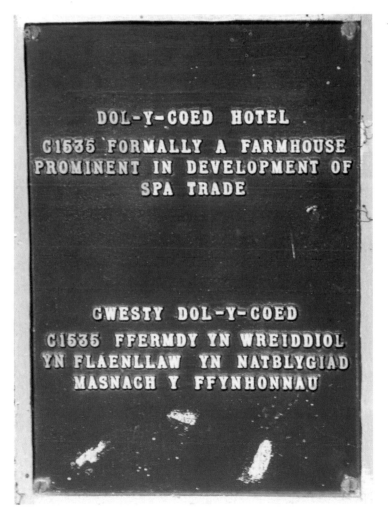

058

Cwmtydu and Traeth Pen-y-graig

SN 360580

Gerald Morgan, author of *Llwybr Arfordir Ceredigion / Ceredigion Coast Path* (2008), the official guide to the path 'From the Teifi to the Dyfi', asserts that 'Llangrannog is surely the most charming of all Ceredigion's coastal villages'. Picturesque it may be, but it is spoilt by a surfeit of holiday homes devoid of life for the greater part of the year. The village occupies one of the many breaks in Ceredigion's cliffy shoreline and is worth a visit if only because it's a convenient starting point from which to follow the anomalous, seven-kilometre-long and, in places, steep-sided valley that forms an unbroken link between Llangrannog and Cwmtydu, whose few houses are set well back from the shore dominated by a restored limekiln.

On no account is it possible to attribute the depth, narrowness and sinuosity of the atypical valley to the erosive action of the few streams that occupy its floor. Nowhere is that more evident than in Cwmtydu, where the valley assumes the form of a channel carved by torrents of glacial meltwater during the time when the huge ice sheet, which once reached this shore by way of the Irish Sea, was

Traeth Pen-y-graig and the site of the Iron Age fort of Castell Bach

rapidly melting and retreating northwards, some 17,000 years ago. An additional legacy of that glacial period are the deposits – chiefly boulder-clay and gravel – piled in places against the channel's lower slopes. Since the disappearance of the ice, the stream has been busily sweeping some of the deposits seaward. Amongst the water-worn stones heaped on Cwmtydu'r beach by the action of storm waves, are numerous examples of foreign rocks: pebbles and cobbles of crystalline granites, blue-grey limestones and red sandstones derived from outcrops in north Wales, the Lake District and north-west Scotland.

Although old, both the glacial deposits and meltwater channel are very recent features when compared to the 440-million-year-old rocks exposed in the cliffs either side of the stony beach. Those outcropping at the foot of Banc Cae'r-llan, on the north side of the bay, are of particular interest, because the thick layers of sandstone are the very oldest strata of the Aberystwyth Grits, a succession of sedimentary rocks no less than 1,200 metres thick, which are the foundation of Ceredigion's magnificent coastal cliffs between Cwmtydu and Y Borth, north of Aberystwyth. This rock sequence was also the first in Britain to be recognized as the depositional product of powerful, submarine currents, known as turbidity currents.

To see such rocks at their best, it's worth climbing Banc Cae'r-llan and walking the Ceredigion Coast Path – part of the 1,400-kilometre-

long Wales Coast Path (Llwybr Arfordir Cymru) opened in May 2012 – as far as Traeth Pen-y-graig, an enchanting embayment cum small island noted for its geological wonders and archaeological interest. The alternating layers of pale-coloured sandstone and dark-grey mudstone are the legacy of early Silurian times when 'Wales' lay about 30° south of the equator. Each bed of sandstone and its associated covering layer of mudstone records one dramatic event.

The original deposits – a mixture of sand and mud – were swept into the sea by rivers flowing north-eastwards off a landmass that lay to the south-west. There the pile of sediments accumulated in the relatively shallow water covering the continental shelf. Every now and then, however, the unstable pile would collapse – perhaps after being shaken by an earth tremor – and hurtle down into the depths of the sea in the form of a dense, turbulent current. On reaching the deep-sea floor, the current would lose momentum and by so doing it would, in the first instance, shed its load of coarse and fine sand, the stuff of sandstone, and ultimately the fine grains of silt and clay, the stuff of mudstone, as the current became ever weaker. It was this repetitive process that led to the formation of the Aberystwyth Grits, probably the finest example in Britain of rocks known as turbidites, the product of turbidity currents.

Originally laid down in near horizontal layers, the alternating pile of sandstones and mudstones was later crumpled during a period of powerful earth movements, some 400 million years ago, as two ancient continents collided with one another. There are no better examples of upfolds (anticlines) and complementary downfolds (synclines) than those at Traeth Pen-y-graig.

Whether such spectacular phenomena were of interest to the Iron Age occupants of Castell Bach is not known but the remains of the promontory fort, established on the gently-sloping, grassy patch of ground above the pebbly beach about 2,500 years ago, is very much in evidence. Its defences consist of two components: two inner banks and ditches and a single outer bank and ditch. Unsurprisingly, part of the outer defences, constructed not on rock but on a foundation of unconsolidated glacial deposits – boulder-clay and thick layers of gravel – have already been lost to the sea. Unfortunately, further loss is inevitable as long as sea level continues to rise.

Mwnt

SN 195519

059

Beloved by holidaymakers, Mwnt's delectable bay-head, sandy beach (Traeth y Mwnt), bounded by the dark-grey cliffs of Hatling Fawr to the south and the rocky knoll of Foel y Mwnt to the north, is one of the gems of Ceredigion's Heritage Coast. Lovely though the beach is, it's not possible to appreciate fully neither Mwnt's current transient charm nor the splendour of the coastal cliffs without climbing the steep path to the summit of Foel y Mwnt.

Underfoot, the 445-million-year old layers of mudstone, which accumulated on the floor of an ancient Ordovician sea, point east–west. To the east, the rugged, indented cliff-line is traceable as far as the bold headland short of Aber-porth, long since despoiled and commandeered by the MOD as a self-proclaimed 'safe environment for the release of land-, air- and sea-launched' missiles. To the west lies Cardigan Island (Ynys Aberteifi), a nature reserve and Site of Special Scientific Interest managed by the Wildlife Trust of South & West Wales. Once the seasonal nesting place of puffins,

Mwnt beach, Foel y Mwnt (76 m) and the whitewashed Eglwys y Grog

exterminated by brown rats that came ashore following the wrecking of the steamer SS *Herefordshire* on the island's rocks in 1934, the breeding seabird population is now dominated by herring gulls and lesser black-backed gulls. The rats were destroyed in the 1960s.

Mwnt's hilltop vantage point is also an excellent place from which to view the seemingly playful antics of dolphins and porpoises, especially between spring and autumn. In fact, the waters of Cardigan Bay (Bae Ceredigion) are home to the largest population of bottle-nosed dolphins – perhaps as many as 250 – in Britain.

Weather permitting, the unmistakeable outline of Bardsey Island (Ynys Enlli), 70 kilometres due north of Traeth y Mwnt, is clearly

Eglwys y Grog and the nearby rocky gorge through which the stream flows and plunges into the sea

visible at the western tip of the Llŷn peninsula. Reputedly the burial place of 20,000 saints, the island was one of the most frequently visited pilgrimage centres in medieval Wales. Prior to setting sail from Traeth y Mwnt, pilgrims would, in all probability, have initially gathered in an earlier church pre-dating the small, austere, fourteenth-century Church of the Holy Cross (Eglwys y Grog), that stands in the shelter of Foel y Mwnt, in order to pray for a safe passage across the oft treacherous waters.

Over the centuries the ever-open door of the solitary church has offered comfort and solace to countless visitors, including well-known Welsh-language poet and author T. Llew Jones, who, in a poem composed in April 1940, spoke of 'leaving behind all of the world's tribulations at the church door'. But the church faces an uncertain future. The National Trust, owners of Traeth y Mwnt and the adjoining land, and publishers of *Shifting shores: Living with a changing coastline* (2007) know full well that 'The sea has immense power, which we ignore at our peril'. Furthermore, in their report they made it abundantly clear that 'In time the road and car park at Mwnt will be affected by erosion'.

The road, car park and church are built on a foundation of unconsolidated deposits, well-exposed in the 25-metre-high cliffs at the head of the sandy beach. All are glacial in origin: a complex accumulation of clay – containing fragments of sea shells and foreign stones of varying colours, shapes and sizes – and folded layers of sand and gravel, which choke the floor of the valley once followed by the stream that now skirts the church, on its seaward journey. Ever since the disappearance of the ice sheet that left the deposits in its wake, the stream that formerly entered the bay was compelled to pursue an alternative course, which involved cutting a rocky gorge through the coastal cliffs and plunging headlong into the sea. In the meantime, as sea level rose following the melting of land-based ice sheets and glaciers at the end of the Last Glaciation, storm waves periodically hammered and undercut the unstable pile of glacial deposits, causing parts of the bay-head cliff to collapse and recede. That process is set to continue unabated as long as sea level continues to rise.

As a result of human induced global warming, triggered by the profligate burning of fossil fuels, the Intergovernmental Panel on

Climate Change foresee that global temperatures are likely to rise between 1.4°C and 5.8°C by the year 2100. Such a change would trigger further melting of the world's ice sheets and glaciers and a rise in sea level of about one metre. If these changes come about, Mwnt's retreating cliff-line will not only threaten the road and car park, but also Eglwys y Grog, which stands a mere 75 metres from the current cliff edge. It has stood for about 700 years but its days are numbered. In time, the rising sea will have washed away the plug of glacial deposits, thereby allowing the diverted stream to repossess its former preglacial course and re-enter the sea at the head of an inlet extending well up-valley of the present high water mark.

060

Teifi Marshes Nature Reserve

(Gwarchodfa Natur Corsydd Teifi) SN 185454

Owned and managed by the Wildlife Trust of South & West Wales, Teifi Marshes is one of the best wetland reserves in Wales. Central to the reserve, within walking distance of Cardigan (Aberteifi), is the Welsh Wildlife Centre (Canolfan Bywyd Gwyllt Cymru), a visitor centre and café deemed worthy of a prestigious award on account of its notable architecture. Within the bounds of the reserve visitors can not only marvel at the wildlife, but also explore the remains of a number of disused slate quarries, or simply enjoy a quiet walk in the fresh air by following one of several footpaths which wind their way through varied and attractive habitats. By far the most popular pathway is a section of the now tarmacked track of the former Cardigan and Whitland Railway, opened as far as the lead mining and slate quarrying villages of Llanfyrnach and Y Glog in 1873 and extended north as far as Cardigan in 1885. Sadly, the line, which closed in 1962, was one of many axed by Dr Richard Beeching.

By visiting the reserve at different times of the year and spending time in the relative comfort of the hides set amidst the extensive

Reed beds and the unmistakeable outline of the Teifi valley no longer occupied by the river

reed beds and nearby woodland, a feast awaits the patient naturalist. He or she can expect to see birds such as Cetti's warbler, kingfisher, marsh harrier and red kite, in addition to a variety of ducks, geese and waders; mammals such as otter, badger and water vole, and even a small herd of water buffalo, introduced to graze parts of the marshy grassland at particular times of the year. One species which

has yet to appear is the osprey but the man-made nest atop a pole awaits its anticipated arrival.

The so-called Fforest slate quarries, cut into the steep-sided, wooded Cilgerran gorge, closed in the late nineteenth century and, as a consequence, trees, ferns, mosses and liverworts have long since clothed their former working faces. Nevertheless, the silent vestiges of all six quarries – Carnarvon [*sic*], Ffynnon, Tommy, Bâch [*sic*], Gigfran and Forever – and their associated waste tips remain to kindle the curiosity of industrial archaeologists and historians alike. Less obvious is the track of the riverside tramway that carted slate slabs from the three largest quarries – Carnarvon, Ffynnon and Tommy – as far as workshops that once stood where the Teifi exits the gorge. Today the peace and quiet of the ravine is the haunt of canoeists, many if not most of whom are blissfully unaware of its past industrial history.

The gorge too is a reminder that the river Teifi hereabouts and elsewhere on its path to the sea no longer occupies its original valley. Indeed, at several locations it abandons its broad valley tract

Blocks of furnace slag edging the track of the former Cardigan and Whitland Railway

in favour of a ravine, such as the meandering Cilgerran gorge which, in places, is over 30 metres deep. Viewed from the old railway track, built on a firm foundation of slate waste from Y Glog and between low walls constructed of blocks of slag, probably derived from Swansea's once world-famous copper works, the outline of the Teifi valley, demarcated by its bounding wooded slopes, is clearly to be seen. But the valley's rock floor lies some 30 metres not only below the surface of the marsh, but also the rock bed of the gorge. Furthermore, the valley's rock floor, deep below the reed beds, is actually some 25 metres below current sea level. A short distance north of Cardigan, the floor of the buried valley is about 40 metres below sea level, a depth exceeded where the Teifi meets the open sea.

To the south of the nature reserve and the old slate quarrying village of Cilgerran, whose ruined Norman castle was the focus of paintings by J.M.W. Turner (1775–1851) and Richard Wilson (1713/14–82), the buried valley floor is traceable eastwards as far as St David's Church, Maenordeifi, situated on the southern edge of the Teifi floodplain, a short distance beyond the point where the river enters the Cilgerran gorge. The Teifi was prevented from following its original course by a thick accumulation of glacial deposits – mainly clay – that choked its valley floor at the peak Last Glaciation, some 20,000 years ago. As the ice sheet that had overridden the area began to melt and retreat, torrents of meltwater released subglacially excavated the five-kilometre-long Cilgerran gorge, a glacial meltwater channel subsequently occupied by the river Teifi following the final disappearance of the ice some 17,000 years ago.

Up-stream of the Cilgerran gorge, similar conditions gave rise to a sequence of gorges and associated buried valleys at Cenarth, Newcastle Emlyn (Castellnewydd Emlyn), Henllan, Alltcafan, Llandysul, Craig Gwrtheyrn and Llanllwni. Indeed, Alltcafan inspired Welsh-language poet T. Llew Jones (1915–2009) to compose one of his best known lyric poems urging all those who have not stood in awe of the wooded gorge and deep, fast-flowing river to do so without delay.

A ready-made osprey nest

Dolaucothi

SN 664402

061

Largely hidden on the floor and flanks of a col amongst the deciduous trees clothing the north-west-facing slopes of the two hills of Allt Cwmhenog and Allt Ogofâu, near the village of Pumsaint, is the former site of Dolaucothi gold mine, known locally as Ogofâu (caves). It is unique, for it's the site of the only known Roman gold mine in Britain. Gold was much sought after by the Romans and it appears that they headed for Ogofâu because they had become aware of the fact that the native folk already knew of the existence of the highly-prized metal to be found in the late Ordovician–early Silurian black shales and siltstones of the area. However, Roman engineers were the first to develop the mine on a large scale, a venture that persuaded them, in all probability, to establish a fort on meadowland at the nearby confluence of the rivers Twrch and Cothi in order to protect and manage their mining interests during their period of occupation between about AD 75 and 350.

Mitchell adit, named after James Mitchell, the Cornish mining engineer employed by the Johnes family in 1905 to re-establish mining on the site

Dolaucothi gold, which is in the form of tiny grains not normally visible to the naked eye, is to be found either amongst bands of sulphide minerals (pyrite and arsenopyrite) or in association with veins of white quartz, both within the crumpled black shales. After sinking shafts and excavating tunnels, it appears that the Roman miners succeeded in winning some of the gold by finely crushing the quartz in order to separate the heavy metal from the lighter, worthless minerals with the aid of water. But much of the gold produced at Dolaucothi was won by excavating open pits in those places where the shales and bands of sulphide minerals had been

weathered. Utilizing a technique described by the Roman author, Pliny the Elder, in AD 77, enormous quantities of water were used to flush away the weathered rock and minerals, whilst the grains of gold were captured in ditches or boxes lined with fleece or gorse.

On the north-west and south-east slopes of Allt Cwmhenog are the remains of leats and aqueducts used to carry water from the rivers Cothi and Annell, which was stored in tanks and reservoirs above the open pits. It is estimated that this sophisticated hydrological system could deliver over 11 million litres of water a day, ready to be released in one torrent over the walls of the open pits –

a process known as hushing. Ogofâu Pit – site of the current visitor attraction – was the largest excavation, where an estimated 500,000 tonnes of rock and worthless minerals yielded 830 kilograms of gold, processed into coins in the Roman Empire's mint either in Lyon, France, or Trier, Germany.

Following the departure of the Romans, the gold mine lay silent until the end of the eighteenth century when some mining was undertaken at the request of John Johnes, owner of Dolaucothi mansion and the 1,284-hectare estate, including the mine. Ogofâu was quiet once again in spring 1842 when Johnes invited well-known geologist, Andrew Crombie Ramsay, of the Geological Survey of Great Britain, 'to a picnic in one of the caves of the Gogofau'! Two years later, one of the officers of the Geological Survey 'rediscovered' gold on the site, a find that prompted others to try to reopen the mine during the second half of the nineteenth and the early years of the twentieth century. In spite of the efforts of James Mitchell, a Cornish mining engineer who had been employed by the Johnes family in 1905, his endeavours met with little success and the mine closed in 1912.

The formation of Roman Deep Ltd in 1933 heralded the most prosperous period of mining. The shaft sunk between 1905 and 1910 was deepened to a depth of 140 metres and a new mill was erected to process the ore. However, the ore at depth, within the Roman Vein, proved problematic. Because of its high arsenic content, nobody in Britain would smelt the auriferous ore and, consequently, it had to be shipped overseas. Small quantities were shipped to Hamburg in the 1930s but, because of the political situation in Europe, the ore was subsequently exported to Seattle at a cost far beyond the means of the mine owners. In 1938, the year Dolaucothi gold mine finally closed, the workforce of 200 men succeeded in producing 39 kilograms of gold by crushing and treating over 17,140,000 kilograms of ore.

In the early 1940s the National Trust were gifted the entire Dolaucothi estate by the Johnes family. Today, the former gold mine is a popular visitor attraction developed by the Trust, especially during the 1980s when the head-frame and buildings from the Olwyn Goch lead mine at Rhyd-y-mwyn, Flintshire, took the place of the original structures demolished following the mine's closure.

Guided tours now allow visitors to experience the Roman, Victorian and 1930s underground workings, whilst a self-guided trail offers an explanation of the mine's on-site legacy.

Roman adit: its form is similar to other known Roman adits

062

MILITARY DEBRIS
IT MAY EXPLODE AND KILL
YOU

PERYGL
PAN CHANIATAU MYNEDIADAU
MYNEDIAD AR HYD LLWYBRAU
FFYRDD CYHOEDDOS YN YNUG
PEIDIWCH A CHYFFWRDD
UNRHIW GWASTRAFF MILWROL
FE ALL FFRWYDRO ACH LLAD.

Merthyr Cynog and Mynydd Epynt

SN 985375

As though it was not enough to destroy a Welsh-speaking community, the MOD chooses to insult and pour scorn on Welsh speakers by erecting unintelligible warning signs, riddled with linguistic errors (above)

Mynydd Epynt is, to a large extent, *terra incognita*. Ever since June 1940, when it was expropriated by the War Office, it has been 'out of bounds' and, as a consequence, members of the public are denied access to a substantial portion of upland Wales. When not greeted by red flags, most of those who choose to travel along the B4519 between Upper Chapel (Capel Uchaf) and Garth – the only road crossing the Artillery Range – must content themselves with viewing a depopulated and desecrated landscape through car windows.

The upland is, in reality, a dissected, southerly-sloping plateau: nowhere do the northernmost sections of the ridges between the rivers Clydach, Cilieni, Brân, Ysgir Fechan, Ysgir Fawr and Honddu rise higher than about 450 metres or lower than about 350 metres where they overlook the Usk (Wysg) valley. With the exception of one tongue of marine rocks of Silurian age in the vicinity of Lower Chapel (Capel Isaf), the upland is carved out of red mudstones and red, purple, green and grey sandstones, hardened fluvial deposits that originally accumulated on river floodplains during early Devonian times, some 410 million years ago.

Within the sheltered valleys, the red, fertile soils, derived from the disintegration of the rocks, are in marked contrast to the high moorland tracts. Indeed, James Rhys 'Kilsby' Jones (1813–89), eccentric, editor and Welsh Independent minister, was firmly of the opinion that no crow had ever flown over hills more desolate and peat-lands more boggy than those of Mynydd Epynt! To experience the contrast, the visitor need only follow the country road up the Ysgir Fechan valley as far as Pont Rhyd-y-berry, before climbing to the village of Merthyr Cynog, atop the ridge between the Ysgir Fechan and Ysgir Fawr valleys. From there on, the visitor must follow the public footpath to the southern boundary fence of the Artillery Range on Cefn Merthyr Cynog (409 m), a journey that has to be undertaken, more often than not, to the accompaniment of clamorous war games.

St Cynog's Church, Merthyr Cynog

Beyond the boundary fence, the view towards the north-east, north and north-west is an eyesore that bears witness to a shameful chapter in the area's history and is an example of land use that should not be tolerated within the bounderies of a civilized country. Here, on the exposed moorland and in the upper reaches of the uninhabited Mynydd Epynt valleys, young soldiers are taught to handle weapons used to kill their fellow human beings.

The fate of Mynydd Epynt – 16,000 hectares of land noted for its natural beauty – was sealed in the early 1940s when the War Office issued an order informing all those living within the boundary of the proposed Artillery Range that they were required to leave their homes by midsummer. A total of 54 families – some 400 men, women and children in all – were forcibly driven out of their homes. As a consequence, a Welsh-speaking community was destroyed; their homes were demolished; their lands were despoiled; and Capel y Babell, the Welsh Calvinistic Methodist chapel built in 1857 in the upper reaches of Cwm Cilieni, was razed to the ground. Ugly blocks of non-native coniferous trees were planted on the mountain pastures beyond the boundary walls of former farms. A number of watchtowers were built from where army officers could follow the course of the war games fought. In the late 1980s, during the 'Cold War', a Germanic-looking village – including a 'church' and 'cemetery' – was constructed not far from the remains of Capel y Babell, so that urban warfare games might also be played out. More recently,

Mynydd Epynt is the target of drone strikes. The unmanned aircraft, part of the latest armoury of the armed forces of Britain and the United States of America, are launched on their test flights from MOD Aber-porth, on the shores of Cardigan Bay.

In his collection of essays, *Personau* (1982), Iorwerth Peate (1901–82), first curator of the Welsh Folk Museum (now the St Fagans: National Museum of History [Sain Ffagan: Amgueddfa Werin Cymru]), expressed the hope that the MOD would relinquish its iron grip on Mynydd Epynt in the fullness of time. However, even if that were to happen, he recognised that it would not be repopulated by a Welsh-speaking people whose ancestral roots lay in the area, but rather by English-speaking newcomers. Although Peate's hope is never likely to materialize, the climb as far as the southern end of Cefn Merthyr Cynog is neither a waste of time nor of energy.

Beyond the southern fringe of Mynydd Epynt and the Usk valley the majestic Old Red Sandstone escarpment comes into view. To the south lie the three highest summits of the Brecon Beacons: Cribyn (795 m) and Corn Du (873 m) either side of Pen y Fan (886 m); to the south-south-west, Fan Gyhirych (725 m) crowns Fforest Fawr, and to the south-west, the silhouetted outline of Fan Hir (c.750 m), Fan Brycheiniog (802 m) and Fan Foel (781 m) beckons.

The north-east-facing escarpment of Fan Hir, Fan Brycheiniog and Fan Foel

Garn Fawr and Pen-caer

SM 896389

063

From the relative safety of their hilltop fort, the members of the Iron Age tribe that established the hill fort on the summit of Garn Fawr (213 m), some 2,500 years ago, could keep watch over much of Pembrokeshire. Beyond Pwll Deri, the bay at the foot of the hill, the headland of Penbwchdy directed their sights towards the twin summits of Carn Llidi and Penbiri near St David's Head (Penmaendewi); to the south and south-east, stretched the featureless but wooded landscape of interior Pembrokeshire; to the east, beyond Carn Ingli, lay the Presely Hills (Y Preselau); and to the north, below the dry-stone walls of their fortress home, stretched the near-flat surface of Pen-caer between them and the open sea.

It's not known whether the now ruined walls of the fort, which link a series of rocky knolls on the hill summit, were ever a witness to an occasional bloody skirmish fought between quarrelsome, neighbouring tribes. But the extensive coastal plateau of Pen-caer, a surface levelled by wave action when sea level was 60–70 metres higher than present, was the stage upon which the 'Last Invasion of Britain' was enacted in February 1797, a battle memorably described by Welsh-language author, T. Llew Jones (1915–2009), as the 'greatest military joke of the eighteenth century'. The headland of Carreg Wastad, the disembarkation point of *La Légion Noire*, an undisciplined French force of 600 regulars and 800 ex-convicts under the command of William Tate, is visible from Garn Fawr. There too on Carreg Wastad, four kilometres north-west of Fishguard (Abergwaun), stands a memorial to the abortive assault. Two days after the landing, the French surrendered on Goodwick (Wdig) beach, thanks in part – according to legend – to local heroine, Jemima Nicholas and her red-cloaked women friends, who were allegedly mistaken for British soldiers. Jemima's gravestone stands beside St Mary's Church, Fishguard.

In contrast to the short-lived fracas of 1797, the record of the rocks exposed between Garn Fawr and Fishguard speaks of a much more violent and long-lived geological commotion that occurred during Ordovician times, when 'Pen-caer' was situated some 30° south of the equator. Lava forms the geological foundation of Pen-caer. It's the product of powerful volcanic eruptions that happened some 470 million years ago as two tectonic plates, on opposite shores of an ancient ocean, drew ever closer to one another and ultimately collided. The same process is active today around the shores of the Pacific Ocean, where the boundaries between colliding tectonic plates are characterised by chains of active volcanoes, some on land and others beneath the sea.

The layers of black, basaltic lava exposed in the coastal cliffs of Pen-caer are known to be the product of submarine eruptions, for the lava is in the form of untidy piles of pillows. As a stream of molten lava is emitted from a submarine opening (like toothpaste from a tube), its surface is cooled rapidly as it comes into contact with cold sea water. As a result, a glassy skin forms around the core of large blobs of molten lava, which are capable of movement (like a balloon filled with water) until the entire mass cools and solidifies.

Columnar-jointed dolerite, Garn Fawr

Part of the ruined walls of Garn Fawr hill fort

Pillow lava: a pile of spherical and ellipsoidal blobs of basaltic lava (right)

The rugged coastline of Pen-caer

Wonderful examples of pillow lavas are evident in the cliffs near the Strumble Head lighthouse atop Ynys Meicel. In places, the pillows are in contact with layers of dark-grey mudstone; mud that was baked and hardened by the once red-hot lava.

The lava pile in the vicinity of Strumble Head is about 1,300 metres thick, but when traced towards Fishguard it thins rapidly, which suggests that the centre of volcanic activity lay somewhere between the lighthouse and Garn Fawr. It's possible that the rocky knoll besides Caer-lem, the farmhouse at the foot of Garn Fawr, denotes the location of one of the volcanic pipes up which flowed the molten rock (magma) that fed one or more of the submarine volcanoes.

The rock (dolerite) forming the foundation of Garn Fawr and neighbouring Garn Fechan, Garn Gilfach, Garn Folch and Y Garn is also the product of volcanic activity. But in contrast to the lava that cooled on the sea floor, a layer of magma was, in this case, intruded into the midst of older rocks, where it slowly cooled, crystallized and contracted. Contraction led to the development of cracks (joints) at right angles to the top and bottom surface of the magma layer. As a consequence, the dolerite was divided into columnar segments, each column possessing six sides when perfectly formed. Columnar jointing is seen at its best at places such as Giant's Causeway on the coast of Antrim in Northern Ireland and Fingal's Cave on the island of Staffa, off the west coast of Scotland, but there's no need to travel further than the summit of Garn Fawr to see excellent examples of the phenomenon. The hexagonal columns were known locally as *torthe ceinioge*, penny loaves, presumably on account of their shape and not their hardness!

197

064

The Presely Hills and their tors

(Y Preselau a'r carnau) SN 145325

Perhaps because of their isolation, standing back as the Presely Hills do from the rest of the Welsh mountains, the westernmost high summits of Wales have acquired a unique quality and character in the minds of many writers and archaeologists alike. Variously described as 'magic mountains', a place of 'innate holiness' and 'home of the gods', the upland has the distinction of being mentioned in 'Culhwch and Olwen', one of the earliest Arthurian tales recorded in the Mabinogion. The tale tells how Culhwch won the hand of Olwen with the aid of Arthur and his knights, who were required to do battle with Twrch Trwyth, the wild boar, on the Presely Hills, an epic bloody encounter recollected in the area's place-names.

Bedd Arthur, 'Arthur's grave', 16 small monoliths arranged in the form of a horseshoe, is situated high on the eastern slopes of Talfynydd and downslope of Carn Bica, from where the 'spotted bluestones' were acquired to construct the monument of unknown date. Near to the king's supposed resting place lies Carn Arthur, 'Arthur's Rock', and on the moorland between Talfynydd and Foel Cwmcerwyn (536 m) stand Cerrig Meibion Arthur, 'the stones of Arthur's sons', two monoliths which, according to tradition, mark the graves of two warriors killed by Twrch Trwyth. The row of small, jagged tors – Cerrig Marchogion – situated atop the ridge between Foel Cwmcerwyn and Talfynydd commemorate Arthur's knights, whilst Foel Dyrch (368 m; 'summit of the wild boars [*tyrch*]'), south-east of Bedd Arthur, recalls Twrch Trwyth.

Place-names apart, the most characteristic feature of the Presely landscape are tors, craggy outcrops of mainly dolerite – a hard, crystalline igneous rock – that seemingly puncture the otherwise

Bedd Arthur, Carn Meini (right) and Foel Drygarn (left)

treeless, grass covered summits and slopes of the hills sculpted from less resistant mudstones and slate, which originally accumulated as layers of mud on the floor of an ancient Ordovician sea. The tors, most numerous in the vicinity of Carn Meini to the north of the dispersed village of Mynachlog-ddu, are the surface expression of thick sheets of molten rock intruded into the midst of the mudstones and slates during Ordovician times, about 470 million years ago. But in contrast to most blue-grey dolerites, that which forms the frost-riven summit tor of Carn Meini and nearby similar tors of Carn Breseb and Carn Goedog, high on the north-facing slopes of the upland, is spotted in appearance due to the presence of small clusters of a white mineral called feldspar.

According to one oft-quoted hypothesis, Carn Meini was the main source of 80 boulders of so-called 'spotted bluestones' which were transported to the site of Stonehenge on Salisbury Plain and used to construct the monument's inner circle and inner horseshoe. That prodigious feat was supposedly accomplished some 5,000 years ago by Presely people who were not only familiar with the geography of south Wales and southern England, but also well-versed in the task of transporting heavy boulders over land and sea. In the case of the 'bluestones', it's envisaged that they were dragged southwards to the shores of the Milford Haven waterway, then by boat via the Bristol Channel as far as the mouth of the river Avon, and finally overland to Stonehenge.

However, geologists have shown that the 'spotted bluestones' were not derived from Carn Meini but from Carn Goedog (c.300 m), on the northern slopes of the Presely Hills. Furthermore, it's also known that some of the small stones found in the soil in and around

Frost-riven 'spotted dolerite' of Carn Meini

Stonehenge came from Craig Rhosyfelin, an outcrop of volcanic lava near Brynberian, at the foot of the north-facing slopes. To transport the 'bluestones' southwards over the crest of the Presely Hills beggars belief, so too a sea voyage from Newport Bay (Bae Trefdraeth), north-west of Carn Goedog and Craig Rhosyfelin, for that would have involved sailing around the entire wave-lashed Pembrokeshire coast. Mike Parker Pearson, well-known archaeologist and author of *Stonehenge: A New Understanding* (2012), is now firmly of the opinion that the monoliths were transported about 350 kilometres via a circuitous overland route through woodland and scrub, across bogs and rivers, by an imagined taskforce of 'thousands' who were presumably fed, watered and offered shelter *en route* by friendly but bemused Neolithic tribesmen and women.

But stones large and small, derived from a variety of sources in south-west Wales are found on Gower and the Vale of Glamorgan. Rocks from south Wales are found in glacial deposits in Somerset. In the light of such firm geological evidence it's difficult, if not impossible, not to attribute the transport of a mixed load of 'bluestones' as far as the western fringes of Salisbury Plain to a vast ice sheet that covered the whole of Wales and the greater part of England north of the Thames valley, about 450,000 years ago. That said, the supposed feat accomplished by the superhuman 'bluestone' carriers is a tale, like that of Culhwch and Olwen, worthy of inclusion in the Mabinogion!

Carn Goedog, main source of the Stonehenge 'spotted bluestones'

Craig Rhosyfelin: frost-shattered volcanic lava

Llanfyrnach and Y Glog

(Llanfyrnach a'r Glog) SN 225315

065

Even today it would be misleading to describe that part of the Taf valley between Llanfyrnach and Y Glog as being rural in character, for Llanfyrnach is the headquarters of Mansel Davies and Son Ltd, one of Wales' largest road haulage companies, which also owns the former Glog slate quarry. Neither was the area rural in character during the adolescent years of John 'Brynach' Davies (1872–1923), poet and editor of the Welsh-language section of the weekly *Cardigan and Tivyside Advertiser*, despite the fact that he waxed lyrical about the incomparable virtues of his rural birthplace. In reality, his home stood beside Llanfyrnach railway station and within a stone's throw and earshot of the Llanfyrnach Silver-Lead Mine, which employed some 100 workers in the 1880s. At about the same time, between 30 and 50 men were employed in the Glog slate quarry, an industrial enterprise audible to the residents of both Y Glog and Llanfyrnach.

Little is known about the early history of the Llanfyrnach mine. It's not known when or who discovered the mineral-rich veins within the local grey-black mudstones, originally deposited on the sea floor during Ordovician times, some 465 million years ago. Nevertheless, several attempts were made to raise commercial quantities of lead ore (galena) from valley-floor pits during the eighteenth century, although the mine was idle when Richard Fenton visited the area a short time prior to the publication of his substantial volume, *A Historical Tour through Pembrokeshire* (1810). Indeed, he records that 'several gentlemen of the first rank and fortune ... derived great wealth from this little Potosí [a town in Bolivia famous for its tin and

Remains of the buddles, machines for separating finely-crushed ore from worthless minerals and rock fragments

silver mines]' but apparently the 'sleeping partners' in the enterprise 'had not even lead for their gold'!

Prospects were equally unpromising during the first half of the nineteenth century but things took a turn for the better in the 1850s. Under the direction of a small group of experienced Cornish miners, who hailed from the Falmouth area, a Cornish beam engine was erected on the banks of the Taf. As a consequence, from 1860 onwards it was possible to raise water from the underground workings even when there was insufficient water in the river to turn the waterwheels previously employed to drain the shafts and levels over 100 metres below the valley floor. By the time that the Cornish miners left the area, sometime before 1871, about 60 workers – men, women and a few children – earned their living in the mine. A sure sign of optimism was Brick Row, two rows of six back-to-back houses, built by the mine owners early in the 1870s to house at least some of their employees. But the good days were short-lived. Failure to locate productive lodes resulted in the production of a mere eight tonnes of lead ore in 1877.

Then, in the summer of 1878, an exceedingly rich vein of ore was discovered. Between 1879 and 1886, 10,000 tonnes of lead ore, valued at £130,000, was produced. During the years of plenty, no longer was it possible for Nant-y-mwyn, near Rhandir-mwyn, by far the most productive lead mine in south Wales, to compete with Llanfyrnach. But within the space of ten years, the miners lost track of all productive mineral veins within the faulted and folded strata and that at a time when the price of lead also began to fall. For those employed in the mine, its closure in 1891 spelt disaster. In 1881 Brick Row housed ten families and of the 56 residents, 11 worked in the mine. Five families remained in 1891 and amongst the 17 residents, only one male was older than 16 years of age. Men sought employment elsewhere.

However, some work was to be had in Glog slate quarry developed by John Owen and his son John (1818–86), two local entrepreneurs, between the 1850s and 1880s. The son, too, was largely responsible for promoting the Whitland and Taff Vale Railway (later renamed the Whitland and Cardigan Railway following its extension to Cardigan [Aberteifi] in 1886) that reached Llanfyrnach and Y Glog in 1873 and provided the means of drawing the quarry's

Ruins of the Cornish beam engine house

products to a wider market. Because of the slate's imperfect cleavage, slabs rather than roofing slates were the main output. For a brief period following the First World War the workforce numbered 80 but the venture did not survive the depression of the 1920s.

The quarry closed in 1926, three years after the death of Brynach who had chosen to ignore the fact that his 'paradisiacal rural birthplace' had been a hive of industrial activity. In the meantime, Mansel Davies, youngest son of John Davies, the mine's blacksmith who had established a business selling coal and lime following the works' closure, was busily developing a company whose maroon-and-grey coloured lorries and tankers are familiar on the highways and byways not only of Wales, but also Britain, Ireland and the continent.

Poisonous waste which only supports particular species of lichen and mosses (below and upper right)

The former Glog slate quarry

066

Carn Llidi and St David's peninsula

(Carn Llidi a Phentir y Sant) SM 738280

It's impossible to experience fully the allure and charm of the St David's peninsula without making for the craggy summit of Carn Llidi (181 m), a hill, mountain-like in appearance, that overlooks Wales' westernmost headland and Ynys Dewi, later called Ramsey by Norse invaders. It was to this hilltop that Waldo Williams (invariably known by his Christian name alone), one of the leading Welsh-language poets of the twentieth century and committed pacifist, came one summer's evening in the early 1930s and underwent a strange experience of a mystical nature. He felt that he had become one with the world around him, a preternatural experience that inspired him to compose a traditional, long Welsh poem (*awdl*) entitled 'Tŷ Ddewi' (The House of David), adjudicated second-best in the competition for the Chair awarded at the National Eisteddfod held in Fishguard (Abergwaun) in 1936.

Whitesands Bay (Porth Mawr) and Ramsey Island (Ynys Dewi)

Waldo's *nom de plume* was Clegyr Boia, the name of the largest and most conspicuous of the smaller rocky islands that overlook the gently undulating coastal plateau of the peninsula, some three kilometres south of Carn Llidi. Though very old, the 470-million-year-old igneous rocks of Carn Llidi are some 130 million years younger than the multicoloured Precambrian volcanic ashes and lava sculpted to form Clegyr Boia. Those rocks, the product of violent eruptions, not only form the core of the peninsula, but also of an enormous upfold (anticline) traceable from one side of the peninsula to the other.

On the southern flank of the anticline, layers of purple, green and grey sandstones and bright red mudstones, all of which accumulated on the sea floor during Cambrian times, some 500 million years ago, plunge steeply southwards along the southern shores of the peninsula. They are best seen between Porth Clais and the two attractive bays of Caerfai and Caerbwdi, where the builders of St David's Cathedral obtained supplies of purple Caerbwdi sandstone to construct the west wall of the building and parts of its interior. The same Cambrian rocks are visible in the coastal cliffs between Porth Stinan, opposite Ynys Dewi, and Whitesands Bay (Porth Mawr), where they dip towards the north-west on the north-western flank of the St David's Anticline.

From his vantage point on Carn Llidi, Waldo witnessed the waves pounding Trwynhwrddyn, the small headland at the northern end of Whitesands Bay, which denotes the boundary between the Cambrian rocks and those of Ordovician age, the most volcanically active period in the geological history of Wales. Today, Ynys Dewi – the former home of Stinan, St David's confessor – is an RSPB nature reserve famous for its populations of seabirds and its rocky shores that are the breeding grounds of grey seal in the autumn. But some 470 million years ago, it was the centre of explosive, submarine volcanic activity, of lava flows and pyroclastic flows (hot mixtures of volcanically fragmented rocks and gas) that accumulated on the sea floor. At the same time, thick sheets of molten rock forced their way amongst layers of older Ordovician mudstones, where they slowly cooled and crystallized. The resultant hard, dark, coarse-grained igneous rock (gabbro) is not only the foundation of Carn Llidi and Penbiri (175 m) and the intervening row of lesser craggy hills, but

One of two collapsed Neolithic burial chambers on the flanks of Carn Llidi

Penbiri and in the background, Garn Fawr and Pen-caer

The tower of St David's Cathedral visible from Carn Llidi

There is less uncertainty about the area's glacial history and legacy. An ice sheet overwhelmed the peninsula about 20,000 years ago, when the Last Glaciation was at its peak. The southerly-flowing ice smoothed and scratched rocks exposed on the summit of Carn Llidi and scattered boulders of gabbro over the ground to the south and south-east of the hill. Some were incorporated in the walls of St David's Cathedral and associated buildings, which nestle on the floor of Glyn Rhosyn, a deep, meandering channel carved by huge volumes of meltwater released during the disappearance of the ice sheet and now occupied by the diminutive river Alun. Precambrian volcanic rocks quarried on the flanks of Glyn Rhosyn were the main source of building stones used in the construction of the cathedral whose tower alone is visible from Carn Llidi.

also the rocky ridge between St David's Head (Penmaendewi) and Penllechwen.

In contrast to its rocks, the peninsula's landforms were fashioned in 'recent' geological times. The most prominent feature is the undulating coastal plateau, a product of probable marine erosion that can be traced at an altitude of some 35–50 metres above present sea level across the mainland and neighbouring Ynys Dewi. Topographic islands such as Carn Llidi–Penbiri and Clegyr Boia on the mainland, and Carn Llundain (136 m) and Carn Ysgubor (101 m) on Ynys Dewi testify to the fact that only the most resistant igneous rocks – their building blocks – could withstand the onslaught of the waves. However, there is considerable uncertainty as to when the topographic islands of today were surrounded by the sea. The current best estimate is some five million years ago. Sometime later the land rose to its present elevation above sea level.

Solva harbour

(Harbwr Solfach) SM 804242

067

There are relatively few sheltered natural harbours around the coastline of Wales and three of the best anchorages are to be found in Pembrokeshire. The largest and most well-known is the Milford Haven waterway (dyfrffordd Aberdaugleddau), a harbour which was, in the opinion of the English naval commander, Horatio Nelson, one of the finest he had ever seen. Porth Clais, the harbour that served the monastic community and cathedral church at St David's (Tyddewi), is the smallest anchorage, whilst Solva (more properly Solfa; f in Welsh is pronounced like the English v) is the most attractive harbour, especially at high tide when the sea reaches the point where the river Solfach empties its waters into the tidal channel.

Like the Milford Haven waterway and Porth Clais, Solfa harbour is a fine example of a ria, a valley partially drowned as sea level worldwide gradually rose and attained its present level about 7,000 years ago. The rise was triggered by the melting and retreat of the vast ice sheets that covered the greater part of the North American continent and north-west Europe – including most of Wales – during the Last Glaciation, which was at its peak some 20,000 years ago. The torrents of glacial meltwater that flowed off the St David's peninsula were also largely responsible for carving the 6.5-kilometre-long, winding channel between Cerbyd and Solfa (a distance of 3.8 kilometres as the crow flies), subsequently occupied by the river Solfach, following the disappearance of the ice.

Trinity Quay

The four limekilns at the foot of the wooded slopes of Y Gribyn

Although the harbour entrance is made treacherous by two rocky islets – St Elvis Rock and Black Rock – John Leland, who journeyed through parts of Wales between 1534 and 1543, was in no doubt that Solfa was the best creek on the shores of St Bride's Bay (Bae Sain Ffraid) for small trading vessels and fishing boats. By the end of the eighteenth century shipping had greatly increased. In 1848 the passenger ship *Cradle* sailed directly from Solfa to New York and eight years later, the formation of a local trading company boosted the further development of Lower Solfa (Solfach Isaf).

Butter and corn were the main exports. Limestone and coal were the main imported goods and on the beach at the foot of Y Gribyn, a ridge topped by a dilapidated Iron Age hill fort, stands four of the dozen limekilns built in Solfa during the eighteenth century. To produce the lime used to sweeten the acid soils of local farmland, limestone was imported from the West Williamston quarries on the shores of the Milford Haven waterway and coal, the fuel to fire the kilns, from the pits of Nolton Haven on the shores of St Bride's Bay. In the early years of the nineteenth century, a century before the lime trade came to an end, it is said that Solfa would have been 'a most delectable place', were it not for the noisome smoke, noxious fumes and dust emitted by the kilns.

During the 1770s, Solfa also witnessed the assembly of the first 'Heath Robinson' lighthouse to be erected on 'the Smalls', a cluster of wave-washed, rocky islets about 35 kilometres west-south-west of the harbour. By 1856, however, work had begun on constructing a more substantial stone-built lighthouse, some 38 metres in height, which would not 'sway alarmingly in rough weather'. Under the direction of Sir James Douglass, chief engineer of Trinity House, the first task involved the building of Trinity Quay on the western shore of the ria, a landing place for the use of steam tugs and barges that transported 3,755 tonnes of silver-grey Cornish granite from the famous De Lank quarries on the western flank of Bodmin Moor, to Solfa at a cost of £50,125. On the quay, each block of granite was trimmed to size before being shipped to the building site, where Douglass and his workers were hard at work during spring and summer months. Nights were spent aboard a ship anchored nearby. The vessel would only return to the shelter of Solfa harbour during very stormy weather.

Lower Solfa

With the exception of the lighthouse, the only memorial to the remarkable achievement and bravery of James Douglass and his workforce is one, small, square pillar of the 275-million-year-old De Lank granite which, although weathered, still retains a measure of its former silvery brilliance. The pillar stands at the foot of a public footpath linking the seaward end of Trinity Quay and Upper Solfa (Solfach Uchaf) but most walkers pass it by without a second glance

and, if challenged, few of the many thousands of visitors and pleasure-boat owners who flock to Solfa every summer could offer an explanation for the two letters and year inscribed on the face of the pillar: 'T[rinity] H[ouse] 1856', the launch date of the enterprise that reached its climax in 1861. It was then that the lantern of the new Smalls lighthouse – the tallest and most graceful of all the lighthouses of Wales – was lit for the first time.

068

Newgale Sands

(Traeth Niwgwl) SM 847223

In 1188 Gerald of Wales (Gerallt Gymro) spent six weeks in the company of Archbishop Baldwin on a preaching tour undertaken to gain support in Wales for the Third Crusade. Whilst travelling from Haverfordwest (Hwlffordd) to St David's (Tyddewi) they were required to cross Newgale Sands in the north-east corner of St Bride's Bay (Bae Sain Ffraid), a journey that prompted Gerald to call to mind and to record in his diary details of a 'curious phenomenon' that Henry II witnessed, in the winter of 1171–2, in the wake of a fearful storm that lashed the coast of south and south-west Wales.

According to Gerald's account 'the shores of South Wales were completely denuded of sand' and, as a consequence, 'Tree-trunks became visible, standing in the sea, with their tops lopped off ... and the sea-shore took on the appearance of a forest grove, cut down at the time of the Flood, or perhaps a little later, but certainly very long ago, and then ... swallowed up by the waves'.

A long time ago, indeed, for it is now known that the sea drowned the forest and the dark, peaty soil which sustained the trees about 6,500–7,000 years ago, as sea level worldwide rose

Newgale Sands and storm beach, and the vulnerable buildings alongside the A487

following the melting of the ice sheets and glaciers of the Last Glaciation, which came to an end 11,500 years ago. Rarely, however, does the buried forest come into view. It's only exposed at low tide and after winter storms, such as those of January and February 2014, have denuded the beach.

The vast expanse of Newgale Sands, a 2.5-kilometre-long, 200-metre-wide intertidal sandy beach, is a favourite haunt of kite-surfers and surf-riders alike, especially in autumn and winter when the waves are at their largest and the prevailing south-westerly winds at their strongest. In summer it attracts hordes of holidaymakers but neither they nor the venturesome surfing fraternity pay scant attention to the enormous bank of rounded cobbles and pebbles that has accumulated at the back of the beach and along that part of St Bride's Bay exposed to the full force of the elements. It is, unquestionably, the finest example in Wales of a storm beach whose crest rises five metres above high water mark. Most of the wave-rounded stones are chunks of sandstone derived from nearby cliffs but amongst them are numerous exotic rocks, glacial erratics deposited on the floor of the bay when the ice sheet that had overran the adjoining St David's peninsula 20,000 years ago, melted.

The marshland on the banks of Brandy Brook (Nant Breudeth) (above)
Layers of black peat that sustained the 'forest grove' (right)

The site of the former Trefrân colliery near the southern end of Newgale Sands

As the ice disappeared, sea level rose and, as a consequence, storm waves gradually moved the countless tonnes of cobbles and pebbles, piled high in the form of a ridge, in a landward direction. That movement has persisted unabated over the centuries.

Whilst there's no truth in the tale that Newgale's storm beach was formed during the infamous storm of 25/26 October 1859 that battered the Welsh coastline and shipwrecked the *Royal Charter* on the east coast of Anglesey (Ynys Môn), the breaking waves would undoubtedly have hurled hundreds of tonnes of stones over the ridge's crest. That certainly happened post 1887, the year that officers of the Ordnance Survey produced the first detailed, large-scale maps of the area. In 1887 the Bridge Inn – renamed the Duke of Edinburgh after Queen Victoria's youngest son who, in 1882, passed by *en route* to St David's – stood at the foot of the storm beach's landward side. It's not known for how many years the hostelry survived the onslaught of storm waves but it was totally destroyed in October 1895. It is said that the innkeeper and her daughter escaped via an upstairs window but not before pocketing 20 gold sovereigns that allowed them to build a new tavern on the opposite side of the road!

Although the present public house is in less danger than the Bridge Inn, the Duke of Edinburgh and other buildings did suffer considerable damage during the tempest of 17 December 1989. In addition to the barrage of stones flung at the walls of the tavern and nearby bungalow, the waves that overtopped the storm beach swept vehicles across the marshland landward of the A487. The scene was repeated during the winter storms of 2014 and, as long as sea level continues to rise, the storm beach will continue on its unstoppable landward journey. In July 2015 Pembrokeshire County Council published its *Newgale Adaptation Plan: identifying potential options*. Although numerous options were proposed (including 'Do nothing' and 'The indefinite repair and renewal of existing bank'!) the only viable, cost-effective and relatively long-term option requires the wholesale relocation of threatened buildings; the building of a viaduct inland to carry the A487 across the marshland, and the abandonment of the marshes to the sea. That's the price that has to be paid for human-induced global warming and resultant sea level rise.

Tywi Valley: Dinefwr–Dryslwyn

(Dyffryn Tywi: Dinefwr–Dryslwyn) SN 612217

069

That stretch of countryside between Llanarthne and Llandeilo is repleat with vantage points from which to marvel at the scenic delights of the Tywi valley. Unsurprisingly, poet and painter John Dyer (1699–1757), chose the summit of Grongaer, for Aberglasney (Aberglasne), his family's home (its gardens, renovated in the 1990s, are now a major visitor attraction) stands at the foot of the hill that inspired his poem 'Grongar Hill'. In it, wrote renowned art historian Peter Lord, Dyer 'described with the precision of intimate acquaintance the beauty of the landscape in which he had grown up'. No less striking is the view from Gelli Aur, an early nineteenth-century mansion, now the focal point of Gelli Aur Country Park, situated on the southern slopes of the Tywi valley, almost opposite Grongaer.

Impressive, too, is the panorama from Paxton's Tower, a neo-Gothic folly erected in honour of Horatio Nelson by Sir William Paxton, owner of Middleton Hall that stood in the grounds of what is now the National Botanic Garden of Wales. From the first-floor room of his tower, Paxton's guests could not only enjoy a repast, but also feast upon the loveliness of the valley between Dryslwyn Castle and Dinefwr Castle, two fortresses which occupy a place of great affection in the minds and traditions of the Welsh people, for both were founded by the Welsh rulers of Deheubarth, the medieval principality of south-west Wales.

But there is no better place to appreciate the form of the valley, and the processes that have left their imprint upon it, than to stand on the walls of Dinefwr Castle, within sight of Dryslwyn Castle, six

The Tywi floodplain beneath the walls of Dinefwr Castle

The meandering Tywi at the foot of the hillock on which stands Dryslwyn Castle

Newton House, centrepiece of Dinefwr Park. The house was extensively modernized in 1856–7.

kilometres down-valley. The stronghold stands atop a hill whose summit is some 75 metres above the river's floodplain meadowlands. Nowhere is the near-flat valley floor less than 600 metres wide, a feature attributable to the ceaseless work of the river, which has been busily recycling and redistributing the glacial deposits left behind following the retreat of the Tywi glacier, some 17,000 years ago. The process of eroding the outer banks of the river's meandering channel and the formation of new land on its inner shores continues unabated as the Tywi meanders across its entire floodplain, except where it is prevented from doing so by the firm foundations of the dismantled Carmarthen (Caerfyrddin)–Llandeilo railway.

The Llandeilo Flags

Apart from one prominent horseshoe bend, that part of the river channel beyond Dinefwr Park is devoid of numerous meanders. That, too, was the state of affairs immediately down-valley of Dryslwyn Castle as recently as 1946. At that time, the river channel between the road bridge, Pont y Dryslwyn, and its confluence with the river Dulas measured 1.6 kilometres in length. However, over the intervening years, complex meanders have added over 600 metres to the river's length, thereby transforming the floodplain's appearance and destroying farmland.

Traces of former meanders also speak of a period when that section of the river channel visible from Dinefwr Castle was far more sinuous than at present. Furthermore, the steep wooded slopes below the castle wall recall a time when the Tywi was actively undercutting the south-facing valley-side.

To the north of the castle's enormous keep, visitors may glance Newton House, originally built in about 1660, and now the centrepiece of Dinefwr Park, an eighteenth-century landscape park, enclosing a medieval deer park, now owned and maintained by the National Trust. In December 1697, Edward Llwyd (Lhuyd), Keeper of the Ashmolean Museum, Oxford, and his companions visited Newton House, the home of Sir George Rice, whilst on their tour around Wales and the Celtic countries between May 1697 and April 1701. Llwyd was an avid collector of fossils and in a 'stone pit' near

the house he made a remarkable discovery: 'flat fish [which represent] one of the greatest rarities hitherto observ'd by ye curious in such enquiries. We found', he added, 'plenty of them (thô few fayr specimens)'. What he had discovered in the thinly-layered calcareous sandstones was the remains of trilobites. Indeed, Llwyd was the first person, in all probability, to discover and portray such marine crustaceans that thrived in a shallow sea during Ordovician times, some 470 million years ago.

The sandstones containing the trilobites were named the 'Llandeilo Flags', after the town of Llandeilo, by Roderick Impey Murchison, who had been elected President of the Geological Society of London six years prior to the publication of his masterpiece, *The Silurian System* (1839). The volume includes a detailed description and illustration of Llwyd's 'flat fish', named *Asaphus Buchii* by Murchison but now known as *Ogygiocarella debuchi*. But why feature an Ordovician trilobite in a book about the Silurian period? In the 1850s the boundary between rocks of Cambrian age and those of Silurian age was the subject of acrimonious debate. The dispute was not resolved until 1879 when Charles Lapworth defined the Ordovician system for the very first time, a period made up of Upper Cambrian and Lower Silurian rocks, including Murchison's 'Llandeilo Flags'!

Coed y Castell Nature Reserve, Dinefwr Park

070

Carreg Cennen and Llygad Llwchwr

SN 668191

Nowhere in Wales is there a more dramatically sited castle than that which stands aloft on the summit of Carreg Cennen, an enormous block of limestone whose sheer south-eastern flank rises some 100 metres above the floodplain of the river Cennen. Less steep are the slopes on the other three sides of the romantic, picturesque ruin that can, at times, appear menacing, judging by J.M.W. Turner's painting of the fortress that appears in his sketchbook, dated 1798. He chose to set the castle's bare outline against a backdrop of a glowering, leaden sky.

The building, in its present form, dates to the late thirteenth century or early fourteenth century and was constructed of local grey limestone, although that hard rock, difficult to carve and dress, did not satisfy all of the stonemasons' demands. Hence, blocks of

softer, reddish sandstone are the dressed stones that appear around the widows, above an occasional doorway arch and forming the row of corbels high on the inner wall of the inner ward built on the highest portion of the crag.

Beds of sandstone, together with siltstones, outcrop along the path which leads from the farm and café to the castle's entranceway. Furthermore, layers of red sand and silt, evident in the banks of the meandering river Cennen, also testify to the presence of Old Red Sandstone rocks which actually encircle the Carboniferous limestone crag of Carreg Cennen. Until about 300 million years ago the crag was part of the Carboniferous limestone's outcrop, encountered about a kilometre south of the castle and traceable in an almost unbroken line from Llandybïe and beyond in the west to

Dan yr Ogof and beyond in the east. The now isolated crag was physically disconnected from the main outcrop as a result of a tectonic collision between two ancient landmasses lying in the vicinity of the equator. Indeed, Carreg Cennen is bounded by two fractures immediately north and south of the limestone island, tears that are but a small section of a large fault system traceable from Pendine (Pentywyn) on the shores of Carmarthen Bay (Bae Caerfyrddin), through Sennybridge (Pontsenni) in the Usk (Wysg) valley and on towards Church Stretton beyond the Welsh border.

When the collision between the two tectonic plates was at its peak, the area would have experienced many powerful earthquakes. That restless period has long since ended but lines of structural weakness remain. On Monday evening, 27 October 1999 the area around Sennybridge was shaken by an earth tremor. The residents of Llandeilo, five kilometres north-west of Carreg Cennen, experienced a similar but more severe event on the evening of 30 October 1868, although that disturbance, which was felt over a wide area and set the 'pheasants and fowls [of nearby Glanbrydan Park, Maenordeifi] screaming', is now known to have been caused by an earthquake centred upon Neath (Castell-nedd).

The person who recorded the earthquake in Llandeilo and the surrounding area was Thomas Jenkins (1813–71), a 'Carpenter and Diarist' according to his headstone in St Teilo's churchyard. The description does not do him justice, for he was also an architect, an astronomer, a scientist and a speleologist. He regularly visited Carreg Cennen Castle and was familiar with the underground passage,

The castle and passageway that leads into the cave

ingeniously created within the brink of the precipice, which he followed in June 1837 'to see the cave under the castle, [which] is about 159ft. [48.5 m] long and has a fine spring of clean water near the further extremity'. Jenkins too was the first to examine thoroughly nearby Llygad Llwchwr and prepare a map of the cave (dated 18 August 1843), which Edward Llwyd had also visited during the 1690s. There in the limestone Llwyd found examples of 'St Cuthbert's Beads', the small circular discs that are the fossilized stems of crinoids, creatures that thrived in the warm, tropical, Carboniferous seas, some 350 million years ago.

Two years prior to preparing his map, Jenkins, in the company of four friends, spent five hours in Llygad Llwchwr on 1 May 1841 but were prevented from penetrating further than about 172 metres from the entrance by a deep pool. Undeterred, he revisited the cave in August and again in September 1843, when he and his friends, in the dim light of candles, succeeded to detect 'two branches where no human being had been before'. On 9 September 1844, after discovering the new branches, Jenkins set about making a coracle, which could be readily taken apart and reassembled. On the following day he and six companions spent a further five hours in Llygad Llwchwr and, after having 'made up the coracle', they 'proceeded down the stream over very deep pools through several magnificent caverns where man never dared to go before'.

By today, cavers with the aid of divers, have mapped about 1.6 kilometres of passageways. Thomas Jenkins, whose fascinating diary spans the years between 1826 and 1870, is recognised as south Wales' first true speleologist.

A window frame made of dressed blocks of reddish sandstone

The river Llwchwr emerging from Llygad Llwchwr cave

Llyn y Fan Fach

SN 803218

071

Bannau Sir Gâr (summits of Carmarthenshire; 677–747 m), that most westerly portion of the Old Red Sandstone escarpment traceable as far east as Hay Bluff (Penybegwn), to the south of Hay (Y Gelli Gandryll), are the most remote summits of south Wales. Relatively difficult to access and blessed with few intrusive footpaths, the mountains form part of the Fforest Fawr Geopark, Wales' first 'geological park' that became a member of the European Geoparks Networks in 2005 and is now one of the 120 members of the UNESCO Geoparks Network, formally established in November 2015. The designation is a means of recognising the rich geological heritage of the park's protected landscape, coterminous with the western half of the Brecon Beacons National Park, designated in 1957.

But geoparks are also to do with people, their relationship to the land and its use over the centuries, and their folk legends, such as the romantic but heartbreaking tale of the 'Lady of the Lake' (Morwyn Llyn y Fan Fach [Maiden of Llyn y Fan Fach]).

One day, according to tradition, there appeared out of the dark waters of the lake, occupying a semi-enclosed, cliff-bound basin, a beautiful maiden who, after many trials and tribulations, finally

Llyn y Fan Fach and the summits of Picws Du (749 m; centre) and Fan Foel (781 m; left)

Llyn y Fan Fach ceased to function as a reservoir serving Llanelli in 1993

agreed to marry the shepherd of nearby Blaen Sawdde farm. The young couple settled in Esgair Llaethdy, a farm near the village of Myddfai, and there raised three sons. But then, after many blissfully happy years of marriage, the husband was guilty of breaking a promise given to his wife prior to marrying, namely that he would never strike her, however gently or accidentally, with an iron object on three separate occasions. Following the third blow, she returned to the mountains in the company of all the animals she had received as a dowry at the time of her wedding and disappeared into the depths of Llyn y Fan Fach, reputed home of the fairy folk, known as *'Gwlad y Tylwyth Teg'*.

In spite of its mythological associations, the lake basin is a natural phenomenon. The rock basin, forming the floor of the craggy amphitheatre (cirque), is the product of the erosive power of an 'ice age' glacier, part of the ice sheet that covered virtually the whole of Wales at the height of the Last Glaciation, 20,000 years ago. That glacial period came to an end about 15,000 years ago, and for some 2,000 years Wales was ice free. A sudden drop in temperature, however, triggered the formation of small glaciers that developed in the shade of the high, north-facing cliffs and did not finally disappear until about 11,500 years ago. As a consequence of its bulldozer-like behaviour, the terminus of the Llyn y Fan Fach glacier is marked by

220

an arcuate, hummocky ridge (moraine) of glacial deposits, a natural dam behind which accumulated the lake waters. Similarly, morainic ridges at the foot of the 100–150-metre-high escarpment, between Llyn y Fan Fach and Fan Foel (781 m), testify to the former presence of two additional but much smaller glaciers. Following their disappearance, two place-names – Pwll yr Henllyn (former lake hollow) and Sychlwch (dry lake) – indicate that water once filled the basins behind the moraines.

Despite the relative warmth of the present post-glacial period, echoes of the intensely cold, glacial conditions of the past are to be found on the cliffs above the shores of Llyn y Fan Fach. There, amongst wild flowers typical of mountain habitats, such as northern bedstraw (*Galium boreale*), rock stonecrop (*Sedum forsterianum*) and lesser meadow-rue (*Thalictrum minus*), are cushions of mossy saxifrage (*Saxifraga hypnoides*) and clusters of roseroot (*Sedum rosea*), both being arctic-alpine species.

In Welsh, roseroot is called *pren y ddannoedd*, 'toothache wood', for in years gone by it was used to ease toothache. The remedy brings to mind the Physicians of Myddfai (Meddygon Myddfai), because tradition has it that the Maiden of Llyn y Fan Fach disclosed vital information regarding the medicinal properties of plants to Rhiwallon, her eldest son. Rhiwallon, with his three sons, was not only the doctor of Rhys Gryg, son of the Lord Rhys (d. 1197), but it was he who also established the lineage of the Physicians of Myddfai, which finally came to an end following the death of David Jones (d. 1719) and his son John Jones (d. 1739). Their gravestone stands in the porch of St Michael's Church, Myddfai.

A darker chapter in the history of Llyn y Fan Fach dawned when an Act of Parliament in 1912 empowered Llanelli Rural District Council to convert the lake into a reservoir. The construction of a water works, an access road as far as the lake shore and a dam wall in order to raise the water level was largely accomplished by 150–200 First World War Conscientious Objectors between 1916 and 1918. Unfamiliar with hard manual labour and under appalling physical circumstances, it was they who were compelled to complete the arduous task begun in 1914.

072

Cwm Llwch and the Brecon Beacons

(Cwm Llwch a Bannau Brycheiniog) SO 002220

During the 1960s and 1970s, the contrast between the mad scramble of walkers on the popular paths homing in on the honeypot peak of Snowdon (Yr Wyddfa) in summer and the relative solitude of the summits of the Brecon Beacons (Bannau Brycheiniog), was striking. Not any more. Regrettably, no longer is it possible to experience the seclusion once guaranteed on the ill-defined paths and highest grass-topped summits – Pen y Fan (886 m), Corn Du (873 m), Y Cribyn (795 m) and Fan y Big (719 m) – of the magnificent Old Red Sandstone escarpment of the Brecon Beacons National Park.

So severe is the annual wear and tear of paths triggered by the tens of thousands of walkers who have their eyes set on conquering one or more of the highest mountains of south Wales, that the National Trust, the landowners, has been compelled to act. The remedial measures have involved paving substantial sections of the two most popular paths leading to Corn Du and Pen y Fan, the one from Pont ar Daf in the upper reaches of Cwm Taf Fawr and the other from Storey Arms Outdoor Education Centre, alongside the busy A470(T).

The moraine-dammed lake of Llyn Cwm Llwch

The path that heads upwards from Storey Arms, via Y Gyrn (619 m), is by far the most scenic. It's also the hardest, especially the final steep ascent to the summit of Corn Du. But the slow, strenuous walk up the ridge of Craig Cwm Llwch, a climb of about 170 metres over a distance of 800 metres, provides interested walkers with an opportunity to ponder the processes that have led to the formation of the Old Red Sandstone rocks and to wonder at the forces that have shaped today's dramatic landforms.

About 390 million years ago, this fragment of the Earth's crust lay about 20° south of the equator and to the south of a chain of mountains of Himalayan proportions that overlooked a semi-arid lowland tract. As the intense heat of the day and chill of night shattered the rocks, the debris – mainly sand and mud – was periodically swept away by flash floods, before accumulating layer by layer on the surface of an extensive plain at the foot of the highlands. Such events gave rise to the so-called Brownstones, a massive, alternately-layered pile of red sandstones and mudstones visible in the high cliffs below the summits of the north-facing escarpment. Resting upon the Brownstones are layers of harder, more resistant sandstones known as the Plateau Beds, to which can be attributed the characteristic table-top appearance of both Corn Du and Pen y Fan. Unfortunately, the layers of peat that formerly covered the Plateau Beds have long since disappeared under the trample of innumerable walkers. The ruined Bronze Age cairns atop the two highest summits have suffered a similar fate.

Originally unremarkable, the upper reaches of the rivers Llwch, Sere, Cynwyn and Menasgin were transformed into enormous horseshoe-shaped cirques by the erosive power of 'ice age' glaciers. And beyond the cirques, the once V-shaped river valleys have been

The bare summit of Corn Du

gouged into a series of steep-sided glacial troughs separated from one another by sharp mountain ridges. However, the retreat of the glaciers about 17,000 years ago did not herald the end of the glacial period. As a result of a rapid cooling of climate 13,000 years ago, small glaciers re-established themselves at the foot of the coldest, sunless slopes within the larger cirques. One such glacier lay beneath the shadow of Craig Cwm Llwch and, around its snout, at a height of about 580 metres, mounds of broken and pulverized sandstone and mudstone accumulated. Following the disappearance of the ice about 11,500 years ago, a lake filled the nine-metre-deep basin between the moraine dam and the steep backwall. To this day Llyn Cwm Llwch, the most perfect of all the moraine-dammed lakes of Wales, bears witness to the end of the Last Glaciation.

However, echoes of the glacial interval that resulted in the formation of the lake have not escaped the notice of plant lovers.

Growing here and there on the shady, cirque backwalls, thanks to the presence of minute quantities of lime within the layers of mudstone, are a few species of lime-loving arctic-alpine plants such as purple saxifrage (*Saxifraga oppositifolia*), mossy saxifrage (*Saxifraga hypnoides*) and roseroot (*Sedum rosea*).

The current climate of the Beacons is noted for its unpredictability, even during summer months. Extreme weather has claimed the lives of several walkers, including five year-old Tommy Jones. A month after his disappearance on 4 August 1900, his body was found close to the site of the obelisk that stands on the lip of Craig Cwm Llwch. Although his grandparents' home, Login farm, was not far from the lake, it seems that he lost his way in the disorientating mist of that fateful summer's evening. Surprisingly, his memorial, unveiled in July 1901, is a pillar of Shap granite, from Cumbria, rather than a slab of local red sandstone.

The Plateau Beds, the foundation of the table-topped summit of Corn Du reached via a paved trackway

The Vale of Ewias and Cwmyoy

(Dyffryn Ewias a Chwm-iou) SO 299233

073

One of the many places visited by Gerald of Wales (Gerallt Gymro) on his journey through Wales in the company of Archbishop Baldwin in 1188 was the delectable 'deep vale of Ewias' on the floor of which stands the Augustinian priory of Llanthony (Llanddewi Nant Hodni) 'in solitude and far removed from the bustle of everyday existence'. Although over 800 years have elapsed since Gerald's visit, relatively little has disturbed the tranquillity or despoiled the incomparable beauty of the area. For that, thanks are due mainly to the narrow country road that winds its way from the village of Llanvihangel Crucorney (Llanfihangel Crucornau), past the tiny hamlets of Cwmyoy (Cwm-iou) and Capel-y-ffin, and on through Gospel Pass (Bwlch yr Efengyl) between two of the high summits of the Black Mountains (Y Mynydd Du), before heading down to Hay-on-Wye (Y Gelli Gandryll) that hosts the annual Hay Festival of Literature and Arts.

According to Gerald, nowhere is the Vale of Ewias 'more than three arrow-shots in width', a narrowness attributable to its glacial history. The dimensions and form of the vale were transformed by the erosive power of a valley glacier that flowed southwards during the Last Glaciation, some 20,000 years ago. As the 'river of ice' ground and pulverized the local red-brown, purple and green sandstones and mudstones, the valley floor was deepened and its sides straightened to such an extent so as to assume the form of a deep, steep-sided trough, bounded in places by high cliffs. The greater part of the valley's bedrock floor is obscured by a thick coating of glacial deposits, an unsorted mass of clay, sand, gravel and boulders that was dumped and left behind as the 'ice age' glacier melted, receded and vacated its trough about 17,000 years ago. Following its disappearance, the river Honddu reoccupied the valley and promptly set about reworking the glacial deposits, a process that resulted in the formation of the fertile, floodplain meadows on either side of its meandering course.

As a consequence of its glacial history, one of the vale's most obvious aspects is the instability of its steep, valley-side slopes. Under the shadow of Tarren yr Esgob, near Capel-y-ffin, the hummocky appearance of the land surface is attributable to a series of age-old landslides. Similar threatening signs of instability visible on the slopes overlooking the ruins of Llanthony priory are also much in evidence below the cliffs of Darren on the west-facing slopes of Hatterrall Hill (Mynydd y Gader), especially at Cwmyoy. There, on a landslip and near its terminus, about 40 metres above the Honddu floodplain, stands the crooked, twisted church of Saint Martin, a building like no other elsewhere in Britain.

Nowhere, either outside or inside the church, parts of which date from the twelfth and thirteenth centuries, is there a vertical wall or walls at right-angles to one another, and it is said that the tower,

The romantic ruins of Llanthony priory, the subject of paintings by J.M.W. Turner (dated 1794) and John Piper (dated 1941)

225

buttressed in two directions, tilts at an angle greater than the world-famous tower of Pisa, which used to lean at an angle of 5.5° prior to the completion of restoration work between 1990 and 2001 that reduced the tilt to about 4°. Part of the church roof sags, whilst windows and interior arches are distorted. Furthermore, the alarming cracks in the interior wall of the nave appear to confirm the views of British Geological Survey officers who believe that the ground beneath the building's foundations occasionally creeps a little further downslope.

According to a local legend, the landslip was triggered by the earthquake that shook the Earth following the crucifixion of Christ. Needless to say, that was not the case. The spectacular slip owes its

existence primarily to the nature and disposition of the rocks, and the steep, valley-side slopes. The mudstones and siltstones forming the foundation of the slope on which the church stands tilt southwards. But they are overlain by a sequence of sandstones forming the foundation of the upper slopes and summit of Hatterrall Hill (531 m). Water is able to percolate through the permeable sandstones but not through the underlying impermeable rocks. Instead, it lubricates the junction between the permeable and impermeable strata, potentially causing enormous blocks of sandstone and broken rock debris to slide downslope under the influence of gravity. As long as the glacier occupying the Vale of Ewias remained in position, it buttressed the unstable slopes, but its removal triggered the Cwmyoy landslide.

It's possible, however, that the continued, slow, downslope creep of the slide is attributable, at least in part, to those who built the church, builders guilty of overloading extremely unstable ground. So, without undertaking expensive engineering work to stabilize the church, its future is less certain than the ruins of Llanthony priory, a place, according to Gerald of Wales, 'still called today Llanddewi Nant Honddu [sic] by the local inhabitants', before adding, 'The English have corrupted the name to Llanthony'.

The prominent gash high above the church formed as a huge slice of the hillside slipped downslope

074

Ysgyryd Fawr

SO 331183

The Reverend William Coxe, author of *An Historical Tour of Monmouthshire* (1801), was unaware of the experiences that awaited him on 'the narrow and desolate ridge' of Ysgyryd Fawr (thankfully 'Skirrid', the mangled English rendition of 'Ysgyryd', no longer appears on contemporary Ordnance Survey maps). Had he known, it's doubtful whether he would have ventured to trek as far as the summit of the isolated hill on the eastern edge of the Black Mountains (Y Mynydd Du), to the north-east of Abergavenny (Y Fenni). The 'horror and delight' that he endured surpassed that which he had experienced 'in the Alps of Switzerland'! On reaching the southern end of the ridge 'he threw [himself] exhausted upon the ground'. Near the summit, Coxe suffered bouts of giddiness as he 'looked down the precipitous sides' of the hill and found that he was no longer able to stand by the 'great fissure' that scars the western slopes of Ysgyryd Fawr (486 m).

Although Coxe's account of his eventful trek beggars belief, the walk along the path – stony in places – that leads to the defunct triangulation pillar atop the summit is physically demanding, for it involves a climb of 270 metres over a distance of about two kilometres from the parking spaces alongside the B4521. Nevertheless, it's well worth the effort, if only to admire an unbroken view of the surrounding countryside and to stand in awe of the 'great fissure' that alarmed Coxe.

According to one tale, the fissure developed 'when the earth did shake; and the rocks were rent' following Christ's crucifixion. Others believed that it was formed by Noah's enormous ark, as the keel of the heavily-laden ship struck the hill and excavated a deep furrow at a time when 'the waters prevailed upon the earth; and all the high mountains that were under the whole heaven were covered'.

However, it was neither an earthquake nor any defective nautical skills on the part of Noah, but a landslide that caused one enormous slice of the upper part of the western flank of the steep hillside to move downslope under the influence of gravity. The fact that the landslide and a number of smaller slips to the south of the 'great fissure' are a feature of the western slopes of the hill, is attributable to the disposition and nature of the Old Red Sandstone rocks from which Ysgyryd Fawr is carved.

The hill and surrounding farmland are, for the most part, underlain by layers of red mudstones and siltstones, but they are capped by layers of purplish sandstones. Water is able to percolate through the permeable sandstone but not through the impermeable mudstones and siltstones. As a result, it lubricates the interface between them, and since that surface and all the overlying strata are tilted westwards, the rocks inevitably slide towards the west. In contrast, the east-facing slopes of Ysgyryd Fawr are far more stable, for the underlying rocks dip down into the earth.

The date of the landslide is not known but it was probably

The remains of St Michael's Chapel beside the old triangulation pillar

Ysgyryd Fawr: the crag denotes the uppermost scar of the 'great fissure' (facing page)

triggered by the vast quantity of meltwater that was released as the glaciers that occupied the area during the last 'ice age' melted and retreated, some 17,000 years ago.

Although the two biblical accounts of the origin of the 'great fissure' are apocryphal, Ysgyryd Fawr formerly enjoyed repute as a holy mountain, revered by local folk. Farmers would gather a small amount of soil off its slopes and scatter it over their land to ensure a good harvest. The soil was also scattered atop the coffins of departed friends. Sometime during the Middle Ages a small chapel was established on the summit of Ysgyryd Fawr, one of the many St Michael's mounts up which pilgrims trudged in medieval times. Today, very little remains of St Michael's Chapel but during the seventeenth century it was here that local members of the Roman Catholic Church would celebrate Mass in secret. Indeed, in 1676 Pope Clement X promised indulgences to those who visited the sacred site on 29 September, St Michael's Day.

That part of Gwent within sight of the 'holy mountain' was not only one of the strongholds of Roman Catholicism in Wales, but also the home of John Arnold, Member of Parliament and Justice of the Peace who lived in the nearby village of Llanvihangel Crucorney (Llanfihangel Crucornau). Arnold, a hot-headed Protestant and anti-Papist, persecuted those who worshiped in St Michael's Chapel and it was he who oversaw the execution of Father David Lewis (1616–79), a Welsh Jesuit priest and native of Abergavenny, who was hanged and posthumously disembowelled in Usk (Brynbuga) on 27 August 1679. In 1970 he was canonized by Pope Paul VI. In Usk, opposite the Catholic church dedicated to St Francis Xavier and St David Lewis, stands a memorial bearing the following inscription in Welsh and English: 'Near this spot Saint David Lewis S.J. Catholic Martyr was executed for his faith 1679'.

The 'great fissure'

Sugar Loaf

(Mynydd Pen-y-fâl) SO 273188

075

The old Welsh proverb correctly asserts that 'a woodcock cannot be identified by the shape of its beak' (*Nid wrth ei big mae adnabod cyffylog*): judge not by appearances. By the same token, a volcano cannot be identified on the basis of its external appearance. Although the symmetrical conical form of Sugar Loaf (596 m), a National Trust property acquired in 1936, is reminiscent of some volcanic cones, especially when viewed from the nearby summit of Ysgyryd Fawr (486 m), goodness only knows what possessed the authors of the revised edition of *The National Trust Guide* (1977) to assert that 'the Sugar Loaf is an extinct volcano'! Neither does the hill mass that overlooks the market town of Abergavenny (Y Fenni) assume the form of a sugar loaf, namely a tall cone with a rounded top, the usual form in which refined sugar was produced and sold

until the late nineteenth century. The hill's name in Welsh is Mynydd Pen-y-fâl (the valley-head mountain), for it lies at the head of the deeply-incised Cwm Trosnant, south of the summit.

Sugar Loaf is an outlier of the Black Mountains (Y Mynydd Du), sculpted from a sequence of rocks known as the Old Red Sandstone, although not all are sandstones or red, for that matter. But walkers choosing to follow the path that heads for the summit from the parking ground on the southern flank of Mynydd Llanwenarth, would not be aware of the red sandstones and mudstones of the so-called Brownstones – a division of the Old Red Sandstone – beneath their feet, because the rocks are hidden under a carpet of bracken, heather and bilberry. However, at the foot of the steep slope, immediately below the rocky summit of Sugar Loaf,

patches of red, sandy soil and scree testify to the presence of the Brownstones beneath the surface, although they are nowhere to be seen on the summit. There, around the base of the defunct Ordnance Survey triangulation pillar, layers of grey-green sandstones, eroded by the trample of countless hill walkers, are evident.

Despite the fact that the grey-green sandstones and the underlying Brownstones are tilted southwards, the sand and mud that gave rise to them was deposited layer by horizontal layer by ancient rivers that meandered their way across extensive, arid plains, when 'Wales', during Devonian times, lay some 20° south of the

Pen Cerrig Calch

equator. Nevertheless, there's a striking difference between the age of the red and grey-green strata. The Brownstones were formed during Lower Devonian times, about 390 million years ago, whilst the grey-green sandstones are late Devonian in age, a geological chapter that came to an end some 360 million years ago.

As the name suggests, the rocks atop the 'limestone-topped summit' of Pen Cerrig Calch (701 m), north-west of Sugar Loaf, are very different in character to the underlying Devonian strata. Furthermore, the Carboniferous limestone itself bears a small cap of 'Millstone Grit' sandstones. In reality, the small island of Carboniferous rocks is all that remains of the Carboniferous limestone and 'Millstone Grit' outcrop that today underpins Mynydd Llangatwg, Gilwern Hill (441 m) and Blorenge (Blorens; 561 m) to the south of the river Usk, strata that in times past extended well to the north of the Usk valley.

In spite of its appearance, the limestone escarpment of Craig y Cilau and Darren Cilau, forming the northernmost boundary of Mynydd Llangatwg on the northern edge of the south Wales coalfield, is not entirely natural, because during the eighteenth and nineteenth centuries the limestone cliffs were extensively quarried. From thence the stone was transported via a tram-road to the Nant-y-glo ironworks in the upper Ebwy Fach valley. But the rocky amphitheatre of Craig y Cilau is now a National Nature Reserve not only on account of its rich plant life – including the rare lesser whitebeam (*Sorbus minima*) not found elsewhere in Wales – and the raised bog of Waun Ddu, but also its renowned cave systems, deep within the bowels of Mynydd Llangatwg: Agen Allwedd (32.5 km) and Ogof Darren Cilau (27 km) are two of the longest in Wales.

Natural wonders aside, vestiges of former industrial activity are also much in evidence on the flanks of Gilwern Hill and Blorenge overlooking Cwm Llanwenarth, to the south of Sugar Loaf. With the exception of the old limestone quarries of Pwll-du, at the head of the valley, the industrial scars are barely visible, but situated on the western slopes of Blorenge is the site of the Garnddyrys forge, opened in 1817, and the track of Thomas Hill's tram-road. The latter not only provided the link between the forge and Blaenavon (Blaenafon) ironworks – the most productive works in Wales and possibly in the world by the 1810s, and today a World Heritage Site – but also Llanfoist (Llan-ffwyst) on the Brecon and Abergavenny Canal, at the foot of the incline on the northern slopes of Blorenge. The forge and tram-road closed in 1860–61 and Pwll-du quarry ceased production following the closure of the ironworks in 1904.

The Grwyne Fawr valley and Black Mountains, north of Sugar Loaf

076

Pen-twyn and Pontsticill

SO 055145

Cwm Taf Fechan can boast more lakes than any other valley in south Wales, although none are natural. Of the four reservoirs, the oldest and one of the earliest in Wales is that of Pen-twyn, created in 1858 to satisfy the demand for clean drinking water by the inhabitants of Merthyr Tydfil (Merthyr Tudful), where cholera had claimed the lives of over 1,500 people in 1848–9. Five years after the opening of the reservoir, it was possible to access the valley not only on foot and horseback, but also by train following the opening of the stations at Dôl-y-gaer and Torpantau on the Brecon and Merthyr Railway.

Above all else, it was the opening of the railway that gave rise to the annual summer regattas held on Llyn Dôl-y-gaer, as the reservoir was known locally. At such times, shops and businesses in Merthyr would close at 1 o'clock in the afternoon, allowing members of the gentry and the *hoi polloi* to head in their thousands to the upper reaches of Cwm Taf Fechan in order to escape, if only for a day, the smoke, noise, stench and squalor of the iron manufacturing capital of the Industrial Revolution, home to almost 52,000 people in 1861.

Pontsticill reservoir

On 7 July 1866, for example, two years before the opening of the railway between Merthyr and Pontsticill that would offer easy access to Dôl-y-gaer for those living in the town centre, the *Merthyr Express* reported that 'nearly 11,000 people had congregated on the grassy slope at the side of the lake when the sports had begun. To minister to their pleasure and to their appetites, marquees, booths and stalls had been erected which did a thriving trade.' Honoured guests from 'Bristol and Cardiff ... were entertained most sumptuously in Mr. [Robert Thompson] Crawshay's private tent [where] a repast of a solid nature was flanked up by the choicest fruits, including new figs, bananas, peaches etc., from the Cyfarthfa [Castle] conservatories'. The feast was devoured to the accompaniment of the Cyfarthfa Brass Band and a fife and drum band stationed on the shores of Llyn Dôl-y-gaer.

But ever since its completion, the days of the Pen-twyn reservoir were numbered, because from the very beginning it leaked like a sieve. Superficially, the position of the dam wall seemed ideal, for it was built where the valley was at its narrowest. A competent engineer would have sought to establish the reason why the valley was so narrow at Dôl-y-gaer. But much to the embarrassment and shame of Thomas Hawkesly, described as an engineer of considerable fame by one *Merthyr Express* reporter, he authorized the building of the dam wall where a large and complex fault, traceable from Neath (Castell-nedd) to well beyond the Welsh border, crosses Cwm Taf Fechan. Associated with the fault at Dôl-y-gaer is an enormous 'island' of hard limestone implanted within the local red sandstones and mudstones of the Brecon Beacons (Bannau Brycheiniog). Notwithstanding its hardness, limestone is soluble in acidic rain and river water and, as a consequence, it's riddled with water-worn fissures and caves formed over a period of millions of years.

As a result of the problems posed by the Pen-twyn reservoir and Merthyr's increasing population, two additional reservoirs were built in the upper reaches of Cwm Taf Fechan: Neuadd Isaf was established in 1884, a short distance up-valley of Llyn Dôl-y-gaer, and Neuadd Uchaf or 'the Zulu', as it was known locally, because the reservoir, situated immediately south of the twin summits of Corn Du (873 m) and Pen y Fan (886 m), was completed in 1902, the year the Boer War ended.

In the meantime the Pen-twyn reservoir was losing 50,000,000 litres of water a day! According to the *Merthyr Express*, 'serious attempts were made to bring the Pentwyn mischief under control, and thousands of pounds were spent on it again and again, unfortunately with only miserable temporary success'. Since there was no means of solving the intractable problem, it was decided to build, on far firmer foundations, a new reservoir further down-valley that would retain the water escaping from the ill-fated Pen-twyn dam. Had it not been for the outbreak of the First World War, that halted the construction of the dam wall across the valley floor in the vicinity of the dispersed settlement of Pontsticill, the new Pontsticill reservoir would have been completed long before 1927.

The official opening, Thursday, 21 July 1927, 'was by no means an ideal summer's day, for heavy grey clouds hung low, almost touching the mountain tops on either side of the valley beautiful': so said the *Merthyr Express* reporter. The inclement weather, however, was in keeping with the heartbreak of those residents who, as a consequence of the engineer's incompetence, had to abandon their homes on the valley floor. There, hidden from the gaze of today's visitors, are the lands of eight farms, a few cottages and smallholdings, the fifteenth-century church of Dôl-y-gaer and a Welsh Congregationalist chapel.

Llyn Dôl-y-gaer and the summits (left to right) of Craig Gwaun Taf, Corn Du and Pen y Fan

077

Pen-wyllt, Cwm Tawe

SN 855157

Once known as Bryn Melin, Craig-y-nos, a Gothic mansion built in the upper reaches of the Swansea valley in the early 1840s, was transformed and enlarged following its purchase in 1878 by the world-famous opera singer Adelina Patti (1843–1919), born in Madrid, of Italian parents, and brought up in New York. It was there that Patti, in the company of French tenor Ernesto Nicolini, whom she married in 1886, decided to spend the rest of her life, knowing that its sequestered, rural location offered her an escape from the pressures of fame and periods of privacy and tranquillity.

Tranquillity, perhaps, but not silence, because at the time Craig-y-nos was in earshot of the nearby industrial community of Pen-wyllt, situated high on the eastern slopes of Cwm Tawe. During the first half of the nineteenth century, long before Patti and Nicolini settled

in Craig-y-nos, the area's limestone was extensively quarried and burnt in the limekilns of Twyn-y-ffald, Twyn Disgwylfa and Pen-y-foel, all built between the 1820s and 1860s. The lime was transported as far north as Sennybridge (Pontsenni) via the Fforest Fawr tram-road, in order to satisfy the demands of local farmers, and south to the ironworks of Ynysgedwyn and Ystalyfera further down the Swansea valley.

The limestone quarries, served by a network of tram-roads, were later extended and several short rows of cottages were built not only to house quarrymen and those in charge of limekilns, but also employees of the Pen-wyllt silica-brickworks and the Neath and Brecon Railway. Both the railway and the brickworks were opened in the 1860s. The firebricks, used to line industrial furnaces, were

Part of the limestone quarries of Pen-wyllt. The morainic ridge is visible at the foot of Fan Hir.

by her, and in return the Neath and Brecon Railway provided the diva with her own private railway carriage, which, at her request, could be coupled to any train and take her to any destination within the United Kingdom. She also paid for the construction of a private road and telephone line linking the opulence of her mansion home to the station, renamed Craigynos [*sic*] in 1907.

From the station, on a fine day, Patti could turn her back on the scarred industrial landscape and gaze in awe at the surrounding mountains; the grandeur of Fan Hir to the north and the rocky escarpments of Carreg Lwyd and Carreg y Cadno to the east.

At the foot of Fan Hir (c.750 m), south of Llyn y Fan Fawr, lies one of Wales' most striking and enigmatic landforms. Over the

Carreg Cadno: ice-scratched and polished Basal Grit

Pwll Byfre, site of the silica sand quarry and where the stream – Byfre Fechan – enters Ogof Ffynnon Ddu

manufactured from silica sand, quarried at Pwll Byfre, about two kilometres north-east of Pen-wyllt.

Patti was well-acquainted with the industrial landscape of Pen-wyllt, for she took full advantage of the railway. The remote Penwyllt [*sic*] station provided access to all the major towns and cities of Britain, America via the port of Liverpool, and the countries of north-west Europe via London. Indeed, the station building, which included a lavishly furnished private waiting-room, was partly funded greater part of its length, the 1,200-metre-long steep-sided ridge stands 30 metres above the 'trench' that lies between it and the east-facing Old Red Sandstone escarpment. Despite its unusual, elongated form, the ridge, which is in contact with the scarp at its southern end, is a moraine that accumulated at the snout of a glacier between 13,000 and 11,500 years ago, a short-lived glacial period that signalled the end of the last 'ice age'. Prior to 13,000 years ago, the whole of Wales had been ice free for some 7,000 years but, 20,000 years ago, when the Last Glaciation was at its peak, the entire area was submerged beneath a vast ice sheet, which left its stamp on exposed layers of the so-called Basal Grit – a hard quartzitic sandstone – that overlies the limestone in the vicinity of Carreg Lwyd and Carreg y Cadno. As the ice sheet flowed southwards, rock fragments held fast in its sole, scraped clean, scratched and polished the layers of Basal Grit, all minor features of glacial erosion which would not have survived the ravages of post-glacial times were it not for the intrinsic hardness of the rock. Their survival is in marked contrast to the demise of the area's industries.

The production of refractory bricks ceased in the late 1930s. The limekilns finally closed in 1959 and all passenger services were withdrawn by British Railways three years later. Although one of the limestone quarries reopened for a brief period in 2007–8 and again in 2009 they too are silent. By the 1990s the row of back-to-back workers' cottages called Patti Row was in ruins, but not Powell

Street. That former row of back-to-backs, ten cottages in all, is now the headquarters of the South Wales Caving Club established in 1946. In the same year, two of its members discovered Ogof Ffynnon Ddu, a labyrinthine cave system, over 60 kilometres long and 300 metres deep, within the limestone deep beneath Pen-wyllt and the surrounding area.

The frieze is part of Adelina Patti's theatre built in 1890

Craig-y-nos railway station

239

078

Dan yr Ogof, Cwm Tawe

SN 839161

For those seeking the solitude of desolate countryside, the Black Mountain (Y Mynydd Du) west of the upper reaches of Cwm Tawe – the Swansea valley – is without equal. With the exception of sheep, there is little or nothing to remind walkers of man's imprint and were it not for the myriad shake-holes – whose significance is a mystery to many – few are the signs of the area's wonderful subterranean world, so typical of Carboniferous limestone country.

Stalagmite, two calcite curtains, a pillar and flowstone (© Dan yr Ogof)

Most of the funnel-shaped pits, some of which are water-filled, indicate those places where parts of the roofs of invisible caverns have collapsed. Other pits on the high moorland, such as Sinc y Gïedd, where the river Gïedd, a tributary of the Tawe, disappears underground for a short distance, are more appropriately known as swallow-holes.

Dan yr Ogof is the entranceway to the underworld, that timeless place which is, with the exception of the most venturesome cavers, well beyond the reach of the majority of people. But thanks to the heroic efforts of generations of fearless adventurers that have been responsible, ever since 1912, for exploring the complex network of caves and caverns deep beneath the Black Mountain, the tens of thousands of people who annually visit Dan yr Ogof – the National Showcaves Centre for Wales – are now able to marvel at the natural wonders of one of Britain's finest showcaves.

Historian Theophilus Jones, author of *History of the County of Brecknock* (two volumes, 1805 and 1809) was one of the first to draw attention to the cave out of which flows the Llynfell, a tributary of the Tawe, at the foot of Darren yr Ogof, 'the cave's cliff'. It was by way of this entrance that the Morgan brothers – Edwin, Tommy and Jeff – of Aber-craf made their dramatic discovery in 1912. Though ill-prepared by modern standards, the three succeeded in mapping a kilometre-long passageway with the aid of a coracle used to cross the four lakes they encountered, and candles to light their way.

Although the journey to the far end of the Showcave, at a depth of about 90 metres below ground, is no more than about 500 metres, both the passageways and caverns are adorned with a bewildering array of rock formations whose existence is attributable to the nature of Carboniferous limestone, formed from the skeletal remains of marine creatures that flourished in the warm, shallow waters of a tropical sea, some 350 million years ago. Despite its hardness, the rock dissolves when in contact with mildly acidic water.

Cathedral Cave (© Dan yr Ogof) (right)

As rain and river water slowly trickles through cracks in the soluble limestone, its slow dissolution leads to the formation, over many millions of years, of passageways, large and small caves, and caverns, whose dimensions are further enlarged by the erosive power of underground rivers.

In addition to dissolving the limestone, a proportion of the dissolved calcium carbonate in the underground water is deposited within the cave in the form of the mineral calcite. Each droplet of water on the roof of a cave will deposit a tiny quantity of calcite before it falls to the floor, a process which, over time, will result in the formation of a slender stalactite. When the droplet falls to the floor, yet more calcite is deposited, leading to the creation of a stumpy stalagmite. When a stalactite and stalagmite join and become one, the outcome is a pillar.

Stalactites (sometimes in the form of fragile, slender straws), stalagmites and pillars, some stained red or yellow by the presence of iron minerals in the water, are the most common formations seen within the Showcave and Cathedral Cave (Ogof y Gadeirlan), an enormous cavern discovered in 1953. On the basis of their form, some of the incredibly beautiful calcite creations have been likened to fingers, an angel, a flitch of bacon and a dagger! Both caves also contain splendid examples of flowstone – layers of calcite resembling frozen waterfalls deposited by flowing water on the walls and floors of passageways – and calcite curtains, not dissimilar to rashers of streaky bacon, formed by water trickling at an angle from a cave roof and depositing a succession of very thin layers of calcite.

Only a few kilometres of passageways are known to lie beyond the upper end of the Cathedral Cave, but beyond the end of the Showcave there is a complex maze of passageways, constricted crawl-ways, caves and caverns of varying shapes and sizes that experienced cavers and speleologists have traced over a distance of about 16 kilometres deep below the surface of the Black Mountain. However, it's known that water, which disappears underground near Twyn Tal y Ddraenen, some four kilometres north-west of the Showcave, takes 48 hours to reach the mouth of Dan yr Ogof. Such evidence suggests that part of what is already an extensive cave system, one section of which was designated a National Nature Reserve in 2004, remains to be discovered.

Calcite pillar (© Dan yr Ogof)

Craig Derwyddon and Pant-y-llyn

SN 606167

079

Orth-west of Llandybïe, near the village of Pentregwenlais, the rocks of the south Wales coalfield give way to Carboniferous limestone, whose narrow outcrop is traceable to the east and west of Craig Derwyddon, a limestone cliff that overlooks the anomalous valley of Pant-y-llyn. Both landforms are part of Carmel National Nature Reserve and are key features of Cernydd Carmel Site of Special Scientific Interest and Special Area of Conservation designated in 2004 and traceable westwards almost as far as Llyn Llech Owain, near Gors-las.

Craig Derwyddon hit the headlines in August 1813 when the *Carmarthen Journal* reported that quarrymen had discovered a cave, Ogof Craig Derwyddon (also known as Ogof Pant-y-llyn and Ogof y Penglogau, 'the cave of skulls'), within which lay 12 human skeletons, in addition to a copper vessel and the bones of elk and wild boar. Unfortunately, most of the finds were either destroyed or lost, except for one skull which was brought to the attention of William Buckland, a pioneer geologist and palaeontologist who, in 1813, was appointed Reader of Mineralogy at the University of

Site of the Pant-y-llyn turlough and one circular swallow-hole

Oxford. He, in turn, gave the skull to the university museum and there, presumably, it remains, forgotten amongst countless other treasures.

In the meantime, the human bones became the subject of one of the most remarkable and incredible folk legends of Carmarthenshire (Sir Gaerfyrddin). According to historians, Owain Lawgoch, a Welsh soldier of fortune and a great-nephew of Llywelyn ap Gruffudd ('Llywelyn the Last', d. 1282), was killed during the siege of Mortagne-sur-Gironde, near Bordeaux, in July 1378. But according to the legend, Owain and his men were said to be sleeping in Ogof

Craig Derwyddon, awaiting the call to awake and destroy the enemies of the Welsh. It is also said that one careless act on his behalf led to the formation of Llyn Llech Owain, 'the lake of Owain's stone', for after quenching his thirst Owain forgot to replace the stone slab covering the spring, which promptly overflowed and filled the lake basin.

Although quarrying destroyed the former bone cave, the entrance to one small cave is to be seen in the shadow of Craig Derwyddon and above the floor of Pant-y-llyn, alongside the path that encircles the reserve and the abandoned Glangwenlais

Glangwenlais quarry

limestone quarry. Caves are a common characteristic feature of Carboniferous limestone country but on the floor of Pant-y-llyn lies a fine example of a turlough, a landform not found elsewhere in Wales, England or Scotland. However, turloughs, a name derived from the Irish *tuar loch*, 'dry lake', are a common feature of the lowland limestone terrain of The Burren of Clare and also Galway in the west of Ireland. A turlough is neither fed nor drained by a stream or river and the water that normally fills the lake basin during wet, winter months, disappears following the onset of drier summer weather.

The Pant-y-llyn turlough occupies a depression on the floor of a narrow valley carved by glacial meltwater during the Last Glaciation along the course of the Betws Fault, a line of weakness between Craig Derwyddon and Craig y Ddinas, site of the large Cilyrychen limestone quarry. Although the limestone forming the bed of the channel is hard, its dissolution by the action of mildly acidic rainwater percolating through cracks within the rock results in the formation of large and small caves and passageways which, at depth, are full of water throughout the year, whereas those nearer the surface only fill to overflowing in winter. As groundwater emerges through swallow-holes and other fissures in the limestone in winter, it alone slowly fills the 400-metre-long lake basin to a maximum depth of about three metres. As winter gives way to spring, the process is reversed and by midsummer only one or two solitary pools mark the location of the largest swallow-holes down which the lake waters disappeared. Needless to say, the transient nature of the lake is not to the liking of fish, but the habitat does support a healthy population of frogs, toads, newts and other small aquatic creatures.

During the 1980s it was feared that any scheme involving the enlargement of the nearby Glangwenlais quarry would interfere with the flow of subsurface water within the limestone, thereby posing a threat to the long-term survival of the unique turlough. Thankfully, that was avoided when Tarmac, owners of the site, decided to close the quarry that had been idle since the 1970s and the area was subsequently designated a National Nature Reserve.

Besides the impressive limestone cliffs, the reserve's thin calcareous soils not only support the ash woodland surrounding the quarry, but also a rich ground flora; wild flowers such as mezereon (*Daphne mezereum*), toothwort (*Lathraea squamaria*), lily-of-the-valley (*Convallaria majalis*), herb-paris (*Paris quadrifolia*), dog's mercury (*Mercurialis perennis*), bluebell (*Hyacinthoides non-scripta*), wood anemone (*Anemone nemorosa*) and ramsons (*Allium ursinum*), all of which are at their most attractive and colourful best in spring and early summer.

Cave entrance under the shadow of Craig Derwyddon

080

Landshipping Quay

(Cei Landshipping) SN 009109

According to industrial archaeologist and railway historian, M.R. Connop-Price, Wales can lay claim to one 'forgotten coalfield'. The history of the north-east Wales coalfield, extending from Chirk (Y Waun) to the Point of Ayr, on the shores of the Dee estuary, is relatively well-documented. Better known by far is the history of the south Wales coalfield that extends from Pontypool (Pontypŵl) in the east as far as the Gwendraeth Fawr valley in the west. But the Pembrokeshire coalfield, traceable as a broad band from Amroth–Saundersfoot, on the shores of Carmarthen Bay (Bae Caerfyrddin), to Little Haven–Newgale (Niwgwl), on the shores of St Bride's Bay

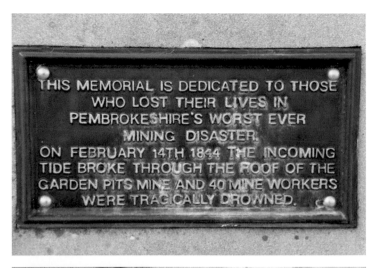

levels, the tracks of former tramways, ruined pit-head buildings and some enigmatic signs that appear to have little or no connection with the coal industry.

The narrow road heading west from the hamlet of Landshipping comes to an abrupt end at Landshipping Quay, on the eastern shores of the Daugleddau, a short distance south of the confluence of the Cleddau Wen and Cleddau Ddu rivers. But between the last quarter of the eighteenth century and the late 1860s, the land around the shores of the attractive and remote bay was the focal point of Landshipping colliery, whilst the bay itself functioned as a harbour, from which anthracite and culm, raised from the colliery's many shallow pits, was exported.

The coalmine was owned by the Owen family of Orielton, one of the principal country houses of Pembrokeshire, and in the early years of the nineteenth century Sir Hugh Owen invested a considerable amount of money in the venture. In 1800 a steam engine was purchased – the first to be used in the Pembrokeshire coalfield – in order to drain the pits; a new road embankment and bridge across Landshipping Pill was built, in addition to a new quay on the headland, on the southern shores of the bay. Ten years later, a tramway linking the colliery's pits and new quay was in place. In the wake of these improvements, the colliery annually exported about 10,000 tonnes of coal and culm in sailing vessels bound not only for the small harbours along the shores of the Milford Haven waterway (dyfrffordd Aberdaugleddau), but also ports such as Cardigan

(Bae Sain Ffraid), remains largely forgotten, in spite of the publication of *Pembrokeshire: The Forgotten Coalfield* (2004), Connop-Price's splendid book that records its fascinating history.

When Hook colliery, on the banks of the Western Cleddau (Cleddau Wen), closed in 1948, the 600-year history of coalmining in Pembrokeshire came to an end. Nevertheless, the landscape still bears tell-tale vestiges of the industry, such as old spoil heaps and

Stem of fossil Coal Measure plant (Calamites)

(Aberteifi) and Barmouth (Y Bermo), on the shores of Cardigan Bay (Bae Ceredigion). A lucrative trade developed between Landshipping and Aberdyfi, and during the week 27 March–3 April 1835, ten of Aberdyfi's sailing ships visited Landshipping Quay.

Although the anthracite mined was of high quality, producing little smoke and ash, the coal-seams to be found amongst the intensely folded layers of sandstone and mudstone forming Pembrokeshire's Coal Measures, were both thin and broken. Furthermore, several of the underground roadways and coalfaces, such as those of Garden Pit located near the headland on the south side of the bay, lay at a shallow depth below the tidal waters of the Daugleddau; so shallow that some folk claimed that miners below ground could hear the dipping of oars from boats passing above!

On St Valentine's Day 1844, 58 men, women and children were hard at work in that section of the pit that lay beyond the shoreline. Mid-afternoon, disaster struck. According to the report published in the *Carmarthen Journal* two days after the tragedy, those working near the pit-head became aware of a very 'powerful current of air making up the pit ... [whilst] the water at a little distance from the shore, became much agitated, eddies being visible to a considerable extent', as the ensuing torrent thundered its way through the subterranean roadways. With the exception of the four men and 14 boys rescued, there was no escaping the terrifying flood. The names of the 40 miners who died, including one 'unknown miner', are recorded on a memorial unveiled in 2002. It's possible that the 'Miners' whose Christian names and ages are not recorded were women and children who, under the terms of the 1842 Act of Parliament, should not have been employed underground. The bodies of the dead were never recovered. The disaster, the worst of its kind in Wales, was attributed to the negligence of colliery managers.

All efforts to revive the fortunes of Landshipping colliery in the 1850s and 1860s failed. Bits of the old quay walls survive. One house bears the name, 'Garden Pitts [*sic*]', whilst rocks on the bay's foreshore contain fossils of Coal Measure plants, whose 310-million-year-old remains gave rise to the coal-seams exploited in the infamous Garden Pit.

Landshipping Pill

Laugharne

(Talacharn) SN 301107

081

In 1937, the poet and prose-writer, Dylan Thomas (1914–53), married Caitlin Macnamara and in the month of May the following year settled in Laugharne, the village on the shores of the Taf estuary that would become synonymous with his name. Following his untimely death on 9 November 1953 in New York, his body was returned to Laugharne, where he was buried in St Martin's graveyard, not far from the Boat House, his home for the last six months of his life, and the shed in which he wrote. From his shed, much visited by literary tourists, he was in sight of the splendour of the 'heron Priested shore' and the adjoining area that was the background to many of

his later poems, such as 'Poem on his Birthday'. In fact, 'Laugharne' was the subject of Dylan Thomas' last radio talk, broadcast five days before his death, a place memorably described in words like no one else, as that

> ... forgetful, important place of herons, cormorants (known here as billy duckers), castle, churchyard, gulls, ghosts, geese, feuds, scares, scandals, cherry trees, mysteries, jackdaws in the chimneys, bats in the belfry, skeletons in the cupboards, pubs, mud, cockles, flatfish, curlews, rain and human, often all too human, beings ...

Standing firm on Old Red Sandstone rocks, outcropping on the

The salt-marsh fringing the shores of the Taf estuary

shores of the river Coran, is the imposing twelfth-century Norman castle, once known as Castell Coran. Below its walls, the river offers a safe anchorage to a few boats as it winds its way through a patch of salt-marsh, alongside which the lane, part of Dylan's Birthday Path, climbs steadily through the trees clothing the steep, eastern slopes of Sir John's Hill, south of the village. The path is well worth following, especially on a fine summer's day, for it offers unrivalled views of the scenically stunning Taf estuary and that portion of Carmarthen Bay (Bae Caerfyrddin) where the rivers Taf, Tywi and Gwendraeth merge into one another. The view is at its best at low tide. At such time, it's possible to follow the river on its meandering journey through an ever-changing pattern of sandbanks as far as its confluence with the other two rivers between the sandy beaches of Laugharne and Cefn Sidan.

Laugharne Sands (Traeth Talacharn) is an extension of Pendine Sands (Traeth Pentywyn), where proud Welshman and racing car driver, J.G. Parry Thomas, was tragically killed in March 1927 during his attempt to better Malcolm Campbell's record and become, once again, 'the fastest man on Earth'. Landward of the two sandy beaches is a broad, unbroken line of sand dunes. Although most of the salt-marsh that developed in the lee of the dunes has long since been reclaimed from the sea and utilized as agricultural land, a small strip remains seaward of the embankment that extends from the easternmost tip of the dunes (Ginst Point) as far as the steep, south-east-facing slopes of Sir John's Hill. By far the most common salt-marsh species occupying the flat ground between the bewildering network of muddy, tidal channels and isolated salt pans is sea-purslane (*Atriplex portulacoides*). In contrast to its dull grey-green leaves and the fleshy green, edible stems of common glasswort (*Salicornia europaea*), the purply flowers of common sea-lavender (*Limonium vulgare*) and sea aster (*Aster tripolium*) impart a splash of colour during summer months.

The caves and recesses in the cliffs at the foot of Sir John's Hill, part of a cliff-line traceable westwards as far as the seaside village of Pendine (Pentywyn), were fashioned, in all probability, about 125,000 years ago, during the warm interglacial period that preceded the Last Glaciation, when sea level was some eight metres higher than at present. However, the rocks forming the old sea cliffs are very much older. For the most part, they are beds of red sandstone and mudstone that represent indurated layers of sand and mud originally deposited by rivers on an extensive plain during the Devonian period, about 390 million years ago.

In marked contrast to the red rocks is the mass of hard, blue-grey limestone that is the foundation of the prominent headland a short distance west of Sir John's Hill. Regrettably, quarrying the 350-million-year-old bedrock has been responsible for destroying Coygan cave, the only known site in Wales occupied by man during the Middle Palaeolithic period. The earliest archaeological excavation, the results of which were published in 1867, was conducted by Dr Henry Hicks, a Welsh-speaking physician and native of St David's (Tyddewi) elected Fellow of the Royal Society for his geological research work. The results of subsequent digs suggest that Neanderthal people made use of the shelter between 60,000 and 40,000 years ago. Then, about 30,000 years ago, during the cold period that preceded the Last Glaciation, a pack of hyenas occupied the cave, scattering within it the gnawed bones of their prey, which included woolly mammoth and woolly rhinoceros, now extinct.

Abandoned sea caves at the foot of Sir John's Hill

082

Mynydd Llangyndeyrn and Cwm Gwendraeth Fach

SN 487134

It's not known whether the prehistoric inhabitants who left their imprint on Mynydd Llangyndeyrn were impressed by the magnificent views of the surrounding countryside which greeted them on clear days, but from their vantage point, 262 metres above sea level and well above the marshy floor of Cwm Gwendraeth Fach, the panorama included the summits of the Black Mountain (Y Mynydd Du) to the east, the Gower peninsula (Penrhyn Gŵyr) to the south, the shores of Carmarthen Bay (Bae Caerfyrddin) to the south-west, and the Presely hills (Y Preselau) to the west. Though well short of 600 metres (2,000 feet), the minimum height of a 'mountain' according to some authorities, Mynydd Llangyndeyrn is part of the watershed between the rivers Gwendraeth Fach and Gwendraeth Fawr, an upland tract that was the centre of considerable human activity during Neolithic and Bronze Age times.

Mynydd Llangyndeyrn and the Black Mountain

Bwrdd Arthur, 'Arthur's table' and Gwâl y Filiast, 'the female greyhound's lair', two ruinous Neolithic burial chambers a short distance east of the old triangulation pillar, are the earliest monuments. Built about 5,500 years ago, both nestle at the foot of one of the hard rock ribs characteristic of the upland's southern flank. Each rib corresponds to the outcrop of layered, quartzitic sandstone ('Millstone Grit'), slabs of which were used in the construction of the two, small megalithic tombs.

Far more numerous are monuments attributable to the Bronze Age, although many, and especially ring cairns, are not readily identified amongst the accumulated blocks of frost shattered quartzitic sandstone at the base of the rock ribs and amidst the marshy vegetation between successive ribs. In contrast, the menhir that stands on a strip of land between two rock ribs is unmissable. The 3.8-metre-high standing stone, which was prostrate until 1976 when excavations revealed its stone hole, was probably erected about 3,000 years ago. Less conspicuous is the low, flat-topped cairn, 11 metres in diameter, in the centre of which stands the triangulation pillar.

The north-west-facing scarp slopes of Mynydd Llangyndeyrn, east of the village of Crwbin, are in part breached by three large Carboniferous limestone quarries, namely Crwbin, Torcoed-fawr and Torcoed. Crwbin and Torcoed were the only two in operation during the late nineteenth century and both were primarily involved in the production of agricultural lime. Currently, Torcoed is the only working quarry but Tarmac Ltd, its owner, has recently been granted permission to extend its workings so as to include the long since inactive Torcoed-fawr and Crwbin quarries. The much enlarged quarry is expected to have a life of about 40 years.

Below the steep Carboniferous limestone escarpment, the gentler valley-side slopes of Cwm Gwendraeth Fach, underlain by older red sandstones and mudstones of Devonian age, are a patchwork of green fields, agricultural land that would have largely

Llangyndeyrn village

Bronze Age menhir formed of one rough pillar of quartzitic sandstone

disappeared underwater had the reservoir planned by Swansea Corporation been constructed. Residents of Cwm Gwendraeth Fach, including Llangyndeyrn village, first heard word of the scheme to drown the beautiful valley in February 1960. The intention was to build a dam wall at Llangyndeyrn and create a six-kilometre-long reservoir that would have extended north-east as far as the village of Porth-y-rhyd. Had it have been completed it would have had a devastating impact on about 40 farms, including the demolition of five properties and the drowning of 400 hectares of land. It would also have resulted in the break-up of a Welsh-speaking community.

Local residents responded by establishing a Defence Committee whose members and supporters were determined to employ every means at their disposal, including direct, non-violent action, to thwart Swansea Corporation's stated objective. The battle came to a climax on 21 October 1963 when residents succeeded in preventing engineers and officers of the Corporation from gaining access to the land and surveying the area by locking and blocking farm gates. Their unyielding stubbornness and determination won the day and, as a result, Swansea Corporation abandoned their plans, but not a word was received to inform local residents that their homes and livelihood were no longer under threat.

In 1983, a memorial standing alongside the village hall was unveiled in Llangyndeyrn 'to remember the long battle between 1959 and 1964 [1960 and 1965 according to *Cloi'r Clwydi* (1983; 'locking the gates') and *Sefyll yn y Bwlch* (2013; 'standing in the breach'), two Welsh-language books recounting the battle] to prevent Cwm Gwendraeth Fach from being drowned by Swansea Corporation and out of respect for the two leaders Mr William Thomas and the Reverend W.M. Rees [Chairman and Secretary, respectively, of the Defence Committee]'. But the residents' victory came at a price. Swansea Corporation turned their attention to the upper reaches of the Tywi valley, about 14 kilometres north of Llandovery (Llanymddyfri). Despite fierce local opposition and the hard-fought battle waged by the Tywi Valley Defence Committee, their opposition proved futile and the 'unproductive' valley land was drowned. The official opening ceremony of Llyn Brianne Reservoir, now a tourist attraction, was held in May 1973.

The Cynheidre 'super pit'

083

(Glofa Cynheidre) SN 495073

On a piece of land that was once the property of Cynheidre Fawr farm stand two rusty, lonely pipes, both set within shallow, grassy depressions where once stood the iconic pit-head frames of Cynheidre colliery. For many years, this so-called 'super pit', overlooking the middle reaches of Cwm Gwendraeth Fawr, north-north-west of Llanelli, was the pride of the National Coal Board. But besides a few sections of concrete roadways and indistinct traces of the colliery's vast sidings alongside the path of the Llanelli & Mynydd Mawr Railway, the only visible signs of the former anthracite mine, once the largest in western Europe, are the two rusty pipes, silent witnesses to a venture which failed dismally to live up to its much vaunted expectations.

On St David's Day 1954 work began on sinking the two shafts (Cynheidre 1 and 2) to a depth of about 725 metres with the intention of exploiting the rich, deep seams of high-quality anthracite. It was envisaged that the colliery, officially opened in November 1960, would employ over 3,000 men and produce a million tonnes of coal a year over a period of 100 years. By the early 1970s both the Pentremawr drift mine, three kilometres north of Cynheidre, and the Cwm Sinkings mine, site of Cynheidre shafts 3 and 4 some four kilometres to the north-east of Cynheidre, had become part of the 'super pit'. However, it did not succeed in employing half the projected number of men and neither did it produce more than about 470,000 tonnes of coal a year. By 1980 things had taken a turn for the worse: the number employed had fallen to about 1,000 and the output barely exceeded 200,000 tonnes.

One of Cynheidre's problems was the inappropriate and uneconomical method adopted to win the coal. Opening long coalfaces with the aid of large, moveable coal-cutting machines was an appropriate method where the coal-seams were not severely folded and faulted. But that was not the case with regard to the coal-bearing rocks in the Cynheidre area. One moment the machines would be working their way through thick coal-seams and the next through worthless layers of sandstone and mudstone. Relocating the 'lost' seams was no easy matter.

Another serious problem affecting the Big Vein coal-seam in particular, in each section of the mine, were the numerous 'outbursts', when hundreds of tonnes of coal dust mixed with methane gas were suddenly and violently injected from a coalface and adjoining strata into the underground roadways. As a

consequence of one such event that occurred on 6 April 1971, the deadliest outburst ever recorded in Britain, six colliers lost their lives and 69 were injured.

Despite the problems, Cynheidre colliery was the site chosen for the development of the Carway Fawr drift mine, British Coal's last major investment in the south Wales coalfield. The £30-million project commenced in 1986 and the two drift entrances were situated near the Cynheidre 1 and 2 compound. However, three years later, after hitting the targeted Carway Fawr seam and spending £19 million, the Coal Board announced that it intended to mothball the mine. In 1992, the mine, which never produced a single lump of coal, was sealed.

In the meantime, intractable geological problems were mainly responsible for the Coal Board's decision to close Cynheidre colliery in January 1989, 71 years short of the 100-year life span that the Board's false prophets had predicted for the 'super pit'. Not that their decision came as a surprise to those familiar with the research work of H.K. Jordan, a geologist who, in the early years of the twentieth century, had come to the conclusion, on the basis of the area's complex geology, that the establishment of a coalmine in the vicinity of Cynheidre would be a waste of money.

After the 1,043 men employed on closure had bid farewell to the 80 kilometres or more of underground roadways and 70 or so coalfaces that had been opened to exploit five different seams during the life of Cynheidre colliery, work began on clearing the site. The two pit-head frames, with their winding gear set within box-like structures atop each tower rather than in a separate building, were demolished. The rails of the Llanelli & Mynydd Mawr Railway, once the area's main artery for coal distribution, were lifted and its former track-bed is now a public footpath and cycle track. The only visual reminder of the former busy industrial railway, earlier known as the Carmarthenshire Tramroad – claimed to be 'the earliest operational public railway in Great Britain' – is the Cynheidre Heritage Project. The brainchild of the Llanelli & Mynydd Mawr Railway Company Ltd established in 1999, this highly ambitious project aims to create a visitor and industrial heritage centre – 'a vital educational resource for future generations' – and reopen a section of track 'over half a mile [c.800 m] in length'.

084

Ffos Las, Trimsaran

SN 458062

Ever since the land of Wales was first peopled in prehistoric times, humankind has had an ever-increasing influence on the outward appearance of the country's landscape. By today the imprint of their multifarious activities is indelible, to such an extent that the character of most of the national nature reserves is a function of human intervention. That said, up to now at least, man's direct or indirect impact on the Welsh landform – on the pattern of its coastline and valleys, hills and mountains – has been relatively small. Although the large slate quarries of north-west Wales, at centres such as Bethesda and Llanberis, have made an enduring impression on the Welsh landform, their impact pales into insignificance when compared to the astounding topographical changes that have characterised that part of the Morlais valley west of Five Roads (Pump-hewl) and between the villages of Carway (Carwe) and Trimsaran, about seven kilometres north-west of Llanelli.

Large-scale Ordnance Survey maps (1:10,560; 6" to one mile), published in the early years of the last century, indicate that the land south of the meandering and wooded course of the river Morlais rose gently southwards, before steepening on approach to the summit ridge of Mynydd Pen-bre (192 m). To the north, the valley-side slopes were gentler. The intervening marshy valley floor was a patchwork of small fields that were, in all probability, the property of the owners of the Plas Trimsaran estate, but were farmed by some of their tenants living in a number of small, local farmsteads. The ruined seventeenth-century mansion (*plas*) stood nearby Trimsaran colliery (comprised of three main drifts [driven at an angle below ground]), which opened in 1858, and in the valley-bottom fields there were several old pits sunk in order to exploit the seams of anthracite coal that lay relatively close to the surface. After the closure of two of the drifts in 1934, the remaining drift became part of Trimsaran New drift colliery, opened in 1944. Ten years later it closed, during a period which witnessed the opening of opencast coalmines following the establishment of the Opencast Executive by the National Coal Board in 1952.

As emphasised by Phil Cullen, author of *Gwendraeth Valley Coal Mines* (2010), opencast mining not only allowed 'for the exploitation of shallow and highly disturbed coal-seams which would be impossible via deep mining methods', but also for large private contractors to enter the industry. In no time at all, the opening of opencast mines was responsible for the complete transformation of the Morlais valley between Trimsaran and Carway. During its short

life the Carway mine (1953–7), occupying a 33-hectare site, was the largest and deepest (c.67 m) in Britain. Then, in 1983, the vast 405-hectare Ffos Las opencast mine, opened alongside the site of the old Carway mine and excavated to a depth of about 150 metres, obliterated all signs of previous mining activity and changed the configuration of the Morlais valley. During its 14-year period of production it laid bare 11 coal-seams, each one the legacy of the tropical forests that flourished during Carboniferous times, some 310 million years ago, when 'Wales' sat astride the equator. Although severely folded and torn apart by faults, by far the most important seam was the 'Big Vein', which accounted for two-thirds of the mine's output. In 1988, its workforce of 150 men produced 220,000 tonnes of anthracite.

The closure of what had been the largest and most productive opencast mine in Europe heralded further dramatic landform and landscape change. The huge pit was first filled with an estimated 14 million tonnes of overburden that had been removed prior to mining and then flattened to create the Ffos Las Racecourse, consisting of a 12-furlong course, grandstand, car parks and other associated facilities, at a cost of about £20 million.

Yet further changes have occurred since the opening of the racecourse in August 2009. Within a stone's throw of the main entrance a substantial number of the 528 homes, all of which had been granted planning permission by 2012, have already been built. In March 2013 the 20,000 solar panels of the 12-hectare Ffos Las Solar Farm, established south of the western end of the racetrack, began generating clean electric power. In 2014 the 49-hectare site of Coed Ffos Las, situated close to Ffos Las Racecourse and on the outskirts of Carway village, was bought by the Woodland Trust in order to create a Centenary Wood to honour the part Wales played in the First World War. By 2018 the Trust hopes to plant as many as 90,000 native trees and to establish within the woodland flower-rich glades, ponds and wild flower meadows, in addition to a formal place of remembrance. Coed Ffos Las will also link with woodland planted at Ffos Las Racecourse during the 2010s to provide valuable wildlife habitats destroyed by coalmining.

Sgwd Henryd–Nant Llech

SN 855119

085

The single-leap waterfall of Sgwd Henryd is the highest and most graceful in all of south Wales. Immediately beyond the lip of the cliff encountered by Nant Llech as it heads westwards towards the Tawe valley, the stream drops 27 metres into a deep plunge pool at the foot of the fall. Although at its most dramatic following a prolonged period of heavy rain, the spectacle is no less attractive during dry weather. At such times it's possible to follow the narrow path as far as the rock shelf, between the fall and the cliff face, and there admire not only the view down-valley through a translucent curtain of water droplets, but also to marvel at the mosses, ferns and liverworts that adorn the many thin layers of rusty-coloured sandstone at the back of the shelf.

Similar plants, including very rare species such as Wilson's filmy-fern (*Hymenophyllum wilsonii*), flourish on rock faces permanently blessed with shadowy dampness in the deep, wooded ravine downstream of Sgwd Henryd. Oaks clothe all the upper slopes of Coed Graig-llech, the steep woodland that belongs to the National Trust, but ash trees are more numerous along the more fertile lower slopes beside the stream. There, too, grow birch, alder, rowan and small-leaved lime trees.

Most striking is the contrast between the densely wooded gorge and the open, treeless valley above the fall, a dissimilarity that is largely attributable to the geology. The cliff over which Nant Llech falls corresponds to one small portion of the Henryd Fault, a tear or fracture in the rocks, traceable over a distance of 4.5 kilometres to the north and two kilometres to the south of Sgwd Henryd. Forming the upper third of the cliff is a thick layer of sandstone, known as the Farewell Rock by south Wales' coalminers, because it marks the lowermost boundary of the productive Coal Measures below which no coal-seams were to be found. But the Farewell Rock is also encountered at a much lower elevation near the confluence of Nant Llech and the river Tawe, indicating that the rock succession west of

Floor of the wooded gorge of Nant Llech

the fall has been lowered along the line of the fault to such a degree that the Nant Llech ravine is actually carved through the productive Coal Measures. Within the gorge, those rocks are mainly a succession of soft, dark-grey mudstones containing occasional layers of hard sandstone that have given rise to several small waterfalls along the course of the stream.

The Coal Measures exposed along the banks of Nant Llech became the focus of attention and much geological excitement during the 1830s. In 1837, William Edmond Logan (1798–1875), a highly-gifted amateur geologist discovered several large fossil trees within the rocks, trees that once grew prolifically in the dense tropical forests of Carboniferous times, some 310 million years ago. Two of the *in situ* trees were excavated: a four-metre-high trunk and a small stump that stood upright amongst layers of sandstone with their roots buried in a layer of mudstone representing the soil in which they originally grew.

Under the direction of Henry De la Beche, first director of the Geological Survey established in 1835, the fossil trees were taken to Swansea (Abertawe) and placed to stand outside the Royal Institute of South Wales (Swansea Museum today). There they remain, silent witnesses to the painstaking research undertaken by Logan, who had been appointed secretary and curator of the Institute's geological department in 1836. He, too, was the first to recognize that coal-seams were the remains of ancient tropical forests and that their roots were invariably found in fossil soils. Furthermore, his detailed geological map of that part of the south Wales coalfield west of Neath (Castell-nedd) was considered a masterpiece by the foremost geologists of the nineteenth century.

In 1842, Logan, who was of Scottish descent but had been born in Montreal, returned to Canada. There he founded the Geological Survey of Canada and became its first director. In January 1855 he was knighted for his contribution to the British Exhibition of 1851, and in 1856 'his brother geologists [bestowed] upon him their highest distinction, the *Wollaston Medal*'.

Prior to 1842, Logan had spent ten years in Swansea as manager of a family copper-smelting and coalmining venture, and after settling in Canada he revisited Wales on several occasions. Much time was spent in Castell Malgwyn, on the banks of the river Teifi at Llechryd, the home of his sister Elizabeth, wife of his '"great" friend and brother-in-law, Mr. A[bel] L[ewes] Gower'. Following his retirement in 1870 his health deteriorated. Logan's visit to Castell Malgwyn in the winter of 1874 proved to be his last. He died on 22 June 1875 and was buried in the Gower family grave in St Llawddog's cemetery, Cilgerran. On the centennial of his death the Geological Association of Canada placed a plaque on Logan's grave, the 'father of Canadian geology'. Canada's highest mountain, Mount Logan (5,959 m), also bears his name.

The largest of the two fossil tree-trunks

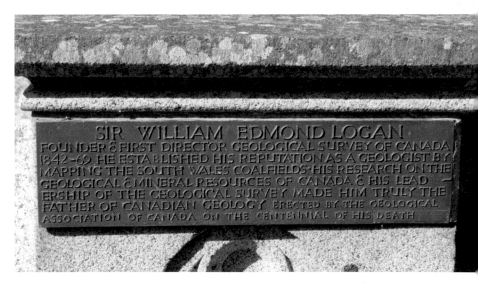

086

Porth yr Ogof, Ystradfellte

SN 928124

The most striking feature of Porth yr Ogof, situated a kilometre down-valley of the village of Ystradfellte, is the enormity of the cave's entrance at the foot of a grey limestone cliff that rises high above the boulder-strewn bed of the river Mellte. Measuring 15 metres wide and five metres high, the colossal entranceway is without equal elsewhere in Wales. Little wonder, therefore, that this cave, that leaves the beholder in silent admiration, annually attracts visitors in their tens of thousands and budding cavers in their thousands to this part of the Brecon Beacons National Park (Parc Cenedlaethol Bannau Brycheiniog).

The enduring appeal of Porth yr Ogof was no less amongst early naturalists and travel writers. In July 1698 it was visited by Edward Llwyd (1660–1709), Keeper of the Ashmolean Museum, Oxford, considered by many of his contemporaries to be the most accomplished naturalist in seventeenth-century Europe. Nevertheless, the cave's impressive dimensions made little impact on him. Judging by the contents of a letter that he wrote to his botanist friend John Ray, Llwyd's sights were fixed on the limestone and the

myriad fossils contained therein. Indeed, he was at pains to stress that 'on the sides (as well as bottom) of a noted cave calld *Porth Gogo* at *Ystrad Velhte* in Brecknockshire, I have observd sevral remains of cockles half worn by the swift current of the River *Melhte* wch runs through this cave and polishes its limestone'.

However, the true significance of the fossil sea shells, not dissimilar to present-day cockles, was a mystery to both Llwyd and most of his peers. Although he acknowledged the possibility that the Biblical Flood, as recorded in Genesis, might have been able to sweep such creatures into Porth yr Ogof, he dismissed the idea that the raging floodwaters could have caused them to adhere firmly to both the roof and sides of the cavern.

In reality, the fossils are the remains of shells, corals and crinoids (also known as 'sea lilies', despite the fact that they are not plants) that accumulated layer by layer on the floor of a shallow, tropical sea, during early Carboniferous times, 350 million years ago. Although rock-hard, the limestone dissolves when in contact with acidic water (weak carbonic acid) and over a period of many millions

Porth yr Ogof (left) and the fissure-like cave beyond which the river continues down-valley

264

of years the acidified waters of the river Mellte have slowly enlarged the natural cracks and fissures within the rock to form a complex system of large and small passageways and caverns – some virtually bone-dry and others partly or wholly submerged. The larger passageways have been traced over a distance of 2.5 kilometres either side of the river's main subterranean course.

During a period of dry weather, when there was little water in the river, English travel writer Benjamin Heath Malkin (1769–1842), author of *The Scenery, Antiquities, and Biography of South Wales* (1804), records that he and his companion 'penetrated about an hundred yards [91.4 m], as far as any glimmering of daylight from the mouth

directed us: and this specimen of Stygian horror was amply sufficient to satisfy all rational curiosity'. One such 'curiosity' was the pillar of white calcium carbonate that lay beyond the small lake called Llyn y Baban. According to some, the pillar is not unlike a child's naked figure but others have likened it to a horse! However, compared to many of the other caves of Wales, Porth yr Ogof is devoid of the stalactites and stalagmites that adorn caverns such as Dan yr Ogof in the upper Swansea valley.

No visitor to Porth yr Ogof should bid it farewell before following the public footpath that heads down-valley from the country road that crosses the cliff-top above the cave's

The smooth, water-worn rocks of the old river bed (above and right)

dangers. It's deep, cold-water pools and powerful currents have claimed the lives of several inexperienced cavers.

Porth yr Ogof is not the only place in the vicinity of Ystradfellte where the river Mellte seemingly plays hide-and-seek as it crosses the outcrop of the Carboniferous limestone. More often than not, much of the boulder-strewn river bed between the cavern and the road bridge crossing the Mellte near the church at Ystradfellte is bone-dry, for within a stone's throw of the bridge lies a sink-hole where the water disappears underground before reappearing near Porth yr Ogof.

entranceway. Over a distance of about 200 metres, the path follows the former bed of the river Mellte, situated several metres above its present course. Although the river abandoned the rocky channel tens of thousands of years ago, the smooth, water-worn rock surfaces and vestiges of old potholes bear testimony to the erosive power of the river before it forsook daylight and adopted its subterranean course.

But geologically, the old river bed is a transient feature. Already, portions of the channel floor have collapsed and in such places it's possible to hear the eerie roar of the underground river which reappears through a small, fissure-like cave, notorious for its

Blaina's landslides

(Tirlithriadau'r Blaenau) SO 205075

087

The main impact of the powerful glaciers that occupied the valleys of the south Wales coalfield during the Last Glaciation, which lasted from about 60,000 to 11,500 years ago, was to straighten the sides and deepen the valley floors of the rivers Afan, Garw, Ogmore (Ogwr), Rhondda, Cynon, Taff (Taf), Bargod Taf, Sirhowy (Sirhywi), Ebbw (Ebwy) and Llwyd, thereby transforming them into impressive steep-sided glacial troughs. Indeed, never before had T.I. Ellis, author of the travel book *Crwydro Mynwy* (Wandering Monmouthshire), published in 1958, encountered streets steeper than those of Abertillery (Abertyleri) on the eastern side of Cwm Ebwy Fach, whose unstable over-steepened slopes have been a source of worry and grave problems to both residents of valley-side homes and the local authority.

Though uncomplicated, geology coupled with high rainfall totals is the root cause of slope instability. The high moorlands of Mynydd James and Mynydd Carn-y-cefn, 260 metres or so above the banks of the Ebwy Fach, are fashioned from Pennant sandstone, which in the past yielded building stones required to construct the valley's terraced houses, chapels and churches, pubs and clubs and industrial premises. However, the multilayered and crack-ridden

The Bournville landslide

The Pen-twyn landslide

sandstone overlies predominantly weaker Coal Measure mudstones, which incorporate coal-seams formerly worked in levels and deeper pits on the valley-side and floor, respectively. Water percolates relatively unhindered through permeable sandstone but not so through impermeable mudstone. As a consequence, the junction between the two rock types is characterized by a line of springs, whose waters lubricate the surface on which the sandstone rests causing blocks to slip, disengage and collapse downslope. In so doing, the accumulated rock debris may then trigger a landslide, especially after a period of prolonged rainfall, as the entire ground surface slips and slides under the influence of gravity.

With a surface area of about 20 hectares (the approximate size of 26 football pitches), the Bournville landslide located on the eastern valley-side slope, is by far the largest of three almost within a stone's throw of one another. It developed over a period of at least 100 years as the steep, sandstone rock face at the head of the slide collapsed and retreated bit by bit. Even before the end of the nineteenth century the northernmost section of the landslide had moved about 500 metres downslope and by so doing it proved to be a threat to houses alongside the road above the valley floor. Between 1915 and 1946, and again during the 1960s, its size increased dramatically as tongues of unstable ground along the edge of the oldest portion of the slide moved downslope. By the 1980s, when a start was made on draining the land in order to stabilize the landslide whose leading edge was moving towards the main road and houses at a rate of about two metres a year, it was estimated that the Bournville slide, beneath the shadow of Mynydd James, was composed of a million cubic metres of rock debris.

Although much smaller in size, the eight-hectare Pen-twyn landslide, a short distance to the north of the Bournville landslide, was more destructive. The prominent cliff at the head of the slide, which began to develop in January 1954, is now a conspicuous landform upslope of row upon row of terraced housing. Within the space of a fortnight of its initiation, the leading edge of the muddy slide which had formed ahead of the boulder-strewn ground at the foot of the cliff, was within a stone's throw of the uppermost terrace, compelling its residents to abandon their homes. The landslide's inexorable downslope movement persisted throughout

A landslip scar on reclaimed, stabilized land upslope of West Side

the 1980s when work began to immobilize the unstable ground. At about the same time it became clear that the instability was not simply the result of natural processes. The mining of coal in levels on the valley-side slopes during the 1930s and 1940s exacerbated the problem.

Coalmining between 1887 and 1959, in addition to the irresponsible and foolish practice of establishing large coal tips on the over-steepened valley-side slopes, was also partly responsible for triggering at least some of West Side's landslides, situated on the western side of Cwm Ebwy Fach, below the summit ridge of Mynydd Carn-y-cefn. A serious landslip initiated by a tip failure in 1959, which continued to move slowly between 1959 and 1961 at a time when the area experienced an exceptionally wet December, led to the demolition of a number of houses. In 1975, nine years after the Aber-fan disaster, work began on clearing unstable tips and on improving the stability of the hillside above West Side. Although additional schemes aimed at halting ground movements have taken place, relatively recent landslips scar reclaimed land.

The three landslides are amongst 92 recorded within the catchment area of the Ebwy valley during a survey completed in 1980. The majority are stable, but time alone will tell whether wetter winters predicted as a consequence of global warming will reactivate some of them.

088

Six Bells, Cwm Ebwy Fach

SO 221029

Though indefinite and difficult to locate, the source of the Ebwy Fach river is to be found north of Beaufort (Cendl) on the southern margin of the desolate, windswept moorland of Mynydd Llangatwg. A short distance to the south, the river is hemmed in between the steep walls of Cwm Ebwy Fach, one of 12 valleys dissecting the stark Pennant sandstone uplands of the south Wales coalfield, which to the east and west of Nant-y-glo rise to a height in excess of 550 metres above sea level.

Between Beaufort and Llanhilleth (Llanhiledd), 16 kilometres downstream, the Ebbw Fach Trail (Llwybr Ebwy Fach) and cycle route now links a chain of 'oases' in an area once bearing innumerable and seemingly indelible scars of its industrial past. All seven 'oases' have been designated Local Nature Reserves: Beaufort Hill Ponds and Parc Nant-y-waun are the sites of ponds that once served the Nant-y-glo ironworks which, in the early years of the nineteenth century, was one of the largest in the world; Cwmcelyn

'Guardian of the Valleys', Six Bells

Pond and Woodlands is the site of an old colliery feeder pond; Trevor Rowson Park was once a GWR station on the line that linked Bryn-mawr and Newport (Casnewydd); whilst Roseheyworth Woodlands, Cwmtillery Lakes and Parc Arael Griffin are the sites of three collieries that closed in 1985, 1982 and 1988, respectively.

But by far the most remarkable 'oasis' is Parc Arael Griffin on the outskirts of the former coalmining village of Six Bells, near Abertillery (Abertyleri). The park takes its name from the former Arael Griffin colliery, opened on the site of a shaft sunk in 1863. Then, in 1892, work began on sinking two 322-metre-deep shafts in order to reach the rich coal-seams, the organic remains of 310-million-year-old tropical forests, deep below the valley floor. Six years later the mine, renamed Six Bells, began producing its first consignments of coal, transported to Newport on the Newport and Pontypool Railway.

With the exception of one period of inactivity during the depression of the 1930s, the colliery was very productive and, by 1960, it was producing about 1,800 tonnes of coal a day and employing nigh on 1,500 men. But then, at about 10:45 a.m. on the morning of 28 June 1960, tragedy struck. The horror and ordinariness of the event, all too familiar to the inhabitants of the coalmining communities of south Wales, was captured by Gillian Clarke, National Poet of Wales (2008–16), in her poignant, heart-rending poem entitled 'Six Bells, 28th June 1960':

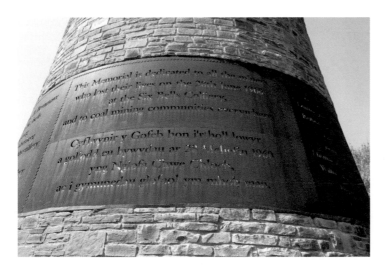

Perhaps a woman hanging out the wash
paused, hearing something, a sudden hush,
a pulse inside the earth like a blow to the heart,
holding in her arms the wet weight
of her wedding sheets, his shirts. Perhaps
heads lifted from the work of scrubbing steps,
hands stilled from wringing rainbows onto slate,
while below the town, deep in the pit
a rock-fall struck a spark from steel, and fired
the void, punched through the mine a fist
of blazing firedamp. As they died,
perhaps a silence, before sirens cried,
before the people gathered in the street,
before she'd finished hanging out her sheets.

The 45 miners working the four-foot, nine-inch coal-seam (c.1.4 m) perished in the inferno.

On the 28 June 2010, half a century after the disaster and 22 years after Six Bells Colliery finally closed, the then Archbishop of Canterbury, Dr Rowan Williams, unveiled a memorial, commemorating those killed, on the site of the coalmine, which is otherwise bereft – unfortunately – of any visible signs of the colliery that was the focal point of the tragedy. The 12.6-metre-high statue of the collier that stands atop a 7.4-metre-high plinth was designed and executed by Sebastien Boyesen, whose home is in the village of Llangrannog on the shores of Cardigan Bay (Bae Ceredigion). Known as the 'Guardian of the Valleys' (Gwarchodwr y Cymoedd), the magnificent statue is constructed of thousands of rusty steel ribbons, and to stand in its shadow, reading the names and nicknames of those who perished, is a harrowing experience.

Ironically, Parc Arael Griffin is today a place to relax but Boyesen's masterpiece is a constant and stark reminder of the terrible price that coalmining communities had to pay as their menfolk ventured their lives underground. Indeed, the iconic memorial commemorating the Six Bells disaster fulfils an important function, for the dignified image of the lone miner serves to remind all visitors to the park of one sobering fact. Major coalmining disasters, such as that at Senghenydd on 14 October 1913 which claimed the lives of 439 men and boys (the worst disaster in the history of the industry in Britain) and that at Gresford (Gresffordd), near Wrexham (Wrecsam), on 22 September 1934 which killed 262 miners, were responsible for only a small proportion of total deaths: 80 per cent of fatal colliery accidents were the result of individual incidents, the so-called 'steady drip-drip of death'.

Mynydd Beili-glas and Craig y Llyn

SN 927031

089

From that point on the outskirts of Hirwaun, where the A4061 turns south and heads for Cwm Rhondda, the proverbial crow need not fly more that about three kilometres in order to reach the roadside vantage point near the summit of Mynydd Beili-glas (505 m). But because it's a climb of 290 metres, an additional two kilometres is added to the path of the A4061 by the presence of two prodigious hairpin bends that make it possible for the road to negotiate the 150-metre-high sandstone cliff of Craig y Llyn.

From the vantage point, at a height of 480 metres, the view north is magnificent, for the west–east panorama incorporates a 17-kilometre chain of summits of the Black Mountain (Y Mynydd Du), Fforest Fawr and the Brecon Beacons (Bannau Brycheiniog): Fan Hir (750 m); Fan Gyhirych (725 m); Fan Nedd (663 m); Fan Llia (632 m); Fan Fawr (734 m); Corn Du (873 m) and, highest of all, Pen y Fan

(886 m). All are carved from Old Red Sandstone rocks, alternating layers of sandstone and mudstone of Devonian age (416–359 million years old) that dip gently southwards and disappear beneath a cover of Carboniferous limestone. They and the succeeding beds of 'Millstone Grit' sandstones and mudstones follow a similar pattern, passing beneath a thick sequence of mainly friable, dark-grey mudstones of the Lower Coal Measures, interspersed with numerous coal-seams, the legacy of tropical forests of Carboniferous times, when 'Wales' lay athwart the equator, some 310 million years ago. It's the Lower Coal Measures that are the foundation of the low ground at the foot of the Craig y Llyn escarpment fashioned from Pennant sandstone of the Upper Coal Measures, a rock infinitely harder and more resistant than the softer underlying strata.

In the early years of the nineteenth century many levels were driven into the coal-seams outcropping at the foot of the escarpment, work that proceeded apace until 1864, when the Tower drift mine was opened on the moorland south of Hirwaun. The mine was named after Crawshay's Tower, a three-storey, nine-metre-high folly and hunting lodge, built on Hirwaun Common by ironmaster Francis Crawshay, second son of William Crawshay II of Cyfarthfa Castle, Merthyr Tydfil (Merthyr Tudful), about 1848. It fell into disrepair when the family left the area in 1859. Tower colliery's shaft was sunk to a depth of 160 metres in 1941 and until 2008 it acted as both a ventilation shaft and one used for access by men and materials.

Following the successful purchase of the colliery by its workforce in December 1994, it remained in operation, producing high-quality anthracite until January 2008. The colliery buildings and the head-frame of what was the last working deep coalmine in Wales remain and are the subject of a preservation order. But the closure of Tower colliery (Glofa'r Tŵr) did not signal the end of coalmining in the area. A new chapter in the industry's history opened in May 2012 when Tower Opencast Mine began working the rich coal reserves down to a depth of 165 metres on and 81-hectare section of the former Tower colliery washery site, south of the junction of the A4061 and A465(T) Head of the Valleys road at Hirwaun. It is anticipated that mining will have ceased and the 300-hectare site fully restored by the end of 2021.

Riches of a very different kind to anthracite coal came to light in the layers of peat on the bed of Llyn Fawr at the foot of Craig y Llyn, between 1909 and 1913, when workers were involved in the task of transforming the small lake into a larger reservoir serving the population of the Rhondda Fawr. What was discovered was a hoard of bronze and iron objects including a number of chisels, sickles and socketed axes, a sword, a spearhead, a razor and horse harness equipment, attributable to the early Iron Age (c.750–600 BC). But the most impressive object was a bronze cauldron, measuring 35.2 centimetres in height and weighing 7.6 kilograms. It appears that the objects were deliberately buried, votive offerings to the gods of the other-world.

Llyn Fawr, at a height of 369 metres, occupies a craggy amphitheatre, initiated as snow accumulated on the floor of a hollow on the shaded, north-facing slopes of Craig y Llyn, during the cold period preceding the Last Glaciation. In the fullness of time, the snow turned to ice, which in turn formed a glacier that flowed downslope under the influence of gravity. By so doing, the glacier's erosive power greatly enlarged and deepened the initial hollow, carving for itself a cirque, a glacially-scoured rock basin with a steep headwall and sidewalls. The lake, that accumulated in the basin after the climate ameliorated and the ice disappeared, is now regularly visited by members of the Upper Rhondda Angling Association with an eye on catching a few brown or rainbow trout.

Craig y Llyn, Llyn Fawr and one of the hairpin bends

090

Clydach, Y Glais and its moraine

(Clydach, Y Glais a'i farian) SN 695004

Copper smelting in the lower Swansea valley (Cwm Tawe), south of Clydach, ceased in 1924. No longer is it possible to identify the sites of all of the 13 copperworks on the banks of the Tawe which, for most of the nineteenth century, smelted virtually all of Britain's copper and much of the world's output. By today the only metal producing works that pre-dates the closure of Copperopolis' copperworks is the Mond nickelworks, Clydach. The refinery, affectionately known as 'the Mond', was established in 1902 by Ludwig Mond (1839–1909), whose bronze statue stands opposite the non-ferrous works redbrick Edwardian entrance and alongside the B4291 that links Clydach and Y Glais, situated on the western and eastern side respectively of the broad Tawe floodplain.

Y Glais is a former coalmining village, the home of many colliers who worked in the nearby mines, especially Birchgrove and Graigola – two collieries eager to claim that they were the source of 'the best steam coal in the world' – and Felin-frân drift mine on the outskirts of the village. However, amongst readers of Welsh literature and Nonconformist chapelgoers the village's name is associated not with collieries but with Thomas Evan Nicholas (1878–1971), Welsh Nonconformist minister, pacifist, Socialist (he joined the Communist Party in 1920), eloquent champion of the working class, newspaper columnist and prolific poet. Following his ten-year period (1904–14) as minister of Seion Chapel he was known as Niclas y Glais, 'Nicholas of Y Glais', despite the fact that he hailed from the Crymych area, north Pembrokeshire.

The name Niclas y Glais would mean little or nothing to non-Welsh-speaking Earth scientists. Yet many if not most of those with an interest in the glacial history of Wales would know of Y Glais, for the village is built in part on the so-called Glais moraine, the largest and finest example in south Wales of a moraine that accumulated at the snout of a glacier that occupied the Tawe valley during the Last Glaciation. To appreciate fully its size and form, it's best viewed either from Heol Gellionnen, the road that heads north-east towards Mynydd Gellionnen from the centre of Clydach, or from the craggy summit of Craig y Pâl, overlooking Y Glais.

This spectacular landform is in the form of an enormous embankment, about 1,300 metres broad and 70 metres wide, that extends across the valley floor between Y Glais and Clydach, thereby compelling the river Tawe near its confluence with the Clydach to flow around the western end of the obstruction. At its highest point, the moraine's hummocky surface is 37 metres above Tawe's floodplain, whose near-flat surface is some 18–22 metres above sea

Y Glais village situated at the foot of Craig y Pâl. The green fields clothe the moraine. Part of the Mond is to be seen standing on the banks of the Tawe (right of photograph).

level. In contrast to the steep, south-facing slopes of the moraine, those that face north-east slope gently down to the banks of the Tawe, opposite the refinery. The entire mound is composed of a mixture of deposits – large and small blocks of Coal Measure sandstones, coarse 'Millstone Grit' (Basal Grit) sandstone and Old Red Sandstone, set in a sandy-clay matrix – derived from the middle and upper reaches of Cwm Tawe.

Despite its great size, the Glais moraine does not denote the terminus of the Tawe glacier, for similar glacial deposits are to be found in the valley well beyond its front edge. Indeed, it appears that the glacier ultimately terminated alongside the neighbouring Neath (Nedd) glacier in Swansea Bay (Bae Abertawe). As it carried its load of deposits southwards, the Tawe glacier was also responsible for eroding a deep basin in the valley's rock floor, which itself is excavated along the line of the Swansea Valley Fault, a line of structural weakness that in all probability accounts for the fact that the floor of the basin south of the moraine was gouged to a depth of 44 metres below sea level.

In reality the Glais moraine marks the point where the Tawe glacier stood stationary for a while during its retreat up-valley at the end of the main phase of the Last Glaciation, between 17,000 and 15,000 years ago. Judging from the size of the moraine, it appears that the glacier stood still for some time, during which huge blocks of ice became detached from the glacier's main body and incorporated amidst the mass of glacial deposits. Melting and disappearance of the ice blocks resulted in the formation of large and small depressions on the moraine's surface, depressions which now appear as marshy hollows. Melting of the glacier also gave rise to streams of meltwater, which were responsible for the deposition of layers of sand and gravel that contributed to the infilling of the rock basin down-valley of the moraine.

It's not known for how long the Tawe glacier remained stationary, but since no other recessional moraine exists between Y Glais and the uppermost reaches of the Tawe valley, it appears that it receded relatively quickly after its temporary halt in the vicinity of present-day Y Glais and Clydach.

The Glais moraine, bathed in sunshine, and Clydach Refinery

Skomer and Skokholm islands

(Ynysoedd Sgomer a Sgogwm) SM 725095

091

When viewed from the mainland, the most striking attribute of both Skomer and Skokholm, the two island National Nature Reserves situated off the south Pembrokeshire coast that once served as impregnable bases for Viking raiders, is their rocky, cliff-bound shores and remarkably flat surfaces. But when observed closely, differences become apparent. At a height of about 50 to 75 metres above sea level, Skomer's surface is not only far less flat than that of Skokholm, but also some 15 to 25 metres higher than its smaller neighbour, contrasting characteristics that can be ascribed in part to their geological histories.

Skomer, Midland Isle and the mainland in the vicinity of Martin's Haven, departure point of the boats that carry visitors to and from Skomer during spring and summer, are formed of volcanic rocks, a tilted pile of thick and thin layers of hard, black basaltic lava that were the product of several eruptions that came to an end in early Silurian times, about 440 million years ago. In contrast, Skokholm, Gateholm Island and the nearby Dale peninsula are fashioned from folded layers of less resistant red sandstones and mudstones of Old Red Sandstone age, deposited on an ancient land surface some 390 million years ago.

However, the plateau surfaces of both islands probably owe their flatness to the erosive power of waves: Skomer to a time when sea level was about 70 metres above its present level (the height of worldwide sea level if all the world's glaciers and ice sheets, including

Wooltack Point, Jack Sound, Midland Isle and Skomer

Gateholm, south-east of Skomer: it echos the form and geology of Skokholm

those of Greenland and Antarctica, were to melt and disappear as a consequence of extreme global warming) and Skokholm to a period when world sea level was some 45 metres above its present level.

Weather permitting, only Skomer is open to the general public and by walking the well-trodden footpaths that criss-cross its windswept, treeless surface visitors are confronted by a landscape relinquished to nature but assiduously managed by the Wildlife Trust of South & West Wales. Other than the restored nineteenth-century farmhouse and outbuildings at the centre of the island, signs of human habitation are restricted to Iron Age field enclosures, lynchets and hut sites. Birds, and especially seabirds, rather than the island's rich and colourful flora, are the *raison d'être* of this National Nature Reserve and there is no better place in Britain to view them in the breeding season.

With an estimated population well in excess of 100,000 pairs, Skomer supports the largest breeding colony of Manx shearwaters in the world, although they are nowhere to be seen during the day. Only at night do these black-and-white petrels emerge from their burrows and head for their fishing grounds far beyond the shores of their island home, prior to returning before dawn. Once fledged, the young birds spend several years in the South Atlantic before heading back to their place of birth.

Burrows, especially abandoned rabbit holes, are also the nesting sites of thousands of puffins, remarkable and likeable on account of their colourful, parrot-like beaks, well adapted to holding several sand eels, their prey. Whilst they raise their chicks below ground, guillemots and razorbills, two other members of the auk family, choose to lay their eggs on exposed cliff ledges. The Wick, a

Atlantic grey seal

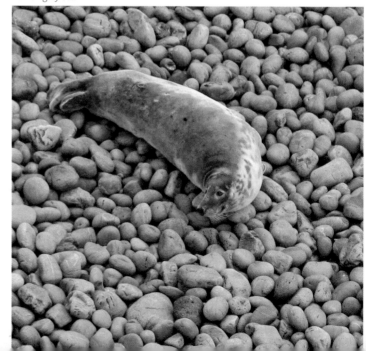

precipice on the southern shores of Skomer is a seasonal, raucous home to both species.

In addition to the hundreds of thousands of Manx shearwaters and auks, both islands are home to kittiwakes, fulmars, European storm petrels, great black-backed gulls, lesser black-backed gulls, herring gulls, shags and cormorants, and a number of resident birds of prey. In light of their ornithological importance, little wonder that R.M. Lockley, a naturalist and native of Cardiff who leased Skokholm for a period of 21 years in 1927, established the first bird observatory in Britain on the island in 1933.

In the same way that day visitors to Skomer are unable to experience the nocturnal habits of Manx shearwaters, the wonders of Skomer Marine Nature Reserve, first designated in 1990 and reclassified as Wales' first Marine Conservation Zone in December 2014, is beyond the reach of all, except scuba-divers. Besides the familiar Atlantic grey seals, dolphins and porpoises, crabs, lobsters and other crustaceans, the waters of the conservation zone that surround Skomer, Midland Isle and the nearby mainland coastline teem with life, including common eelgrass and an enormous variety of seaweeds, sponges, sea anemones and soft corals.

The prime purpose of the Marine Conservation Zone is to safeguard the full range of marine wildlife. Regrettably, however, designating the Skomer Marine Nature Reserve did not serve to safeguard the flora and fauna of this incredibly environmentally sensitive area from the devastating effects of the grounding of the tanker *Sea Empress* in February 1996, on rocks near the entrance to Milford Haven (Aberdaugleddau). Even though most of the migratory seabirds had not yet returned to the area, the spillage of some 72,000 tonnes of crude oil severely affected wildlife and polluted the beaches of south Pembrokeshire.

Puffin

092

The Green Bridge of Wales–St Govan's Head

(Pont y Creigiau–Pentir Sant Gofan) SR 925945

'Probably nowhere else in the British Isles is there so much variety in such a comparatively small area.' So said J.A. Steers of the Pembrokeshire coast in his book entitled *The Coastline of England and Wales* (1946), published six years prior to the designation of the Pembrokeshire Coast National Park. The park, however, is in breach of the two primary objectives of National Parks. The presence of the 2,390-hectare tank and gunnery range does not serve to 'conserve and enhance natural beauty' of the Castlemartin peninsula, nor does its presence 'promote opportunities for the understanding and enjoyment of the [area's] special qualities ... by the public', for walkers are denied access to over nine kilometres of the coastline west of the Green Bridge of Wales (Pont y Creigiau), a splendid natural arch. Furthermore, there is only limited access to the eight-kilometre section of the Wales

Limestone cliffs between the Green Bridge of Wales and St Govan's Head

Coast Path and the unrivalled limestone cliff scenery between the Green Bridge viewpoint, south of Flimston Chapel, and St Govan's Head, near Bosherston.

The cliffs rise to a height of about 45–50 metres above sea level and their profiles are vertical or very steep where the layers of limestone are vertical or inclined landwards, but less steep where they dip seawards. However, the upfolds and downfolds evident in the cliffs are in marked contrast to the land surface, which is as flat as a pancake. Indeed, the most notable feature of the landscape hereabouts is the extensive coastal plateau, levelled, in all probability, by the erosive power of waves when the sea stood at least 50 metres above its present level, perhaps as recently as five million years ago.

Today, the sea is actively undercutting the cliffs and their recession, over the centuries, has given rise to a variety of landforms, including headlands, bays, arches, stacks, blow-holes and geos. The spectacular grey rock arch, inappropriately named the Green Bridge in English, was formed when two caves either side of a small headland united. Sooner or later, the elegant rock bridge is destined to collapse, leaving its seaward limb in the form of a diminutive stack, not unlike that besides the present-day arch. Far more impressive are the nearby Elegug Stacks (Staciau'r Heligog), two limestone pillars that are the unstable remains of long-gone arches.

Elegug Stacks

Huntsman's Leap

The name 'elegug' derives from the Welsh, 'heligog', meaning 'guillemot', which in the company of razorbills and kittiwakes nest in their thousands in the nooks and crannies on the sheer-sided stacks during the late spring–early summer breeding season. Although noted for their 'deafening cries', the call of the kittiwakes is drowned out by the harsh growling of the two members of the auk family.

In contrast to the geologically short-lived stacks and arches, the coastline in the vicinity of St Govan's Head (Pentir Sant Gofan) is noted for its geos, blow-holes and caves. There are no finer examples in Britain of the deep, linear, narrow clefts, known as geos, than Huntsman's Leap (Llam yr Heliwr) and Stennis Ford, both the product of destructive wave action concentrated along faults, lines of structural weakness in the otherwise hard limestone. Stennis Ford, traceable inland over a distance of 180 metres, is by far the longest geo, but the most famous is Huntsman's Leap, named after the eponymous huntsman who apparently died of fright after having accomplished his foolish feat. But the 43-metre-deep chasm is also familiar to rock climbers determined to conquer one or more of the geo's classical climbs.

Amongst Pembrokeshire's other notable features, according to historian George Owen, author of *The Description of Penbrockshire* (1603), are the Bosherston Mere blow-holes, two natural chimneys situated inland of the cliff-line formed by the collapse of part of the roofs of wave-washed caves. During powerful storms, waves are forcibly driven not only through the caves, but skywards via the blow-holes, a sight 'which shows afar off as smoke rising out of a chimney'. Then, as the water recedes, the powerful suction generated is, allegedly, sufficient to draw a 'sheep or what thing soever be found near the brink of the pit … into the gulf' and to its death.

Caves are a feature of limestone country and Ogof Gofan, like others in the cliffs between the Green Bridge and St Govan's Head, was fashioned by a river that has long since abandoned its underground course. It was first examined by archaeologists in 1966 and a limited excavation revealed charcoal and flint waste in addition to the bones of pig, ox, roe deer and sheep, and one piece of pottery. The shard proved to be of late Neolithic age and not part of a vessel owned by Saint Gofan, a contemporary of Saint David (Dewi Sant), the sixth-century patron saint of Wales. According to tradition, Gofan built himself a cell, somewhere near the site of the medieval chapel that stands in the shadow of precipitous cliffs, and spent his life in not-so-quiet contemplation besides a wave-lashed shore.

St Gofan's Chapel

Rhossili

(Rhosili) SS 416881

093

Walkers need only stand atop the long summit ridge of Rhossili Down to appreciate why the Gower peninsula (Penrhyn Gŵyr) was designated an Area of Outstanding Natural Beauty in 1956, the first area in the whole of Britain to be accorded that special status. The seaward and landward vistas are breathtaking: in a southerly direction lies the coastline of Somerset and north Devon, and the distant outline of Lundy Island (Ynys Wair); to the west, Carmarthen Bay (Bae Caerfyrddin) and the cliffs and headlands of south Pembrokeshire (de Penfro), and to the east, that delightful part of inland, rural Gower sandwiched between Rhossili Down and Cefn Bryn, the peninsula's ancient backbone.

More eye-catching, perhaps, and intriguing is the strip pattern of fields characteristic of that portion of the coastal plateau west of the villages of Rhossili and nearby Middleton. Known as 'the Vile', it's one of only a few areas remaining in the whole of Britain of a medieval open-field system, divided into a series of narrow, individually owned strips separated by earthen banks.

No less impressive is the remarkably flat surface of the coastal plateau, traceable as far as the western tip of Worm's Head (Pen Pyrod), a curving but broken finger of land stretching out to sea. Particularly striking is the contrast between the flat, plateau surface and the folded layers of Carboniferous limestone, from which it has

Rhossili beach and the prominent terrace at the foot of Rhossili Down

been carved. On Worm's Head the layers pitch steeply south-westwards, whilst those on the mainland dip north-east. Between the two, the rock floor of the strait, that comes into view at low tide, corresponds to the axis of a large upfold (anticline) no longer evident in today's landscape.

In addition to the wave-cut coastal plateau at a height of 50–60 metres above sea level, there is incontrovertible evidence that sea level has been significantly higher than its present level as recently as 125,000 years ago. The proof is plain to see on the shores of the strait below the old coastguard station. There, above the present beach and resting upon an irregular platform carved from Carboniferous limestone are layers of sand, pebbles and cobbles containing whole and broken shells of limpets (*Patella vulgata*) and common periwinkles (*Littorina littorea*). Vestiges of such raised

beaches are relatively common along the southern coast of Gower and they date from the warm interglacial period that pre-dated the Last Glaciation, when the climate was 1–2°C warmer than present, and sea level at least five metres higher than today.

Unlike the raised beach, which is indicative of a warmer climate, the deposits forming the prominent terrace at the foot of Rhossili Down and at the back of the sandy beach accumulated when the Last Glaciation was at its peak, 20,000 years ago. However, they are not glacial deposits but rather an accumulation of angular, frost-shattered fragments of red sandstone set in a matrix of sand and a little clay, derived from the upper slopes of Rhossili Down, a hill composed of Old Red Sandstone. The terrace built up as more and more debris slid downslope under the influence of gravity. At one and the same time, the ice sheet covering the greater part of Wales extended as far south as Broughton Bay, beyond the northern end of Rhossili Bay. The glacial deposits thereabouts contain fragments of sea shells scooped off the floor of the Loughor estuary (moryd Llwchwr) by the southward-flowing ice.

As the climate warmed, the ice melted and receded, and by the time that Neolithic people set about constructing Sweyne's Howe, two burial chambers not far from the highest summit of Rhossili Down – The Beacon (193 m) – the shoreline and the 4.5-kilometre-long beach had assumed a form not dissimilar to that of today. 'Round the whole coast of Wales', wrote naturalist Bill Condry in 1991, 'there is perhaps a no more perfect beach than the sands which stretch north from Rhossili'. TripAdvisor were in no doubt, for in 2014 it was adjudged to be the finest beach in Britain, the third best in Europe and the ninth best in the world! It is, nevertheless, a terrible place in storms. In the early fourteenth century, the church that stood in the shadow of the cliffs at the southern end of the beach, was overwhelmed by sand. It has also been a scene of shipwrecks in recent centuries.

During the severe storm of 18 November 1840, the paddle steamer *City of Bristol* was wrecked on the beach. On board were 17 crew members, 10 passengers and a cargo of livestock. Except for the ship's carpenter and one cowman, all perished. The barque *Helvetia*, with its cargo of 508 tonnes of timber, suffered a similar fate during the tremendous storm of 1 November 1887. Fortunately, no lives were lost but a few gaunt ribs of the stricken vessel are often to be seen protruding from the sands, a stark reminder of the dangers of Rhossili's seductive beach.

The 125,000-year-old raised beach near the old coastguard station: whole and fragmented shells in a mixture of stones and sand

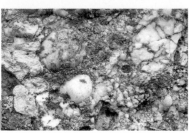

094

Cefn Bryn and Maen Ceti

SS 492900

In 1956 the greater part of Gower (Gŵyr) was designated an Area of Outstanding Natural Beauty and much of its undoubted charm, including that of Cefn Bryn, its prominent backbone, is attributable to its geography and geology. Even so, Benjamin Heath Malkin's description of Cefn Bryn as a 'mountain, the highest in South Wales' in his book, *The Scenery, Antiquities and Biography of South Wales* (1804) was a gross exaggeration. In fact, its highest summit (188 m), at the eastern end of the six-kilometre-long ridge, is five metres short of The Beacon, the high point of Rhossili Down, itself the highest of a cluster of hill summits that rise above the peninsula's gently undulating coastal plateau.

Cefn Bryn and all other Gower hills are carved from layers of Old Red Sandstone conglomerates and sandstones – gravel and sand originally deposited by rivers that meandered across a semi-arid lowland during the Devonian, between 400 and 360 million years ago. Then, early in the succeeding Carboniferous period, the land

Cefn Bryn, Gower's backbone

was submerged, resulting in the accumulation of a very thick sequence of limestone – mainly composed of the remains of marine creatures – on the floor of a warm, tropical sea.

Until about 300 million years ago, the Old Red Sandstone lay hidden beneath a cover of Carboniferous limestone and more recent rocks. That relationship was to change when both the Devonian and Carboniferous strata were folded and faulted during a period of powerful earth movements triggered by the collision of two ancient continents. Cefn Bryn follows the axis of one of Gower's major upfolds (anticlines) and the once hidden Old Red Sandstone rocks resurface in its core, whilst the more recent Carboniferous limestone forms the foundation of the coastal plateau either side of the ridge.

For part of its course, the Gower Way (Llwybr Gŵyr), a long-distance footpath officially opened in 1998, follows the anticlinal ridge of Cefn Bryn. The 56-kilometre-long path extends from Rhossili (Rhosili) at the western end of the ancient lordship of Gower to Penlle'rcastell on Mynydd y Gwair, near Ammanford (Rhydaman). That section which traverses Cefn Bryn is ancient, for many of the numerous cairns along its course are Bronze Age constructions. More impressive, however, are the three Bronze Age cairns near Maen Ceti (Ceti's stone) on the ridge's northern shoulder. The largest, Great Carn (Y Garnedd Fawr), a flat-topped mound of large stones, is 20 metres in diameter.

Maen Ceti, also known as Arthur's Stone and Coetan Arthur (Arthur's quoit), is a Neolithic chambered cairn. It was once thought that the 30–35-tonne capstone was a boulder of local Devonian conglomerate but it's now known to be a glacial erratic, a large lump of Millstone Grit derived from an outcrop on the northern edge of the south Wales coalfield and transported southwards over a distance of about 40 kilometres by ice during the peak of the Last Glaciation, 20,000 years ago. Since the base of the boulder, now broken in two, is at the same level as the surrounding land surface, it's possible that Maen Ceti was never raised above ground level by the builders of the chambered cairn. Instead, it appears that a hollow was excavated beneath the boulder and that nine upright stones were put in place to support its weight. All nine remain in place but, ever since the boulder split in two, the larger chunk now only rests

The Old Red Sandstone of Cefn Bryn

on four. In a sixteenth-century triad, a Welsh form of literary composition, the raising of Maen Ceti was considered to be 'one of the three mighty achievements of the Isle of Britain', the other two being Stonehenge (Côr y Cewri) and Silbury Hill in central southern England. But since it was probably never raised, Maen Ceti can no longer be regarded as a 'mighty achievement'! It is, however, well worth a visit, a vantage point offering views of Gower's north coast and the Loughor estuary (moryd Llwchwr).

At the seaward end of the estuary the finger of Whiteford spit points in the direction of Burry Port (Porth Tywyn), once a centre of copper and tinplate works on the inlet's north shore. Whiteford is a National Nature Reserve whose habitats include not only sandy beaches and sand dunes, but also salt-marsh and mudflats landward of the spit and at the foot of the abandoned sea cliffs between the villages of Llanmadoc (Llanmadog) and Llanrhidian. At least 250 species of flowering plants have been recorded at Whiteford Burrows, making it one of the richest dune systems in Britain, much frequented by botanists. In contrast, the salt-marsh and mudflats, important wintering areas in Wales for waders and wildfowl, are favoured by bird-watchers, for the Loughor is by far the most bird-rich estuary lying wholly in Wales. Sited on its north shore is the Llanelli Wetland Centre, a 182-hectare mosaic of habitats annually visited by tens of thousands of migratory birds.

Millstone Grit conglomerate

Maen Ceti and the Loughor estuary. At some stage Maen Ceti broke in two. The detached slab lies on the ground to the left of the large boulder.

Craig yr Hesg, Pontypridd

ST 076915

095

Designed by William Edwards and built of blocks of rusty-weathering sandstone in 1756, the elegant, single-arch bridge spanning the river Taf in the centre of Pontypridd is an impressive sight, despite the fact that its visual appeal was diminished following the construction of the three-span road bridge alongside it in 1857. Nevertheless, the older bridge still serves as a convenient pedestrian platform from which to admire the wooded slopes of Craig yr Hesg (c.200 m), rising 140 metres above the river and designated a Local Nature Reserve in 2008. Less attractive is the view of the hill from Cefn Eglwysilan (382 m), on the eastern slopes of Cwm Taf. Over a period in excess of 130 years, Craig yr Hesg has been disembowelled by generations of quarrymen charged with the task of extracting enormous quantities of Pennant sandstone, the product of the huge quarry now owned by Hanson, the largest supplier of aggregates in the United Kingdom.

Pennant sandstone is part of the thick sequence of sedimentary rocks known as the Coal Measures, although workable coal-seams are few amongst the layers of sandstone. The once productive seams are to be found amidst the dark-grey and black mudstones of the Lower Coal Measures, deep beneath the floors of the former coalmining valleys of the south Wales coalfield. The period that witnessed the luxurious growth of the tropical forest vegetation that gave rise to the rich coal-seams came to an end about 305 million years ago. Thereafter, as a result of geographical and climatic changes that took place towards the end of Carboniferous times, predominantly northward-flowing meandering rivers spread layer upon layer of sand, for the most part, across the coastal lowlands that previously supported the tropical forests. Eventually, the layers of sand of variable thickness became beds of Pennant sandstone, blue-grey when freshly quarried but weathering rusty-brown when exposed to the elements.

Above all else, Pennant sandstone, the rock from which the valleys of the south Wales coalfield were mainly carved, determined to a large extent the unique townscape of the coalmining

Craig yr Hesg quarry

communities, which persists despite the changes that have occurred following the closure of all the deep mines that sustained the area's inhabitants. Almost every community and colliery had its own quarry which yielded a ready supply of building stones and also flagstones used to pave the long, terraced streets.

By far the largest quarry in and around Pontypridd, the commercial hub of the central part of the south Wales coalfield, was Craig yr Hesg, an undertaking greatly enlarged in the wake of the development of the coal industry in the valleys of the Rhondda Fawr and the Rhondda Fach. The demand for housing between 1851 and 1924, at a time when over 50 collieries were at work, was unprecedented. The period witnessed not only the building of over 30,000 houses, but also numerous chapels and churches, public houses and clubs, welfare halls and shops, in addition to colliery buildings. Craig yr Hesg Pennant sandstone was also in demand in the Elan valley, in mid Wales, where it was used to clad the retaining walls of the reservoirs built by Birmingham Corporation between 1893 and 1904.

Craig yr Hesg quarry was also the source of the large, smooth-hewn blocks of 'Blue Pennant stone', which form the foundation of the splendid memorial, designed and executed by the renowned sculptor Sir William Goscombe John, commemorating Evan James and his son, James James, 'who at Pontypridd', to quote an anonymous reporter of the *Glamorgan Free Press & Rhondda Leader* present at the unveiling ceremony, 'composed the words and music respectively of the Welsh National Anthem, "Hen Wlad fy Nhadau"'. Appropriately, the monument consists primarily of two bronze figures, one representing music and the other poetry. Three days after the unveiling ceremony, held on 23 July 1930 and attended by about 10,000 people, the same anonymous newspaper reporter was pleased to record that, 'Sir W. Goscombe John [was] delighted with the site selected in the Ynysangharad Park [Pontypridd], with the fine background of the Craig-yr-Hesg Mountain'.

In all probability, Craig yr Hesg quarry was also the source of Evan James' gravestone. He died in 1878 and was buried in the cemetery of Carmel Chapel, Pontypridd, but in 1973 the stone was moved and placed at the foot of the memorial in Ynysangharad Park. James James died in 1902 and was buried in the cemetery in

Aberdare (Aberdâr). But, unlike his father's memorial, his gravestone, a slab of white marble from the world-famous quarries of Carrara, Italy, bears not a single Welsh word except for the title of the Welsh National Anthem composed in 1856.

In the village of Langemark in Flanders, four monoliths from Craig yr Hesg quarry, arranged in the form of a cromlech and surmounted by a red dragon designed by artist Lee Odishow, is intended as a memorial 'To all those of Welsh descent who took part in the First World War between 1914 and 1918'. It was unveiled on 16 August 2014.

096

Garth Hill and the Taff valley

(Mynydd y Garth a Chwm Taf) ST 103835

Although many of the scenes in the film *The Englishman Who Went Up a Hill But Came Down a Mountain* (1995) were shot in and around Llanrhaeadr-ym-Mochnant and Llansilin, west of Oswestry (Croesoswallt), the story actually revolves around two Ordnance Survey surveyors dispatched to the village of Ffynnon Garw (Ffynnon Taf [Taff's Well], north of Cardiff, in reality) to measure the height of its 'mountain' in 1917. The two pompous Englishmen caused outrage when they concluded that Mynydd y Garth (Garth Hill) overlooking the village was only a 'hill' because it was 16 feet (4.9 m) short of the necessary 1,000 feet (304.8 m). Undaunted by officialdom, the villagers won the day by constructing an earth and stone mound atop the hill so as to ensure that its summit exceeded the required height.

Today an Ordnance Survey triangulation pillar, which has long since outlived its usefulness, stands on top of the highest of five barrows on the treeless and exposed summit of Mynydd y Garth (307 m). Needless to say, however, not a single mound was constructed during the twentieth century, for all five, strung out in a line along the summit ridge, form the finest surviving group of round barrows in the area. They were built during the Bronze Age, between 3,000 and 4,000 years ago, and their commanding position and the size of the largest (4.3 metres high) suggests that this was the burial place of rulers of the local community.

Impressive though the ancient monuments are, it's the stunning 360° panorama which occupies the attention of most walkers who choose to walk the paths that criss-cross the common land, including a small section of the Ridgeway Walk (Ffordd y Bryniau), a 53-kilometre-long pathway that extends from Margam Country Park (Parc Gwledig Margam), near Port Talbot, to Caerphilly Castle (Castell Caerffili). To the south, on a clear day, the seaside town of Weston-super-Mare on the southern shores of the Bristol Channel (Môr Hafren) is in view, whilst the high summits of the Brecon Beacons (Bannau Brycheiniog) dominate the skyline at the head of the Taff valley.

The Taff valley, looking north from the summit of Mynydd y Garth

The Taff gorge: the roofs of Castell Coch are visible above the disused quarry alongside the A470

Caerphilly at rainbow's end

Apart from resplendent, eye-catching vistas, the area in the vicinity of Taff's Well is of geographical and geological interest on account of the close relationship between its geology and topography. South of Mynydd y Garth, the Taff gorge breaches the prominent ridge of Garth Fach–Fforest-fawr formed of normally blue-grey Carboniferous limestone, here stained red by iron oxides. On the southern slopes of Fforest-fawr stands Castell Coch, the irresistibly appealing 'red castle', whose round towers topped with conical roofs stand proud of the surrounding woodland. The original stone castle was built by the de Clare Lords of Glamorgan during the late thirteenth century but when John Leland saw the building in the 1530s it was 'all in ruins'. The present 'castle of romantic dreams', funded by the third Marquess of Bute, was the brainchild of notable architect William Burges. Completed exteriorly in 1879, it overlooks Cardiff (Caerdydd), largely built on a foundation of glacial deposits and estuarine clays.

High on the opposite side of the valley to Castell Coch, Cemex UK's huge limestone quarry was once the site of an ironstone mine that supplied the nineteenth-century Pentyrch ironworks until it closed in 1888. The area is also noted for its caves, including Ogof Tŷ-nant and Ogof Ffynnon Taf whose walls are coated with orange-stained calcite.

The layered, 350-million-year-old Carboniferous limestone that is the foundation of the Garth Fach–Fforest-fawr ridge plunges steeply

northwards and disappears beneath rocks of the south Wales coalfield before climbing steadily and reappearing a short distance north of Merthyr Tydfil (Merthyr Tudful). In contrast to the Garth Fach–Fforest-fawr ridge, the Mynydd y Garth–Craig yr Allt ridge, which is also breached by the Taff, corresponds to the outcrop of Pennant sandstone that underlies the high moorland of the coalfield. In the past, the rusty-weathering sandstone was extensively quarried in the hills to the north of Caerphilly and utilized by Gilbert de Clare during the thirteenth century to build Caerphilly Castle, comparable to the greatest of Edward I's fortresses in north Wales and ranked as one of the great medieval castles of western Europe. Never before had Pennant sandstone been used on such an extensive scale, a building stone which was destined to put its stamp on domestic, religious and industrial buildings the length and breadth of the coalfield during the nineteenth century.

The lower ground, sandwiched between the Carboniferous limestone and Pennant sandstone ridges, corresponds to the outcrop of softer, readily-eroded mudstones of the Lower and Middle Coal Measures, a sequence of 310-million-year-old rocks incorporating valuable coal-seams mined in small pits and consumed in local nineteenth-century ironworks. Although occupied in part by two small tributaries of the Taff, the two vales north-east of Pentyrch and Taff's Well, respectively, were probably excavated not by streams but by glaciers of the Great Ice Age.

The defunct triangulation pillar stands on the summit of the largest round barrow on Mynydd y Garth

Goldcliff and the Caldicot Levels

(Allteuryn a Gwastadeddau Caldicot) ST 373819

097

'High above the water, and not far from Caerleon, there stands a rocky eminence which dominates the River Severn. In the English language it is called Goldcliff, the Golden Rock. When the sun's rays strike it, the stone shines very bright and takes on a golden sheen': so said Gerald of Wales (Gerallt Gymro) in his account of the journey through Wales in the company of Archbishop Baldwin in 1188.

Today, Goldcliff is a tiny headland but during the early post-glacial period, about 11,000 years ago, it was a hillock of yellowish Jurassic limestone and mudstone, the summit of which stood above an extensive lowland tract criss-crossed by the river Severn (afon Hafren) as it flowed westward towards the open sea. Later, following the disappearance of the world's large ice sheets that had blanketed northern North America and north-west Europe during the Last Glaciation, the slowly rising sea extended across the once dry land, destroying oak woodland in its wake. As a result of the marine incursion, Goldcliff's unremarkable low cliffs now rise above the muddy shores of the Severn estuary (Môr Hafren), and in the layers

The tower of St Mary's Church, Nash

Porch wall of St Thomas' Church, Redwick

St Mary Magdalene's Church, Goldcliff

of mud, visible only at low tide at the foot of the huge sea wall built between 1952 and 1974 to protect the Caldicot Levels, archaeologists uncovered treasures galore.

During the 1990s and the early years of the present century, archaeologists picking their way through the glutinous mud came across an abundance of evidence dating from the Mesolithic period that shed light on the activities of hunter-gatherers who lived in the area between 8,000 and 6,800 years ago. Sites utilized for the cooking of fish and butchering of aurochs (extinct wild oxen) came to light. Also discovered were the bones of pigs and otters, in addition to implements fashioned from wood, bone and antlers. But the site was of particular interest to archaeologists and the media, on account of the human footprints found in the layers of mud, most of them those of young children. Footprints of red deer and cranes, long-legged wading birds no longer native to Britain, were also recorded.

The archaeological evidence indicates that hunter-gatherers visited the muddy shores throughout the year, but especially in summer and autumn, and during the 1,200 years that Mesolithic communities lived in the area, sea level continued to rise a few millimetres annually, thereby adding to the thickness of sediment accumulating along the shores of the Severn estuary. Indeed, the evidence gathered near Redwick, a village situated 4.5 kilometres east-north-east of 'the Golden Rock', suggests that the ten-metre-thick pile of mud began accumulating 8,000 years ago on what was then dry land but is now about five metres below sea level.

The discovery of an inscribed Roman boundary stone near Goldcliff in 1878 suggests that it was the Romans, who had established the fort of Caerleon (Caerllion) about AD 74, that were the first to construct a sea wall in an attempt to protect the rich coastal lowlands from being flooded. Their attempt and similar work undertaken during the Middle Ages was, for the most part, unsuccessful. In 1424 Goldcliff Priory, established in 1113 on the western flank of the headland, was partially destroyed by floodwaters. Although nothing of it remains today, the event led to the construction of the church of St Mary Magdalene further inland, a building that incorporates dressed blocks of Jurassic limestone salvaged from the priory. But the Goldcliff floods of 1424 pale into

insignificance when compared to the damage and deaths caused by the flood of 20 January 1606 (or 1607 according to the Gregorian calendar). The brass plaque on the wall near the altar of St Mary Magdalene's Church records the calamity:

On the XX [20] day of Janvary even as it came to pas it pleased God the flvd did flow to the edge of this same bras [*] – and in this parish theare was lost 5000 od pownds besides XXII [22] people was in this parrish drown

*The plaque is about a metre above the floor of the church and seven metres above sea level

The height of the floodwaters is also recorded on the outer wall of St Thomas' Church, Redwick, and the outer wall of the tower of St Mary's Church, Nash. But the floodwaters were not restricted to the Caldicot Levels. Inundation of the coastal lowlands either side of the Severn estuary led to the death of about 2,000 people and thousands of animals.

Some geologists believe that the disaster was caused by a tsunami, a powerful earthquake-generated wave similar to that which overwhelmed parts of Japan's eastern seaboard in March 2011. In reality, the event was more akin to the North Sea Flood of 1953, a tidal surge caused by a combination of high spring tides and a deep low-pressure system that generated large waves. That flood claimed the lives of over 2,000 people living in eastern England and the Netherlands.

One of the many reens (ditches) draining the Caldicot Levels

098

Dunraven and the Vale of Glamorgan coastline

(Dwnrhefn ac arfordir Bro Morgannwg) SS 885731

Dunraven beach

Anative of the village of Llancarfan in the Vale of Glamorgan, poet, antiquary and literary forger Edward Williams, better-known by his bardic name, Iolo Morganwg (1747–1826), was a scholar of genius who spent most of his life as a stonemason. He was well-acquainted with the geology of his home area, particularly the attributes of its various building stones, and insisted that one of the glories of the Vale was its strikingly beautiful coastal cliffs and rocky shores. The incomparable splendour of the Vale's unspoilt coastline was duly recognized in 1972 when the 22.5-kilometre-long section between Aberthaw (Aberddawan) and Porth-cawl was awarded Heritage Coast status, managed with a view to conserving its natural beauty and wildlife, and promoting its enjoyment by members of the public At its heart are the cliffs of Blue Lias limestone on either side of the popular beach of Dunraven (Dwnrhefn), near the village of Southerndown.

According to the *Handbook of Geological Terms* (1865), 'lias' 'is said to be a corruption of *lyers*, or *layers*', but in *English Rock Terms* (1953) the term is said to be 'Adopted from Old French *liois* … [meaning] a compact kind of limestone'. In truth, Blue Lias limestone is both hard and stratified, each layer – normally no more than 30 centimetres thick – is separated from the next by a thinner layer of grey mudstone. The rocks, which accumulated stratum by stratum on the floor of a warm, shallow sea when 'Wales' was situated about 30° north of the equator, are the youngest in Wales and are noted for their fossils. An inspection of the surfaces of water-worn, beach cobbles and wave-washed layers of limestone on Dunraven beach soon reveals impressions of large and small ammonites, sea shells, corals and crinoids that lived in the sea during early Jurassic times, some 190 million years ago.

Attractive though the beach is, it's not possible to appreciate fully the grandeur of the Heritage Coast without climbing the grassy path that leads to the summit of Trwyn y Witsh (the witch's nose;

The cliffs between Trwyn y Witsh and Cwm Nash (right)

Fossil sea shells

Fossil ammonite

'witsh' is misspelled as 'witch' on the 1:25,000 OS map), a windswept, 63-metre-high headland on the southern side of Dunraven Bay. The path heads past what little remains of Dunraven Castle, originally the site of a medieval house that was replaced during the nineteenth century by a castellated Gothic mansion. Demolished in 1962, the house and its gardens actually stood within the ramparts of an Iron Age hill fort established on Trwyn y Witsh, about 2,500 years ago. Despite the solidity of the headland, strengthened by a core of resistant Carboniferous limestone, the explosive force of storm waves has undermined the cliffs and caused portions to collapse, resulting in the destruction of part of the fort's ramparts. Wave erosion has also accelerated the retreat of the Blue Lias cliffs south of the headland, thereby adding to the width of the extensive rock platform at their foot.

From the cliff-top vantage point the view as far as Cwm Nash (Cwm yr As Fawr), three kilometres to the south-east, is breathtaking. Since the cliffs are retreating faster than the ability of the two streams – Nant Cwm Mawr and Nant Cwm Bach – to deepen their valleys, their waters, at high tide, plunge vertically into the sea. At low tide, the spectacle is more dramatic because the rock platform at the base of the cliffs then assumes the form of a grand geological map. The curved outlines of the hard limestone layers – broken in places by faults – mirror the pattern of folds and faults evident in the face of the cliffs. Although insignificant when compared to the enormous folds and faults created by the powerful tectonic forces that gave rise to the Alps, the creases and tears are, nevertheless, a faint echo of the selfsame Alpine earth movements, a period of mountain building that was at its most intense 25 million years ago.

Even though natural outcrops of Blue Lias are few and far between within the Vale of Glamorgan, the rock has left an indelible stamp on its landscape, a fact that did not escape the attention of Iolo Morganwg. By burning the limestone, he claimed that it was possible to produce lime of the highest quality for use on local farms. Furthermore, Iolo maintained that the rock was not only suitable for the construction of walls, but that it could also be used to fashion ashlar finer than Portland stone or Bath stone. That was a gross exaggeration but it was easily quarried and readily yielded rectangular blocks of valuable building stone. The walls of Cardiff Castle are built, in part, on the remains of the walls of a Roman fort constructed of Blue Lias. The Normans too made use of the same stone in building some of their castles in the Vale of Glamorgan. Indeed, part of the Vale's enduring charm is its sequestered villages, dominated by small grey churches with tall square towers built of Lias limestone.

Ogmore-by-Sea

(Aberogwr) SS 866751

099

There has never been a shortage of building stone in Wales. Until the end of the nineteenth century, builders were largely dependent on securing supplies of stone quarried locally. Nevertheless, that which was available locally did not always satisfy the needs of stonemasons and, during the Middle Ages in particular, a period that witnessed the building of castles, abbeys and churches the length and breadth of Wales, those charged with the task of overseeing such prestigious building projects were required to obtain a supply of freestone. Defined as block stone which can be freely cut in any direction with toothed saws and readily worked with chisels, freestone was used to fashion distinctive architectural features such as door and window jambs, and decorative mouldings.

Although Wales cannot boast freestones of a quality equal to that of Bath stone and Portland stone, quarried near Bath and Weymouth, respectively, the country is not wholly devoid of such material. In south Wales, especially, much use was made of Sutton stone extracted in a number of small quarries situated on the slopes overlooking Ogmore-by-Sea (Aberogwr), an undistinguished little seaside resort, which, in spite of its pretentious English name, is devoid of a single building worthy of attention in *The Buildings of Wales: Glamorgan* (1995), written by architectural historian John Newman.

The old quarries have not survived but the stone, prized by medieval stonemasons, outcrops in the coastal cliffs near the bottom of Pant y Slâd, a prominent dry valley near the southern limit of the resort. Sutton stone is a pitted, whitish-grey limestone, deposited on the floor of an island-dotted sea during Jurassic times, about 195 million years ago. In addition to fragments of shells of creatures that flourished in the warm sea water, the limestone also contains pebbles of 350-million-year-old Carboniferous limestone, the foundation of the islands attacked by the waves of the Jurassic sea and the rock on which lie the thick layers of Sutton stone today.

Without doubt, Sutton stone is the finest of the freestones of Wales and it was in demand not only in the Vale of Glamorgan (Bro Morgannwg) but also elsewhere in south and south-west Wales. For example, early in the twelfth century it was used to fashion the dressed stones to be seen in the keep of Ogmore Castle (Castell Aberogwr), largely built of locally outcropping Carboniferous limestone on the banks of the river Ogmore (afon Ogwr), a short distance from the Sutton stone quarries. The same freestone was extensively employed in the nearby Ewenny Priory (Priordy Ewenni), a church originally commissioned by William de Londres, keeper of Ogmore Castle, who died in 1126. At about the same time, the

The degraded face of one of the old Sutton stone quarries of Ogmore-by-Sea

valuable limestone was also exported eastwards, where it was used to create decorative features in Llandaff Cathedral (Eglwys Gadeiriol Llandaf), the construction of which was begun by Urban in 1120, after the Normans had appointed him as their first bishop in 1107.

Early in the thirteenth century, the monks of Margam and Neath (Nedd) imported a considerable quantity of Sutton stone used by the stonemasons for the ashlar parts of both abbeys and their conventual buildings. Further to the west, dressed blocks of the stone are evident in the splendid arcaded parapet of Swansea Castle (Castell Abertawe), built during the first half of the fourteenth century.

The magnificent sixteenth-century Trinity Chapel screen in St David's Cathedral (Eglwys Gadeiriol Tyddewi) was constructed of yellowish-grey Jurassic limestone imported from two different sources: Dundry stone from the ancient quarries of Dundry Hill, south of Bristol, and Bath stone from quarries near Bath. But within the screen there are also a few crudely fashioned mullions of Sutton stone, which appear to have been used to repair damaged stonework at an unknown date.

However, St David's was not journey's end for all the trading vessels that sailed westwards from the shores of Ogmore-by-Sea. Although Sutton stone is not found in the ruined walls of St Dogmaels Abbey (Abaty Llandudoch), situated close to the banks of the river Teifi near Cardigan (Aberteifi), the small, on-site museum houses part of an elaborate, thirteenth-century arched canopy of Sutton stone and an early sixteenth-century cadaver stone, part of a table tomb originally located, in all probability, in the church's north transept, itself extensively modified in the sixteenth century.

By the late Middle Ages, the golden age of the Sutton stone quarries was at an end. For those wishing to acquire supplies of the esteemed freestone, the only alternative was to recycle material plundered from pre-existing buildings. Caerphilly Castle (Castell Caerffili), built largely of Pennant sandstone, is one of the great medieval castles of western Europe but in 1583 it was dealt an architectural blow when the Earl of Pembroke leased it to Thomas Lewis, with express permission to make free and unlimited use of dressed Sutton stonework for reuse at his nearby house, The Van (Y Fan).

Layers of Sutton stone resting on Carboniferous limestone coated with common orange lichen (Xanthoria parietina) on the southern outskirts of Ogmore-by-Sea

100

Bendrick Rock

(Creigiau Bendrick) ST 134671

Whilst on his journey through that part of the Vale of Glamorgan in the vicinity of Porth-cawl in September 1878, Welsh artist Thomas Henry Thomas (1834–1915), born in Pontypool (Pont-y-pŵl), lingered awhile in the village of Newton Nottage (Drenewydd yn Notais) and wandered around the sixteenth-century church of St John the Baptist. The rays of the setting sun lit up a stone measuring about two square metres. As he drew nearer, the sharp-eyed artist, keenly interested in geology amongst other things, noticed that the block of red conglomerate (a rock containing a mixture of small pebbles and sand) bore the unmistakeable impression of a row of five, three-toed footprints made by some reptilian creature. Although he did not realize it at the time, on that late September day Thomas secured his place in geology's hall of fame, for he was the first to record and describe dinosaur footprints in Wales.

On the basis of the size and the stride length of the creature that created the fossilized footprints, W.J. Sollas, a friend of Thomas and lecturer in geology and zoology at Bristol University, adjudged that

Bendrick Rock's red and pale-coloured Triassic sandstones and siltstones

they were the imprint of a two-metre-tall dinosaur, which he named *Brontozoum thomasi*; thomasi in honour of the fossil's discoverer. In spite of its importance, however, nothing could be said about the creature's habitat because neither Thomas nor Sollas knew from whence the block of conglomerate had come.

In Wales, it was not until April 1974 that several sets of dinosaur footprints were found *in situ* in a succession of colourful rocks exposed in the vicinity of Bendrick Rock (Creigiau Bendrick), on the shores of the Bristol Channel (Môr Hafren), about two kilometres east of the seaside resort of Barry Island (Ynys y Barri). Within an area measuring about 25 square metres, over 400 footprints – some three-toed and others four-toed – could be traced across the surface of layers of reddish sandstone dating from Triassic times, some 220 million years ago. In the absence of bones, geologists are unable to attribute the different kinds of footprints to particular species of dinosaur but, in all probability, the small and large, three-toed footprints were made by small and large, meat-eating dinosaurs which walked on their hind legs, whilst the four-toed footprints may have belonged to a plant-eating dinosaur that walked on all fours.

The deposits that gave rise to the layered rocks accumulated on a hot, dry, lowland plain about 20° north of the equator. Rain fell infrequently but when it did it fell in torrents, resulting in flash floods that swept cobbles, pebbles, sand, silt and mud from nearby barren hills towards the shores of a large, shallow, inland lake or sea that lay in the vicinity of today's Bristol Channel. Ripple marks, similar to those that form between the high and low water marks on a modern sandy beach, characterize the upper surfaces of some of the layers of sandstone, which when still soft gave way under the feet and weight of some of the earliest dinosaurs in the world as they wandered from place to place. Unlike their footprints, their whole or dismembered skeletons have not survived, reduced to dust perhaps under the hot desert sun during the frequent prolonged periods of drought when their bones were not being buried beneath protective layers of river-borne silt, sand and pebbles.

Sadly, the footprints have not only been vandalized on occasions but also plundered by unscrupulous fossil collectors. In 2005, for example, slabs of sandstone on which were a number of fossil footprints were illegally collected from the Bendrick Rock Site of

Water-filled dinosaur footprints

beach, five kilometres east of Bendrick Rock, in spring 2014. It lived at the time when 'south Wales' was a coastal region enjoying a warm, Mediterranean-type climate. Shortly after dying close to the shoreline, it appears that the dinosaur's body was washed out to sea and quickly buried alongside marine creatures, such as sea urchins, in the sediment accumulating on the sea floor. The approximately 200-million-year-old fossil, named in honour of its discoverers and kindly donated to National Museum Wales, is a brand-new species of dinosaur, never seen before. Some 20 million years younger than the anonymous dinosaurs that left their stamp on the Triassic strata of Bendrick Rock, *Dracoraptor hanigani* is probably the earliest Jurassic dinosaur in the world.

Special Scientific Interest and subsequently offered for sale on the internet and in fossil shops and fairs in Britain and the USA. Fortunately, some of the stolen fossils have been recovered and placed in the safekeeping of National Museum Wales (Amgueddfa Cymru). Regrettably, there are no easy means of protecting such a site.

The tale of *Dracoraptor hanigani*, a distant cousin of the much later dinosaur, *Tyrannosaurus rex*, has a more positive outcome. The fossilized skeletal remains of this small, agile dinosaur, probably only about 70 centimetres tall, were discovered by two brothers, Nick and Rob Hanigan, while fossil hunting along Lavernock (Larnog)

Dinosaur footprints (above, right and facing page)

A Glossary of Geological Terms

aeolian: wind-borne

ammonite: an extinct, coiled-shell mollusc

anticline: an upfold similar in form to an arch

ash-flow tuff: a pyroclastic rock formed by the cooling and consolidation of dense clouds of red-hot volcanic dust and ash

basalt: dark, fine-grained lava

boulder-clay: a glacial deposit containing a mixture of boulders, cobbles, pebbles, sand and clay

chalcopyrite: copper ore

cirque: a glacially eroded rock basin with a steep headwall and steep sidewalls, resembling an amphitheatre

conglomerate: a sedimentary rock composed of rounded pebbles set in a matrix of sand

dolerite: a dark-coloured, medium-grained igneous rock that has cooled and crystallized below the surface of the Earth

erratic: a rock transported by a glacier or ice sheet and deposited well beyond its place of origin

fault: a fracture where the rocks either side of the break have moved relative to one another

glacial trough: a valley deepened, widened and straightened by the erosive action of a glacier

gabbro: a dark, coarse-grained igneous rock that has crystallized deep within the Earth's crust

galena: lead ore that occurs in veins, often in association with quartz, zinc blende (zinc ore) and pyrite

granite: a coarse-grained, crystalline, light-coloured igneous rock

Great Ice Age: the period between 2.6 million years ago and the present characterised by a succession of cold, glacial periods, such as the Last Glaciation, alternating with warm interglacial periods, such as the present

hanging valley: a tributary glacial valley whose floor is at a higher level than that of a neighbouring glacial trough

hydrothermal vent: an opening on the ocean floor in the form of a chimney out of which flows mineral-rich fluids

igneous rock: a rock formed as a result of the crystallization of magma (molten rock)

ignimbrite: see **ash-flow tuff**

interglacial: a warm period between two glacial periods

jasper: a microcrystalline variety of quartz, often red in colour

joint: a natural crack in a rock. Joints in igneous rocks, which often assume a columnar pattern, develop as the molten rock cools and solidifies

Last Glaciation: the glacial period that was at its peak about 20,000 years ago

lava: molten rock (magma) that has solidified on the Earth's surface

lode: a mineral vein

magma: molten rock

meltwater channel: a valley eroded by meltwater flowing either ahead of, alongside or beneath a glacier or ice sheet

metamorphic rock: a rock such as slate or schist which was previously sedimentary or igneous but which has been transformed by intense heat or pressure (or both)

moraine: a mound of glacial debris deposited by melting glacier ice

pillow lava: heaped masses of lava resembling piles of pillows formed during the submarine extrusion of lava

pyrite: a mineral composed of iron sulphide, often known as 'fool's gold'

pyroclastic flow: see **ash-flow tuff**

pyroclastic rock: a rock formed by the accumulation of volcanic ash and fragmented lava as a result of a powerful volcanic eruption

raised beach: layers of sand and shingle containing sea shells found well above modern sea level

quartz: a hard mineral formed of silica, common in mineral veins

ria: a river valley drowned during a period of rising sea level

rock basin: a basin excavated by the erosive power of a glacier

schist: a metamorphic rock that tends to split along parallel planes that are the result of the parallel alignment of platy minerals

scree: an accumulation of angular rock fragments of various sizes at the foot of a cliff

sedimentary rock: rocks formed as deposits, such as mud, sand and pebbles, on the Earth's surface

sett: a paving-block normally fashioned from a hard igneous rock such as granite

shale: mudstone that splits into thin leaves

sphalerite: zinc ore

spit: a narrow, elongated, coastal accumulation of sand and shingle projecting into the sea

striations, striae: scratches on a rock surface caused by the abrasive action of a glacier armed with rock fragments

submerged forest: a coastal woodland inundated and killed as a consequence of a rise in sea level

syncline: a downfold similar in form to the cross section of a saucer

tor: a relatively small castellated hill or outcrop, usually composed of a hard igneous rock, rising abruptly from a smooth hilltop or slope

trilobite: an extinct marine crustacean whose body is divided into three segments: a head, thorax and tail

tuff: see **ash-flow tuff**

volcanic ash: a fine-grained volcanic material which is the product of a volcanic eruption

volcanic rock: lava, ash and dust which is the product of a volcanic eruption

The Chief Divisions of Geological Time

Quaternary	
	1.8 million years ago
Neogene	
	23
Paleogene	
	65
Cretaceous	
	145
Jurassic	
	199
Triassic	
	251
Permian	
	299
Carboniferous	
	359
Devonian	
	416
Silurian	
	443
Ordovician	
	488
Cambrian	
	542

Precambrian (the oldest rocks on mainland Wales are some 700 million years old, whereas the oldest on Earth are about 4 billion years old)

y Lolfa

www.ylolfa.com